Recollections & Reflections

Recollections & Reflections

Volume 1

Richard Birney-Smith

Recollections & Reflections © 2024 Fly With Me Publishing and Richard Birney-Smith

Library and Archives Canada Cataloguing in Publications.

Copyright in Ontario Canada.

For permissions contact:
rbs4533@gmail.com

Print ISBN: 978-1-990419-29-4
Hardcover ISBN: 978-1-990419-30-0
1st Edition

Edited by Julia Kollek Creative Services
Cover image: Mbzt (under Creative Commons Attribution 3.0 license)
Cover Design: Meraki Cover Design

To my grandsons

— Christian, Luke, Aaron —

and their descendants

with much love.

Reader Responses

I am enjoying your book. It's almost like you were sitting in my living room talking to me.

2 July 2024

Frank Johnson, choir member

Grace Church, Milton, Ontario

I loved this book; finished it in two days.

It's refreshing to read an autobiography where the author honestly reviews the facts of his life --- both the triumphs and failures. Richard dedicated this book to his grandchildren. What better gift could you give them than the honesty of their family's back story? They will be better people for having read this.

31 July 2024

Larry Paikin, long-time friend

Hamilton, Ontario

I thoroughly enjoyed reading your wonderful new book, Recollections & Reflections. I was really struck by the Reflections section. It was unexpected, but very powerful. Your personal history makes a great story. As I read the book, I could hear your voice. I was aware of your many accomplishments, but mostly in the years after 1981. I look forward to volume two, now that you have set the stage so well.

8 August 2024

Scott Reynolds, Trinity College classmate

Little Falls, New Jersey

Table of Contents

Reflections

FOREWORD

These compelling recollections by my good friend and colleague Richard Birney-Smith are a testament to his inspiring and lifelong dedication to being a church musician. A rich and diverse set of influences during his upbringing cumulate in a storyline which is at once detailed and coherent. Would that I had this degree of memory for past events! Being an ardent francophile and devotee of Pierre Cochereau, I find his chapters on life in France (especially Paris) particularly gripping and evocative. Richard writes with a sense of pride and significant respect for our predecessors which is healthy and admirable, especially in our fast-moving current era, which can sometimes seem overly preoccupied with the present. I commend this colossal project to all those whose life is influenced and nourished by our great instrument, aptly known as *The King of Instruments*.

David Briggs

Artist in Residence, Cathedral Church of St. John the Divine, New York City

International Organ Recitalist, Recording Artist, and Composer

To the Reader

Why *Recollections and Reflections*?

Why not *The Autobiography of Richard Birney-Smith*?

I think autobiography implies a more-or-less chronological history of one's life. Not all of life is interesting. I only want to write about what I find memorable, and what I hope my daughters, grandsons, and as-yet-unborn descendants will also find worth knowing.

I have, on more than one occasion, launched into a story only to be greeted with, "I didn't know that . . . ." The reaction is usually about a detail. "I didn't know that you and mummy ever visited Kansas City together." Or, "I didn't know that you heard Joni Mitchell when you lived in Saskatoon." Sometimes the story gets lost because the detail was a sufficient distraction to change the direction of the conversation. Okay, that's life, and that's how real conversation works.

Memories are often at variance with facts. I have seriously tried to fact-check my recollections, but my life has been shaped as much by memories and impressions as by facts. Fact-checking can offer significant distractions from writing. I have tried hard to keep writing rather than getting lost in the myriad rabbit holes I encountered during the process.

The reflections are opinion pieces, which I hope will be informative and useful.

It is my wish that these books will supply or recall some of those stories and details that will help my daughters, grandsons, their spouses, children of my grandsons, and their spouses know who I am, was, or thought I was.

If anyone else finds this interesting, that will be a bonus.

Feel free to look at the Table of Contents and choose the parts that draw your attention. Do not feel that you must read in the order set out there, as I can guarantee the material was neither written nor lived in that way. However you choose to approach the material, I hope that you will eventually read it all. Some of the information will be personal and some will be professional. Some will be detailed, and some will be snippets. So be it.

A certain amount of musical, liturgical, and French terminology is unavoidable. Rather than trying to explain terms like great organ, Eucharist, and *déjeuner* each time they occur, I have provided a glossary. Racial terminology is also unavoidable. I use words like coloured, Negro, black, and African American as they would have been used in the historical context of the narrative.

I am providing footnotes along the way because I do not want to interrupt the narrative with explanations or background information. You may read the book without referring to the footnotes, or, if you want to know more, you may delve into them as they occur, or later.

Some will find my syntax, grammar, and font choice old-fashioned and somewhat formal.

So be it. I think it important to write in my own voice.

I hope you will enjoy and learn from what you find here.

Begun on 2 January 2018 and revised along the way.

Recollections

My Names

I was born on 29 January 1941 in Detroit, Michigan, USA, the first-born child of Birney Walker Smith Jr. and Jetawyn Barbara Smith (née Solomon). My first name was after Richard Carlyle Johnson, my maternal grandmother's brother who died in 1940. My mother called him Uncle Richard. On both sides of my family, it was frequent for the first son to receive his father's name as a middle name. So, mine was Birney.

I was called Richard throughout my childhood and was usually styled Richard B. Smith on mail and school records. I came to be called Dick at the age of eleven while attending boy scout camp. This nickname stuck with me until 27 March 1963 when I met my future wife, Thalia. She asked me what I liked to be called. I replied, "Richard." From that moment on, I discouraged the use of my nickname. Very few old friends call me Dick anymore. Anybody else who attempts to address me by a shortened form is promptly, and I hope gently, corrected. I also answer to rbs.

Early in my college years, as I became a professional organist, friends pointed out that Richard Smith or Richard B. Smith were entirely too common for a public person. After some wordplay with possibilities like R. Birney Smith (too much like E. Power Biggs, the well-known English-born American organist), we decided to use my full name: Richard Birney Smith. I made this change in 1960 or 1961 and it remained so until 1978. The college chaplain bluntly told me that using my full name was "ostentatious", but we ignored him.

When I arrived in Canada in 1965, I found that the telephone directory, newspapers, and others frequently reduced me to R.B. Smith. That was even more anonymous than Richard Smith. Despite meeting some resistance, I insisted that my name not be abbreviated.

AFTER I MOVED to Dundas in 1967, I discovered that many people of British background assumed that my surname was Birney Smith. This did not bother me, and I seldom corrected them. In 1978, while working as interim music director at the Church of the Holy Saviour in Waterloo, Ontario, people naturally hyphenated my middle and last name together. I then decided to adopt Richard Birney-Smith for professional purposes.

It is perhaps the world's simplest stage name. It is much simpler than the complete name changes adopted by people like Cary Grant, Engelbert Humperdinck, or Tom Jones. A friend and colleague in the '70s and '80s was Allen Stewart-Coates. He had, I believe, the second-simplest stage name. Born Allen Coates Stewart, he was not allowed to use his birth name when he joined ACTRA (the Association of Canadian Television and Radio Actors) because someone was already registered as Allen Stewart. He then reversed his middle and last names to become Allen Stewart-Coates.

Richard Birney-Smith is now my professional name as well as in life. It is on my passport, health card, and tax returns. Only my driver's licence continues with my birth name because the Ontario Department of Transport will not allow the hyphen unless I spend hundreds of dollars for a legal name change.

My daughters' names, Noëlle Lumsden-Smith and Monique

Lumsden-Smith, combined Thalia's surname with mine. Neither the Province of Saskatchewan in 1966 nor the Province of Ontario in 1969 would allow the hyphen. The law at the time stated that a legitimate child had to carry his or her father's surname. This has since been relaxed. I regret that neither daughter uses Lumsden as her middle name.

MY NAME USAGE occasionally causes moments of humour. I once introduced my brother Birney to a friend who looked very puzzled. "Birney Birney-Smith?" he asked.

-2-

Dad

My father was Birney Walker Smith Jr. He was born in Detroit, Michigan, on 21 November 1912, the second child and second son of Birney Walker Smith and Ruth Elizabeth Jordan. On both sides of my family, it is common for the second son to be his father's namesake.

Dad's father was an Episcopalian (Anglican); his mother was Roman Catholic. In those days, couples of mixed denominations had to sign a document promising to raise all children as Roman Catholics. Such children were often called dotted-line babies. At least, that's what my dad called himself.

Dad and his elder brother, Carter Talbert Smith, were raised as Roman Catholics. Their sister, Ina Jane Smith, was twelve years younger than Dad. Ina's daughter tells me that her mother attended a Roman Catholic boarding school but remained Anglican. She could nevertheless pray the Rosary: not uncommon among Anglo-Catholics.[1]

Dad was a devout child who early on became an altar boy and discovered a vocation to the priesthood. Fortunately for my siblings and me, he left the Roman Catholic Church at thirteen to become an Anglo-Catholic. He was later significantly influenced by Father Irwin C. Johnson, who in 1934 became Rector of St. John's Episcopal Church on Woodward Avenue in Detroit. St. John's is less than two miles from the former location (at the corner of St. Antoine and Elizabeth Streets) of old St. Matthew's, the parish church of both of my grandfathers. St. John's was a white parish; St. Matthew's was black.

[1] Thank you Ruth Ezell for sharing your mother's religious upbringing.

It is essential to know that racial separation was the norm in those times. In the southern USA, blacks and whites were segregated by law (*de jure*). In the northern USA, where my parents grew up, separation was a fact of life (*de facto*) enforced by custom. There were black neighbourhoods as well as Polish, Italian, Jewish and other neighbourhoods. There were black schools, black churches, and black businesses.

It is easy for us in the 21st century to overstate, understate, or misunderstand why things were as they were in the early-to-mid-20th century United States. In addition to intentional racial and ethnic separation, churches of the same denomination might be separated by short distances because of class, or because when the buildings were erected, people got around on foot, horseback, or by horse and buggy. What I or anyone else might have experienced in the forties resulted from many forces at play since the 19th century. But I digress.

Uncle Carter wanted to attend Albion College in Albion, Michigan. Grandpa could not afford the tuition there. The Great Depression may have caused this problem, or it is possible that Albion, a private college, was simply too expensive for the family budget. Uncle Carter, a very strong-willed individual, refused to attend anywhere else. He nevertheless had a long and successful career with the Ford Motor Company, eventually rising to the level of foreman at the River Rouge plant. He instilled his college dream in his daughter Ruth Ellen who graduated from Albion in 1959 with a Bachelor of Arts in music.

My dad was more practical and accepted admission to a Negro school, St. Augustine's College in Raleigh, North Carolina. I believe that it took him five years to work his way through. He graduated in 1936 with a Bachelor of Arts degree. He majored in English, a choice that shaped both of us.

He could not afford seminary in 1936, the middle of the depression, so he took a job at the Ford Motor Company. Dad became attracted to my mother around this time. He had possibly known her for some time as they were both members of St. Matthew's Church. Mother was seven years younger than he and would not likely have attracted his attention until after he returned from college.

Dad told me about being laid off at Ford. The personnel manager told him he had to choose between laying off two good men. One was already married; Dad was only engaged, so he got the axe.

My parents postponed their wedding until Dad could find suitable employment. He eventually went to work in a government employment office. They married on 20 April 1938, her nineteenth birthday.

The United States entered the Second World War in December 1941. Dad was 29 years old and of no interest to the draft board. He enrolled in Seabury-Western Theological Seminary in Evanston, Illinois, in the fall of 1943. Soon after he arrived, Dad was visited by the FBI (or similar agency) because a townsperson saw him and thought he might be Japanese. It was a short visit when they discovered that he was an American Negro rather than a Japanese American.

He was assigned a tiny room for his first year in seminary. Two second-year students across the hall, Joseph Turnbull and Roger J. Bunday, both from Minnesota and younger than he was, had a suite and felt that Dad was being relegated to a closet because he was Negro. They therefore invited Dad to use their common room for study whenever he desired. Thus began a lifelong friendship among the three men.

Mother and I visited Seabury, as it was familiarly called, sometime in 1943 or 1944. Children were usually prohibited from addressing adults by their first names in the forties and earlier. These two men, therefore, became Uncle Joe and Uncle Jack to me. I continued to address them as such until sometime after their eightieth birthdays. Only then did I begin calling them by their first names.

I know little of Dad's seminary experience, yet many influences that occurred there indelibly shaped him. He frequently mentioned B.I. Bell, Bernard Iddings Bell, who taught theology there. I remember him visiting our home on at least one occasion when I was less than ten years old. Dad also became and remained a friend of the seminary dean whose name, I believe, was Kennedy.

The music of the seminary chapel was another seminal influence. Dad was a fine musician. Although he struggled unsuccessfully to master the piano, he had a very true yet unpretentious voice. He sang simply, in tune and in rhythm, values that I try to instill in my choristers more than seventy years later. I have never heard a priest chant the Eucharist, daily offices, or any other priestly music, better than Dad, and very few are his equal.

Dr. Thomas Matthews directed chapel music. He was also the organist-choirmaster at St. Luke's Church in Evanston and a music professor at Northwestern University. Dr. Matthews instilled in Dad a love for plainchant (also called plainsong or Gregorian chant) that Dad passed on to me. Dad taught me the principles of plainchant and Anglican chant just as thoroughly as he taught me various roles near the altar: acolyte, server, and thurifer. I mostly learned these things from him between the ages of six and thirteen. Learning, however, never stops.

War rationing was in place during Dad's seminary years. Seminarians were allowed only one teaspoon of sugar at breakfast. He therefore learned to drink black coffee, put salt on his grapefruit, and save the sugar ration for his cereal. I still occasionally put salt on grapefruit because I like it and it reminds me of him.

There was a clergy shortage during the war, as many were serving as military chaplains. Dad was therefore ordained deacon a year earlier than usual, after completing only two years of seminary.

He served the Church of St. Mary the Virgin in Keokuk, Iowa, during his third year. Mother quit her job in Detroit, and we all moved to Keokuk in the summer of 1945. We lived in a ten or twelve-room home rented for us by the church. One entered the dirt-floored basement from an exterior stairway. Coal-fired furnaces were the norm in those days. Finished basements did not become common until after oil or gas heating became the norm. The rent was $25 per month, a very high figure for Keokuk in those days. In the fall, seminary classes resumed and Dad commuted between Chicago and Keokuk. Dad took an overnight train from Chicago each Friday evening and returned by overnight train on Sunday. I remember well riding in our 1936 Chevrolet coupe to the train station, which overlooked a dam on the Mississippi River, each Saturday morning and Sunday evening.

St. Mary's was a black congregation. As I was only four years old, I never questioned how a deacon could lead a congregation. Did the priest from the white congregation across town periodically come to St.

Mary's to celebrate mass, or did Dad periodically receive a supply of consecrated elements or both? It is too late now to learn such details.

I have only a few memories of the church. I sat next to Mother. Once, when Dad was instructing the congregation on the importance of offering envelopes, I waved ours over my head. I didn't understand why everyone laughed or why Mother was embarrassed. Every hymn had two numbers, one from the old hymnal and one from the new. *The Hymnal 1940* was so named because General Convention approved the words that year. It took a couple more years to edit and publish it with music. I suspect the Church of St. Mary the Virgin could not afford to buy a full set of new books and had to make do with a mixture of editions. I also remember that the church had a pump organ and an outhouse.

MY SISTER, MARRIS JANE SMITH, was born on 24 May 1946. Dad soon came home to be with us and missed his final exams. The seminary gave him a Licentiate in Divinity, rather than a Bachelor of Divinity, in recognition of the fact that he had successfully passed his courses. He passed his canonical exams in the Diocese of Michigan and was ordained priest on 23 June 1946.

Dad's sister Ina was engaged to Dr. William Ezell. Grandpa and Grandma Smith were planning a substantial wedding for their only daughter[2], and Dad was expected to officiate. Sadly, Grandma died. She had been in ill-health for years. Aunt Ina was devastated by her mother's death and the wedding plans were cancelled. Dad's first service as a priest was to preside at his mother's funeral. His first act as a pastor was

[2] Thank you Wayman Ezell for filling me in on your parents' wedding plans and other details of the summer of 1946.

to persuade Aunt Ina and Uncle Bill that Grandma would not have wanted them to postpone their wedding. Shortly thereafter, they took a bus from Detroit to Keokuk and were married at the Church of St. Mary the Virgin on 15 July 1946, with Dad presiding. I was the acolyte. If my memory serves me right, my mother was matron of honour and the best man was a parishioner and good friend named William Boyd. Uncle Bill and Aunt Ina moved to Alabama that fall where he became Chair of the Department of Physiology and Pharmacology at the new School of Veterinary Science at Tuskegee Institute.

Dad spent the summer of 1946 with us in Keokuk. I was told that the landlord wanted his house back and that the church could find no other affordable accommodation. I find this much-too-simple explanation hard to believe now. So we moved to Dayton, Ohio, in the early fall of 1946. Dad became Vicar of St. Margaret's Church there and remained until February 1949. I remember two 1948 services in particular: Grandpa Smith married Marjorie Bell from Windsor or Chatham, Ontario (not sure which) and I was confirmed by Bishop Henry Hobson.

DAD BECAME VICAR of St. Andrew's Church, Evanston, Illinois, in February 1949. He had been superintendent of the Sunday School at St. Andrew's during seminary and was called back as their priest when a vacancy occurred. Within a year he raised St. Andrew's from mission to parish status and was appointed its first rector. In September of 1955, Dad was a clerical deputy from the Diocese of Chicago to the General Convention of the Episcopal Church which took place in Honolulu. He was somehow able to scrape together the funds (probably with help from parishioners and other friends) to take Mother along for a vacation. They flew both ways, as the ships sailing from California were beyond their means.

Dad was very dedicated to his priestly vocation. I cannot from this distance say whether or not he might now be termed a workaholic. That word, according to Merriam-Webster, was first used in 1947 and was quite unknown to us in the early fifties. Dr. Bryant, our family doctor in our early years in Evanston, was a private pilot and small aircraft owner. He felt that Dad worked too hard and needed a hobby, so he persuaded Dad to take up flying, paid for flying lessons, and gave him the use of his plane (a side-by-side two-seat Luscombe). Dad's only expense was gasoline.

Soon after earning his pilot's licence, Dad was invited to be Squadron Chaplain, with the rank of Captain, in the Civil Air Patrol, an auxiliary of the United States Air Force. Dad was the only flying chaplain in the entire U.S. military, and within a year, was promoted to Group Chaplain with the rank of Major.

IN THE SPRING of 1956, Dad was appointed rector of St. Augustine's Church, Kansas City, Missouri. He remained there until 1965. St. Augustine's (pronounced AWE-gus-teen) was named after the Bishop of Hippo, author of *Confessions* and *City of God*. Augustine of Hippo is not to be confused with St. Augustine (a-GUS-tin) of Canterbury. Black congregations sometimes took the names of North African saints in the belief that they were black. You will, therefore, find numerous churches named St. Cyprian, St. Augustine, and St. Monica.

Whether or not these individuals were black, white, or tan is of no interest to me.

Dad's major accomplishment while in Kansas City was leading the congregation to build a new church. They had been using a mansion at 2732 Benton Blvd. as church, office, and parish hall for some years. They owned an adjacent vacant property and were ready to take the next step. One of the major parish fundraising projects was an annual fish fry. The parish commissioned a frying pan, six feet in diameter, that was advertised as the world's largest. A wood or charcoal fire was built each summer in a cinderblock pit on the site of the yet-to-be-built church and people came from miles around for a dinner of catfish or buffalo fish, potato salad, soft drinks and desserts. Ground was broken for the new church in 1960. It was dedicated in March of 1962.[3]

My parents separated and divorced in 1965. As the Bishop of West Missouri would not allow divorced or remarried priests in his diocese, Dad had to move. At the time, he was also a representative for Province 7 on the National Council of the Episcopal Church. Not wanting to lose his seat on the council, his choices were seriously limited by geography. He accepted a two-point parish in Galveston and La Marque, Texas.

After serving two years in Texas and completing his term on National Council, he accepted a position as Associate Rector of St. Thomas Church in Philadelphia. St. Thomas, established in 1792, is the oldest black congregation in the Episcopal Church in the USA. Its proud history includes the Rev. Absalom Jones, the first black American Episcopal priest.

[3] https://spirit.diowestmo.org/2021/12/st-augustines-unusual-round-design-dates-back-to-the-4th-century/

IN 1969, DONALD WOODWARD, Vicar of Trinity Church, Wall Street, invited Dad to join the staff of this historic parish in downtown Manhattan. Father Woodward (pronounced WOOD-ard) had been Dean of Grace and Holy Trinity Cathedral in Kansas City during our time there. Dad had the best days of his professional life at Trinity Church. He was a strong liturgical leader and an excellent pastor but administration was not Dad's strength. At Trinity, he could be a full-time priest and pastor. My esteemed colleague, the late Larry King, Director of Music at Trinity Church, said that Dad was pastor to the staff. This was not part of his job description: it just happened naturally. On visits to Trinity Church after Dad's retirement in 1976, Larry and others told me no one ever again filled Dad's shoes as pastor to the staff. He was truly missed. My most recent visit to Trinity Church was in 2012. Even then, I encountered a parishioner who remembered Dad with great affection.

I remember going out with Dad for lunch at a neighbourhood hamburger joint on Church Street behind Trinity. While we were eating, the cook came over to our table to share a personal relationship problem and seek Dad's advice. This moment was, for me, more deeply touching than any other in witnessing my father's professional life over four decades.

DAD WAS GODFATHER to Kurt Carter, son of Lieutenant Colonel Herbert Eugene Carter, a former parishioner from St. Augustine's in Kansas City. Gene Carter was one of the famed Tuskegee Airmen from World War Two. After retirement from the Air Force, he returned with his wife and family to accept an administrative position at Tuskegee University.

One summer in the early 1970s, Dad visited the Carters. While attending a social function with them, he noticed an attractive lady. He asked Colonel Carter about her and discovered that she was a widow. Dad asked to be introduced. Ada Peters was chair of the English Department at Tuskegee. Her late husband, Dr. Jerome Peters, had been head of Radiology at the local Veterans Administration Hospital. The introduction led to friendship, romance, and eventually marriage on 27 December 1974, which was my paternal grandfather's 90th birthday. After several months of long-distance marriage, taking turns flying back and forth between Tuskegee and New York City, Ada retired and moved during the summer of 1975 so they could be together in New York City. After Dad's retirement in 1976[4], they moved back to Tuskegee where they lived very happily.

Dad was a survivor of the 1930s economic depression. It informed his frugality for the rest of his life. Even as long-distance phone calls gradually became less expensive in the early 1960s, Dad always regarded them as a luxury for use only in emergencies. One of the most touching moments of my personal life was to receive a congratulatory long-distance phone call from Dad in Tuskegee after I received my doctorate from McMaster University in 1992.

When they needed a car, Dad and Ada started looking at

[4] Trinity Church, second only to the Vatican in wealth, owned a great deal of property. 1976 was a recession year, and many rental properties were vacant. Trinity Church did some budget trimming and Dad was asked to retire a year earlier than planned. He was terribly disappointed that he would not meet Queen Elizabeth during her bicentennial visit to Trinity Church.

Volkswagens. This did not last long before Ada marched him across the street to buy a Mercedes. I find this story hilarious, but I know that Dad was always quietly embarrassed to be seen driving such an expensive vehicle.

Dad's health started to fail in 1993 or 1994. Ada was his primary caregiver until her sudden and unexpected death in September 1995. Her substantial estate, administered by Gene Carter, provided full-time home care for my father until his death. Noëlle and I flew to Atlanta, were picked up by my brother, attended Ada's requiem and had a lovely final visit with Dad. By then, he was unable to walk unassisted and had severe memory loss. He was, however, able to attend Ada's requiem in a wheelchair. He died on 19 December that same year.

Dad and Ada donated their bodies to the University of Alabama in Montgomery for up to one year of medical research. Their remains were cremated and interred in unmarked graves near the medical school.

My father believed that the sacramental aspects of a requiem mass were important, but that travelling a great distance to attend someone's funeral was a waste of money. He instructed me not to attend his funeral. I told him that this was my decision, not his. He also did not want people to miss work to attend his service. He instructed that his requiem mass be celebrated on a Saturday. The first Saturday after his death was two days before Christmas. His requiem was postponed until 30 December. My brother was able to attend, but Sunday morning duties at St. Peter's Church in Toronto, where I was interim director of music, prevented me from going. In the end, Dad got his wish.

The Bishop of Alabama presided at Dad's requiem at St. Andrew's Church in Tuskegee. Brother Birney told me that the Bishop began his homily as follows: "Father Birney instructed that there be no eulogy. This is *not* a eulogy."

Noëlle and I drove to Tuskegee a few days later to meet with my brother and Gene Carter to begin dealing with Dad's personal effects.

3

Mother

My mother was Jetawyn Barbara Solomon. She was born in Detroit on 20 April 1919, the third child and second daughter of Harry Ordorthel Solomon and Pansy Enola Jones.[1] Their first child, a daughter named Harrizetta, lived but two years and predeceased my mother and her siblings.

Mother told me that her father found her first name in a book. I have never identified that book nor met anyone else named Jetawyn. A Google search reveals that there are few other Jetawyns in the world. The search entry continues: "Your first name of Jetawyn gives you a responsible, self-sufficient, and dependable nature. If you have been given the opportunity, you could do well in business developing your leadership, administrative, and managing abilities. Appreciating quality in all things, you desire to be prosperous. You do not like to relinquish control nor do you accept advice readily."[2] I think that describes my mother pretty well, except perhaps, "you desire to be prosperous." Mother was very frugal and knew how to make the most of what she had. She was happy with enough and, as far as I know, never wanted more than her fair share.

[1] It seems that Grandpa Solomon was named Harry as a child but later adopted Harrison.

[2] https://www.kabalarians.com/name-meaning/names/f/Jetawyn.htm I do not know anything about Kabalarian Philosophy. A Wiktionary entry defines a Kabalarian as "A member of Canadian organisation that advocates changing one's name to improve its numerological value and achieve spiritual balance." My grandfather chose Mother's name because he liked it. I am reasonably sure that his reasons were no more complicated than that.

My mother and her siblings grew up at 4663 McDougall Street in Detroit. The neighbourhood may have been mixed African-American and Polish, or the two communities may have lived close enough to share the same schools. Mother's high school graduation certificate is dated 25 June 1937. I vaguely remember visiting my grandparents' home on McDougall before Grandpa bought a building with four apartments on East Philadelphia Street and downsized into one of them. Grandpa's business remained behind the former family home until he retired.

The Solomon family attended St. Matthew's Episcopal Church on St. Antoine Street. The parish continues, via merger, as St. Matthew's and St. Joseph's Episcopal Church at 8850 Woodward Avenue. The old church location is now beneath a freeway. Throughout my childhood, Mother frequently mentioned the parish priest of her childhood, Father Daniel, with great respect.[3] She always called him Father Daniels, an unimportant but curious detail.

Mother and Dad married in old St. Matthew's on her 19th birthday, 20 April 1938. She later regretted getting married on that day because she felt that the two events mutually diminished each other.

By the time of my earliest memories, Dad was already in seminary in Evanston, Illinois. We were in the middle, at least from an American perspective, of World War II, and my mother worked full-time as a turret lathe operator in an aircraft factory. She worked there until we moved away from Detroit in mid-1945. When my brother shares the story of Mother's wartime employment, many express surprise or

---

[3] Everard W. Daniel was Rector of St. Matthew's from 1921 until 1939. Source: *St. Matthew's and St. Joseph's Episcopal Church (Detroit, Mich.) Records*, Bentley Historical Library, University of Michigan.
https://quod.lib.umich.edu/b/bhlead/umich-bhl-89513?view=text

disbelief that a woman could operate such a piece of machinery.

Mother and I lived in a row housing project with Mrs. Benson and her adult daughter, Jessie. Mrs. Benson was familiarly addressed as Benny. She was my daycare provider. Jessie worked full-time, perhaps in the same factory as Mother. I remember only one friend, a cousin called Pinky, Richard Carlyle Johnson III. I was named after his grandfather, Richard Carlyle Johnson, my mother's Uncle Richard. Uncle Richard's wife was my late maternal grandmother Pansy's sister, Viva (pronounced VIGH-va). I remember that she had suffered a stroke and lived in an assisted care facility. I cannot recall whether the stroke occurred while we lived in Detroit or later. Aunt Viva was important to Mother and every time we returned to Detroit we visited her until her death when I was about ten.

OUR FAMILY MOVED to Keokuk, Iowa, in the summer of 1945. Dad returned to seminary that fall, and we only saw him on weekends until the end of the 1945-46 academic year. Mother and I lived in a large ten-or-twelve-room, rented house. She was now a full-time homemaker and mother.

A congregation member got sick and died during our year in Keokuk. When this was explained to me, I commented that I hoped never to die. Mother very patiently explained to me that everyone dies. She must have done a great job because I have never feared death. I would, of course, like the journey there to be quick and painless, but that is an adult observation.

Mother spent at least three days in hospital when my sister Marris Jane Smith was born on 24 May 1944. Mother's sister, DeMarris

Solomon, familiarly known as Aunt Sis, came several days in advance to care for me. She was fun. In those days, a five-year-old child was not allowed to visit a hospital patient. I sat in a waiting room while Aunt Sis visited Mother and the new baby. Mother chose a shortened form of her sister's first and my dad's sister's middle name for my sister. As a child, Marris was called Sissie. She grew out of the nickname before she entered school.

Dad came home to be with us after Marris' birth and, as a result, missed his seminary final exams.[4]

WE MOVED TO Dayton, Ohio, in the fall of 1946.

Mother loved the sight of water. It didn't matter whether it was a river or a lake. It's a shame we never lived near a coast; she would have adored the ocean. Dayton frustrated her as it had neither river nor lake. There was a pond (perhaps related to water treatment) somewhere in town around which we would occasionally drive. The municipal water came from artesian wells and was as hard as nails. We eventually installed a commercial water softener but it only treated the hot water. We therefore chilled pitchers of treated water in the refrigerator for drinking.

The central event of our three years in Dayton was the birth of my brother. Birney Walker Smith III arrived on 16 March 1948. Mother had an awkward fall down the stairs during the latter stages of pregnancy but, other than that, his arrival was without incident. No one missed exams this time. Birney was the last of three children as Mother was warned by her doctor not to have any more children because she tore rather than stretched during childbirth.

[4] See Chapter 2: "Dad"

WE MOVED TO Evanston, Illinois, in February 1949. We lived with parishioners Bill and Edna Morrison for the first few weeks while the congregation finished renovating the rectory for us. I entered Foster School on Valentine's Day. The teacher took me aside to explain why I had no Valentine's cards. She was being kind, but I was insulted. Did she think that I was too stupid to understand the situation?

Once my brother entered grade one in the fall of 1953, Mother began working part-time as a school crossing guard less than a block from home. In Evanston, crossing guards had no authority to stop traffic, but they provided a margin of safety, escorting children across busy intersections.

Dad was embarrassed by Mother working. It implied, in his mind, that he could not support his family. Taking this job perhaps made her an early feminist, a word that had not yet entered the popular vocabulary.

WHEN WE MOVED to Kansas City in 1956, Mother soon found a job working behind the counter in a short-order restaurant. Kansas City was only beginning the process of desegregation. It was entirely voluntary, except for the schools. My mother had very fair skin and could easily pass for white. Passing was, however, beneath her dignity. The restaurant manager happily hired her but asked her not to advertise her race. His strategy was when in future he hired someone with a darker complexion, he would be able to say, "Why is this person a problem? You've been working with Jetty for a long time." Mother soon found a better job at the head office of Hallmark Cards, where she enjoyed working for many years.

Meanwhile, she was growing increasingly unhappy with Dad. This process began in Evanston, maybe even Dayton, and progressed slowly over many years. Eventually, she fixed on the idea that she would leave him when her youngest child graduated high school. True to her word, she filed for divorce in 1965. Dad did not understand why and refused to cooperate. She subsequently managed to find grounds under Missouri law to avoid a messy trial. She left Kansas City for Chicago in the late summer of 1965.

MOTHER MARRIED JOHN CHUR in a civil ceremony in Illinois en route to Chicago. I don't know long they had known each other. He was a widower and related to her friend June Booker who lived outside Kansas City in Lee's Summit, Missouri. The marriage came as a complete surprise to us, but it seemed to be a match made in heaven. John was nineteen years older than Mother. In fact, he had a daughter who was a few months older than she was. Thalia and I had moved to Saskatoon, Saskatchewan, Canada, in 1965. Letter writing was occasional at best.

Mother soon found a job at the head office of Northern Trust Company in downtown Chicago. There, she delivered mail and other messages from office to office. It was an active job that involved a lot of walking. She particularly enjoyed hobnobbing with some of the bank's officers.

She continued to work after John retired. Thalia and I visited them in Chicago in the spring of 1968. I remember him as a quiet, gentle man who was an enthusiastic Oscar Peterson fan. Sadly, John died in October of that same year during an afternoon nap while Mother was at work.

He was just a month shy of his sixty-ninth birthday. He was buried next to his late wife in Oak Park, Illinois. In many ways, Mother never recovered from his death, and over the years he became more and more perfect in her memory.

The next thirty years of Mother's life were not very pretty. She had battled bipolar disorder for many years, perhaps even since our time in Kansas City. She struggled to make ends meet and, after her retirement, sold the house she had inherited from John.

Despite her struggles, Mother seemed unfailingly cheerful and had numerous friends wherever she lived. This observation is probably overly optimistic because Thalia and I and our daughters only saw her when she was not depressed. When she was, she withdrew into her apartment and was silent. Unknown to us, she also spent money extravagantly when she was manic. She sometimes spent hundreds of dollars on long-distance phone calls, often in the wee hours of the morning. Eventually, she had all toll calling removed from her telephone service.

Mother spent her last years in a senior citizens home on the north side of Chicago. My brother called it a warehouse. We were saddened, even a little ashamed, that neither of us had the resources to help her afford a better place to live.

Mother died in hospital of lung cancer and pneumonia on 30 June 1998. The doctors could treat one or the other but not both simultaneously. My brother and I each drove to Chicago to be with her in her final days. She was comatose by the time we arrived. We could talk to her. She might have heard and understood us, but could not respond. We tried to take turns, staying with her through her final days and nights. After consultation with a medical ethicist, we decided to withdraw treatment. She was hydrated and given morphine for pain but nothing else. Her parish priest came to the hospital and gave her holy unction about thirty-six hours before she died. We celebrated her requiem eucharist in the chapel of the Church of St. Paul and the Redeemer on 2 July. The congregation included my brother and me, Uncle Bruz and Aunt Blanche, John's daughter Harriet and Vera Swan, a friend from Gary, Indiana. We interred Mother's ashes in the same grave as her beloved John, just above his chest.

4

My Parents

Looking back, I am unsure how to sum up my relationship with my father. I suspect many children have a similar uncertainty. Dad only came into my life after he graduated from seminary. My first real experience, other than a few early anecdotes, was to have him usurp my position as man of the house. I was accustomed to answering the phone when it rang; now he did. His return, of course, also changed my relationship with my mother. From then until I graduated from high school, my relationship with Dad was more priest and acolyte or priest and organist than father and son. There was a father-son relationship, but our church relationship overshadowed it. I even called him Father for many years before I switched to Dad somewhere in my pre-teen or early teen years.

Perhaps because of that peculiarity, some of my most precious memories are personal. The two of us going on vacation to Brighton, Michigan, in 1949 or 1950 to spend time with Uncle Carter (Dad's brother), Aunt Billie, and my cousins, Ruth Ellen and Bryan; Dad trying to teach me to swim in Lyons Lake in Brighton Gardens; our going to Wrigley Field for a Memorial Day doubleheader between the Chicago Cubs and the St. Louis Cardinals.[1] We later attended numerous White Sox games at Comiskey Park (only a small consolation to me, a diehard Cubs fan). I still remember the scent of the nearby stockyards.

[1] Unfortunately, it rained somewhere after the mid-fifth inning. The Cubs officially won, but I only saw half a game rather than two complete games. I saw Stan Musial, Red Schoendienst, Ralph Kiner, and Hank Sauer in the same game. I don't remember if Ernie Banks was there. If so, he was a recent addition to the Cubs lineup and had

Another significant memory is flying with Dad. I was his first passenger after he got his private pilot's licence.

I can't recall how often I rode with him in Dr. Bryant's Luscombe, but it probably exceeded a dozen outings. A couple of times while on vacation in Detroit, he also took me for a ride in Neil Loving's Piper Cub. He even invited me to handle the stick during one takeoff. I never landed the aircraft — that required more skill.

Dad was supportive and encouraging while I was growing up, albeit a stern taskmaster at times. He encouraged academic excellence and always attended my concerts and athletic events. In short, he was always there for me.

My relationship with my mother was just as complicated. When in therapy after my divorce from Thalia, my psychiatrist stated that I was also my mother's surrogate husband. I was with Mother when Dad was at seminary. I was the one she talked to when Dad was busy at church. In my pre-teen and teen years, she often poured out her frustrations and disappointments about her relationship with him. She tried hard to prepare me to be a better husband and father than he was. As I grew closer to my dad in adulthood, I became a little less close to her.

Mother was always very supportive. She wanted me to grow up to be "clean and honest". Some people have criticized "clean and honest" but she never intended this to be limiting or judgemental. One could always bathe or shower after work if one had a dirty job. There was never any maternal pressure to become this profession or that. Her music was Nat King Cole and Harry Belafonte, and even though

not yet reached superstar status. Dad and I never returned to Wrigley Field because the Cubs only played day games, and he would not take time off work. I did not return again to Wrigley Field until I was a married adult.

classical music and jazz didn't speak to her, she always encouraged me. When I wanted to quit music lessons, Mother suggested I continue for another six months before we discuss the idea once more. The thought of leaving music never again crossed my mind.

When Thalia and I were ready to buy our first house, Mother lent us half the down payment. She, like Dad, was always there for me.

Relationships between parent and child are unique to each pairing, and judging from my conversations with other people, always seem complex to those involved. I have learned that many people think they come from dysfunctional families. Mine is no different in that respect. I do believe that, on balance, I was blessed to have parents who encouraged, supported, and loved my siblings and me.

5

My Paternal Grandparents

My grandfather Birney Walker Smith was born on 27 December 1884, in Bay City, Michigan. His parents were William James Smith (1857-1937) and Mary Elizabeth Carter (1860-1885). Grandpa told me that "Grandma Carter", presumably his mother's mother, was Scots-Irish. His grandmother's origin may partially account for the relatively light complexions of my Smith relatives.

My brother, Birney Walker Smith III, was a voracious reader of the *World Book Encyclopedia* as a child. He concluded that Grandpa Smith was named after James Gillespie Birney (1792-1857), Bay City abolitionist and twice unsuccessful Presidential candidate (1840 and 1844) for the anti-slavery Liberal Party. James G. Birney was later one of the founders of the Republican Party.[1] From party foundation until the time of Theodore Roosevelt, Republicans were more liberal than Democrats. My brother reported Grandpa's naming so convincingly that I believed it as fact for many years, we however have no documents to support his supposition. We know of few families other than ours in which Birney, a surname with a long lineage, is used as a given name. I am long-distance friends with five descendants of James Gillespie Birney who find our story credible, and accept me as an honorary cousin.

I have always believed that my paternal grandmother, Ruth Elizabeth Jordan, was born in Buffalo, New York, but the Ancestry website led me to a Chicago birth certificate dated 2 March 1888.

[1] https://en.wikipedia.org/wiki/James_G._Birney ; also D. Laurence Rogers: *Apostles of Equality – The Birneys, the Republicans, and the Civil War* © 2011 Michigan State University Press, East Lansing.

Grandpa and Grandma married in 1910 in the parlours of St. Nicholas Roman Catholic Church, in or near Buffalo, New York. The reception followed in her parents' home at 11 Elsie Place in Buffalo. My grandparents had three children: Carter Talbert (1911-1982), Birney Walker Jr (1912-1995), and Ina Jane (1925-2013). Familiarly: Uncle Carter, Dad, and Aunt Ina.

Grandpa Smith's elder brother, William Carter Smith (1883-1948) was the first African-American to graduate from Detroit City Law School, now part of Wayne State University. My dad called him Uncle Willie. I attended his funeral but do not remember ever meeting him.

Grandpa Smith was an active layman and church volunteer all his life. The family parish was St. Matthew's Episcopal Church on St. Antoine Street in downtown Detroit. I have recently learned from Cousin Wayman Ezell that Grandpa was not only a volunteer, "he was on staff as the church's business manager for decades, monitoring budgets and paying all of the bills."[2] The church building, long ago demolished, was where my parents met and married and where I was baptized in March of 1941. I like to think that my baptism was on the 6th of March, the Feast of St. Richard of Chichester. That is however unlikely because the 6th of March was a Thursday in 1941 and baptisms usually occurred on Sundays.

Grandpa worked as a juvenile court probation officer in Detroit for most of his career. He had been a letter carrier before that. My dad said that Grandpa told him that the only difference between his two sons and the offenders in juvenile court was that he and Uncle Carter never got caught. Grandpa was also a real estate agent. He lived and worked in

[2] Personal email of 26 August 2013.

Detroit but also assembled a large tract of land between Lyons Lake and the old US-23 highway in or near Brighton, Michigan. He created Brighton Gardens from this land, a subdivision where black people could own property and build community. After retirement in the early 1950s, Grandpa moved to Brighton Gardens for the rest of his life. There he became a member of St. Paul's Episcopal Church. He would still drive forty miles to Detroit and back every Monday morning to help count the offering at St. Matthew's. In 1960, he was given a silver cross by Bishop Richard Emrich for distinguished volunteer service. When Grandpa died in 1976, my dad inherited the cross. When Dad died, I inherited it, and wear it almost every day.

Grandpa was, in 1916, a charter member of the Urban League of Detroit. He outlived all the other charter members. He served with the Selective Service System during World War Two and received the Selective Service Medal from U.S. President Harry S. Truman — a noteworthy accomplishment at that time for a person of colour.

One of the fascinating sidebars of Grandpa's life was that he was in demand as the announcer at the head of receiving lines for high society events. His role was to take the calling card of each guest in turn and introduce them to the first person in the receiving line. He seldom needed the cards after doing this work for decades because he knew the people by name. Even after he retired, he was called back by the family of Henry Ford II for Charlotte Ford's lavish 1,000-guest debutante party on December 21st 1959 at the Country Club of Detroit in Grosse Pointe. His name and photo appeared in both Life and Time magazines on this occasion. We were so proud to see his picture there. His popularity with the social elite was such that this was not the last time they called him out of retirement.

I have only the vaguest recollection of Grandma Smith. She was bedridden with sleeping sickness in the last years of her life[3], and I never saw her except in bed. She died on 20 June 1946 when I was only five. My dad was ordained priest on 24 June 1946 and his first service as a priest was his mother's funeral. As my mother had just given birth to my sister on May 24th, she and I remained behind in Iowa while my dad went to Detroit for ordination.

In 1948, Grandpa married Marjorie Edith Ball (1907-2003) of Windsor, Ontario. My dad officiated at the marriage service in St. Margaret's Church, Dayton, Ohio, where he was vicar. The local press enjoyed the occasion, publishing a photo with a caption noting that the priest and acolyte were the son and grandson of the groom. The only part of the occasion I remember was Grandpa fiddling to unwrap the ring. He had securely wrapped it in a small box with cellophane tape, and it took forever to unwrap before handing the ring to Dad for blessing. We will never know why Grandpa had not given the ring to the best man, as is customary.

Marjorie was twenty-three years younger than Grandpa. Because she

---

[3] A college friend told me that sleeping sickness was impossible because my grandmother could not have been bitten by a Tsetse fly. I was gullible enough to believe him for over fifty years. My cousin Wayman Ezell, son of Aunt Ina (my father's younger and only sister) and Uncle Bill (a licensed Doctor of Veterinary Science) reports the following: "I remember Dad telling us that sleeping sickness can be asymptomatic for up to 30 years and can be maintained in animal reservoirs. I think he meant transmitted by animals as well. According to Mother, Grandma was infected before she [my mother] was born, yet recovered enough so that she could deliver Mom. That would make it before 1924. The main reason Mom was sent away to boarding school was "so she would not have to witness Grandma suffering so much.""

felt too young to be styled grandma, she asked us to call her "Aunt Marge". My siblings and cousins may have honoured her request, but I always called her Grandma and enjoyed her discomfort.

Grandpa was a proficient violinist. I have the impression that he played in dance orchestras. He also liked classical music and sometimes attended the Detroit Symphony. His love of music was likely sidetracked by Grandma Ruth's prolonged illness and Grandma Marge's lack of interest. He gave my daughter, Noëlle, his violin when she was a toddler. It was not a very good instrument, but I had hoped, at least, to keep it as a family heirloom. The century-old glue gave way early in the 21st century, and the violin came apart. It was not worth repairing.

Sometime in the early seventies, Thalia and I took Grandpa and Grandma Marge to *The Underground Railroad*, a soul food restaurant in Toronto. A waiter named Clarence approached the table as we studied the menu. He and Grandma recognized each other from Windsor, five or so decades earlier. Small world.

Grandpa still had salt-and-pepper hair when he died of prostate cancer in 1976 at 91. Thalia, Noëlle, Monique, and I went to Chicago to share the American Bicentennial Celebrations with my mother. I wanted my daughters to see the unique fireworks display at Dyche Stadium, so much a part of my childhood in Evanston. The 4th of July was on a Sunday that year. I played Sunday morning at St. James Church in Dundas before we headed toward the United States' border. We stayed overnight in a motel in Windsor, Ontario, and watched the televised Bicentennial Celebrations from Boston Common. The climax was a spectacular performance of Tchaikovsky's *1812 Overture* by the Boston Pops Orchestra, complete with multiple cannon, a carillon, and fireworks.

The Dyche Stadium fireworks display in Evanston was not until Monday evening, July 5th. My family, my mother, my sister and her son Christopher Rush Paulk, and perhaps others attended it together. In the late evening after returning from Evanston, we were all relaxing in Mother's backyard when my brother Birney arrived on compassionate leave from air force duty in Taiwan. He rode with us to visit Grandpa in Brighton Gardens on our way home. Grandpa was very sick, in a wheelchair, and barely aware of our presence.

Birney remained behind in the Detroit area when we returned home, staying with Aunt Ina and Uncle Bill. We received a call on Sunday morning from our cousin Ruth Ellen, Uncle Carter's daughter, to tell us that Grandpa had died overnight.

Thalia and I flew (between daily New Chamber Orchestra concerts in Toronto) to play Grandpa's requiem Eucharist at St. Paul's Episcopal Church, Brighton. Birney was a pallbearer. Dad and Ada flew in from Tuskegee. The little church was full to overflowing. I vividly remember the congregation's fervent singing of *O God, Our Help in Ages Past*. Grandpa is buried in Fairview Cemetery, Brighton, next to Grandma Ruth, who predeceased him by three decades.

UNCLE CARTER DIED unexpectedly but peacefully in July 1982. My brother Birney and his wife, Ying Hua, were visiting us in Dundas at the time. The four adults drove to Brighton for Carter's requiem in St. Paul's Church. The little church was once again packed. I played the organ. We stayed for the reception at Uncle Carter's house and were able to visit with numerous relatives, many of whom we barely knew.

Grandma Marge continued to live in the house in Brighton for at least two decades after Grandpa died, before returning to Detroit for the final years of her life. She died on 18 January 2003. She is buried in her family's plot in Ontario.

Rosie (my life partner after 2009) and I visited Aunt Ina in her home in August 2013 when we were in Detroit for Aunt Sis's requiem. Ina died on September 9th.

6

My Maternal Grandparents

Harrison Ordorthel Solomon, my maternal grandfather, was born on 15 October 1892 in Indianapolis, Indiana. I only learned of his birthplace from his funeral order of service. I previously believed he had been born in Chatham, Ontario. My brother even created a story that Grandpa Solomon's dad was the son of a Jewish plantation owner named Solomon and a female slave. According to my brother's supposition, the plantation owner/father helped Grandpa's father escape to Canada via the Underground Railroad.

The Canadian connection in my brother's story was nevertheless true. My great-grandfather, George H. Solomon, was born in Alexandria, Virginia, in 1848. George's sister, Virginia, was born in Chatham, Ontario, in 1865. Their father, my great-great-grandfather George Solomon, was born in Virginia in 1827 and died in Chatham in 1905.

I only recently learned that Grandpa was originally named Harry. He adopted Harrison later in life. His first son was named Harrison Ordorthel Solomon Jr. Uncle Harry's second son, Butch, was Harrison Ordorthel Solomon III. When Butch's older brother Bobby, Robert Harrison Solomon, told me things his father had said or done that irritated him, he would sarcastically refer to his dad as Ordorthel. ☺

GRANDPA MARRIED Pansy Enola Jones in 1913, likely at old St. Matthew's Church. Pansy was born in 1891, and her baptism at St. Matthew's is the earliest family parochial record I know of. Grandpa had previously been Baptist. They had five children: Harrizetta Enola (1914-

1917)[1], Harrison Ordorthel Jr (1917-1997), Jetawyn Barbara (1919-1998), twins DeMarr (1921-2021) and DeMarris (1921-2013). Familiarly: Uncle Harry, Mother, Uncle Bruz and Aunt Sis. Pansy was listed as a dancing teacher in the 1910 US Census, and one other thing I know about her is that, according to my mother, she hated being coloured.

Pansy died in 1929 when my mother was only ten-and-a-half years old. Mother became the woman of the house, cooking and caring for her three siblings. Grandpa seriously courted Joanna Mitchell[2] for a while but she was not willing to give up her teaching career to become a full-time homemaker and mother to four kids.

The children were very attached to Joanna and when Grandpa married Eva Stewart in November 1931, they had a difficult time adjusting to her, as she, according to my mother, had no experience with children. When I think of or mention Grandma Solomon, I mean Eva because Pansy died long before I was born.

Grandpa Solomon was a mechanical dentist. He fitted and made dentures. He was the first African American mechanical dentist licenced in Michigan. He operated his practice from a separate building behind the family home on McDougall Street in Detroit. Aunt Sis worked for him as a technician before she married and for some time after that. At a young age and under my aunt's supervision, I spent time at Grandpa's playing with old teeth, pink wax, and a Bunsen burner.

As he became more affluent, Grandpa purchased and moved to a four-apartment block on Philadelphia Avenue. He and Grandma

---

[1] Most documents seem to call her Harrizette but her gravestone says Harrizetta.

[2] I don't know Joanna's maiden name. She and Mother became lifelong friends. Later in life, she lived in Chicago and we saw her frequently during our Evanston years (1949-1956).

occupied apartment #1 and he rented out the other three. He also rented out the former family home on McDougall while continuing his business in the building behind. When the state of Michigan restricted the prescription and fitting of dentures to licenced dentists, they exempted existing businesses, so Grandpa was grandfathered in. He also made dentures prescribed by licenced dentists.

I remember at least two occasions as a toddler when he took me to Belle Isle, a recreational island in the Detroit River. For the winter visit, he rented a pony-drawn sleigh. I enjoyed slipping and sliding on winter ice and also enjoyed watching the pony slip on the ice. When I purposely guided the pony towards an icy patch, Grandpa patiently explained that I could seriously injure it if it slipped and fell. Lesson learned. We also shared a pony-drawn cart during the summer.

AUNT SIS MARRIED Uncle Warren in the summer of 1948. Dad drove our family to Detroit from Dayton, Ohio. Soon after we arrived, Grandpa judged my planned wedding attire inadequate. He then took me downtown to the J.L. Hudson department store and bought me a new powder-blue suit, white shirt and powder-blue tie.

The wedding was quite an event with many bridesmaids and groomsmen. Mother was matron of honour. My dad's sister, Aunt Ina, and Uncle Bruz's wife, Aunt Blanche, were among the numerous bridesmaids. Cousin Bobby Solomon, who was thirteen months older than I, was the ring bearer. I felt left out because I was in the congregation rather than the procession and ceremony.

The nuptial Eucharist was in the late morning at old St. Matthew's. Only the bride, groom, and presiding priest received communion, as was then the custom. The liturgical discipline of the day also required that the bride, groom and priest fast from midnight. A sumptuous breakfast for the wedding party and family members followed at the Gotham Hotel. A lavish mid-afternoon reception followed the breakfast. To end the day, we accompanied Aunt Sis and Uncle Warren to the docks where they boarded the overnight D&C (Detroit and Cleveland) passenger steamship to Buffalo for their honeymoon in nearby Niagara Falls.

My family lingered in Detroit for a day or two before returning home. Along with our car, we took a daytime D&C steamship across Lake Erie to Cleveland and then drove home to Dayton, arriving late at night. Cleveland was well out of our way, but my mother loved being on or near water.

GRANDPA OWNED a salmon-pink 1953 Mercury convertible for many years, first as his primary vehicle and later as a secondary summer car. He enjoyed driving several hundred miles to show up unannounced for a visit, which happened numerous times when we lived in Evanston. The most recent occasion was a summer visit in the late sixties. He and Eva drove to Hamilton on a Saturday, stayed overnight in a hotel, and showed up for the 8 o'clock Eucharist at St. James' in Dundas. He planned to keep his presence secret until after the 10 o'clock service, but fortunately, someone warned my wife by telephone. Thalia tidied up before attending church with Noëlle and Monique, welcoming Grandpa and Grandma into our home afterward.

Eva died in 1977. I chanted the introit, as the clergy and servers in procession escorted the casket into the church, and played the organ for her requiem at St. Matthew's & St. Joseph's. I did the same for Aunt Sis in 2013. I could not play for Uncle Bruz's requiem in 2021 because the border was closed during the Covid-19 pandemic.

Grandpa Solomon died without warning on 30 June 1980. Thalia, Noëlle, Monique and I were leaving on a non-refundable charter flight to London within a day or two after that. Consequently, I could not play the organ for his requiem at St. Matthew's & St. Joseph's. This angered my cousin Bobby, who could not understand why we did not cancel our long-planned trip to England, Scotland, and France.

-7-

Keokuk & Dayton
(1945-1949)

My mother and I arrived in Keokuk, Iowa, sometime during the summer of 1945, though I have no memory of the trip.

An early memory I do have of Keokuk, however, was entering kindergarten in September 1945. I didn't like it. Kindergarten was not compulsory in Iowa, so Mother allowed me to stay home with her, which was probably more fun than school. She later told me I had overheard a teacher say, "What a cute little coloured boy." I did not want to be a coloured boy. Still don't.[1] ☺

I was also the man of the house as Dad was away at seminary five days each week.

On one occasion, the Bishop of Iowa visited our home. This was likely after some church event that I do not recall. I remember proudly showing Bishop Haines my scrapbook containing many Montgomery-Ward catalogue cutouts, including numerous underwear-clad women. He was amused; my mother was not.

I had an occasional teenage babysitter named Jean Belt. I called her Jean until her eighteenth birthday. I then was instructed by Mother to address her as Miss Belt. It seemed very strange to me then and still does, but that was the proper etiquette of the time.

We had at least four different delivery men come to our house regularly: the milkman, the breadman, the coalman, and the iceman. We did not own a refrigerator; we had an icebox. The iceman came two or

[1] See Reflection #1: "Racism."

42

three times each week and delivered a crystal-clear cube of ice that measured at least a foot high, wide, and deep. He wore a leather apron and used a large pair of tongs to carry the ice from his horse-drawn wagon directly to the icebox. People seldom locked their doors so he could deliver even if you were out. If you wanted ice for a cold drink, you opened the door to the ice compartment, which was above and separate from the food compartment, and used a pick to chip off the desired amount.

The milkman came three times a week and delivered Jersey or Guernsey milk, the difference being the breed of cow. There is, I am told, a discernable flavour difference between the two. The milk came in returnable one-quart glass bottles, and to protect it from spoiling in the sun, most houses had a milk box either outside the door or in a wall near the entrance. Getting the bottles out of the milk box and into the icebox as soon as possible was important. The cream floated to the top of the bottle and needed to be carefully poured and stored separately in the icebox. You could buy a pint of cream separately if desired. I don't know if commercially homogenized milk was available but, if you didn't need the cream, you could shake the bottle and produce your own that way.

The bread man came three days a week, not necessarily on the same day as the milkman. He delivered loaves of white, rye, whole wheat or raisin bread. He also sold fancier baked goods such as cakes, cupcakes, pies, and pastries. I particularly remember that Mother and I liked Boston brown bread.[2]

[2] Boston brown bread is a dark, slightly sweet, steamed bread. It is steamed, rather than baked, in a can or cylindrical pan. Its colour comes from a mixture of flours, usually several of the following: cornmeal, rye, whole wheat, and graham flour, with

Butter was rationed in some parts of the country during the war. We had lots of butter in Iowa, but it was scarce in Detroit, so Mother periodically mailed butter there. Mail was moved and sorted on overnight trains and the service was much faster in those days. A pound of butter mailed via today's inefficient postal services would almost certainly arrive as a molten mess. Chicken was scarce in Iowa during the war, so we frequently ate rabbit.

You could order coal by the ton or fraction thereof, and the coalman came as often as necessary. He carried leather or fabric bags of coal over his shoulder from the truck to the coal chute. He dumped the coal, bag by bag, into the chute through which it fell into the coal bin in the basement. Mother would go down there during the heating season to shovel coal into the furnace.

My first memories of a telephone are from our year in Keokuk. It was a simple thing that sat on a table. While searching for a photo, I learned they are now called candlestick telephones. To place a call, one lifted the earpiece from the pedestal and waited for the operator to answer. You then told her the number you wished to reach (for example Keokuk 325), and she would connect you manually at the central switchboard. You used the telephone only occasionally, maybe less than once a day. Most people had party lines shared with others, which meant you could only make or receive calls when those sharing your line were not using it. Incoming calls rang at all the homes that shared the line. You would know whether the call was for you by the number of rings. It

added sweeteners like molasses or maple syrup. Leavening usually comes from baking soda. Raisins may be included. This abbreviated information is from Wikipedia. I have not seen Boston brown bread in decades.

was quite possible for one party to quietly lift the receiver to listen to another party's conversation. This happened frequently in movie scripts; I don't know how common it was in real life.

I recently attended a baseball game in which my grandson Christian was pitching. I complained to his brother Aaron that I was annoyed by the music and sound effect interruptions. I said, "When I was a little boy, we didn't have these constant interruptions; we just had the noise of the crowd." Later that evening, I realized the memory was from Keokuk. I can't tell you whether it was the summer of 1945 or 1946, but I remember going by car to the stadium to watch a few night games, where the teams were likely amateur. The visiting team on such an occasion came from Des Moines or another nearby town. A little digging on the internet gives me the impression that the Keokuk minor league baseball franchise may have been on hiatus. I can find no evidence of minor league activity there between 1935 and 1947. I remember nothing of the games, but I clearly recall being there. I wonder if this experience planted the seed for my later interest in baseball.

I vividly remember the circus coming to town. In those days, circuses arrived on their own train. The stage crew first set up the main tent and other necessary structures in a large field. Then there was a parade of bands, animals and circus wagons through the town from the train to the circus grounds. I remember attending other circuses later in life, but we did not attend this one. Maybe we couldn't afford it.

Sometime during the spring of 1946, Mother's younger brother, DeMarr Solomon, familiarly Uncle Bruz, stopped in for a few days on his way home from army service in the Philippines. He was readjusting to sleeping in a building after a long time sleeping in tents. Every morning he went outdoors for fresh air. I've always had a soft spot for Uncle Bruz. He was a very gentle person with a reputation for never being in a hurry. Mother said that he was also called "Mo" because he moved slower than molasses in January. She always elongated the first syllable of molasses for dramatic effect. He outlived all three of his siblings, dying at the age of 100 years, two months, and twenty some days in April of 2021.

The other important events of 1946 in Keokuk include my dad's graduation from seminary and Aunt Ina's wedding, detailed in Chapter Two, "My Father," and my sister's birth, detailed in Chapter Three, "My Mother."

That fall we moved to Dayton, Ohio, for Dad to become Vicar of St. Margaret's Episcopal Church. He must have gone ahead by car. We had owned a used 1936 Chevrolet for as long as I can remember. Mother and I travelled by train. I particularly remember walking by a huge — at least to me — steam locomotive while changing trains in Chicago. My baby sister, Marris, must also have been with us but I have no memory of her presence.

We spent a month or so in temporary accommodation while the rectory was being refurbished before we moved in at 407 Dearborn Street. The congregation owned a large property at the corner of Dearborn and McCall[3], which was vacant, and they dreamed of building a new church there next to the rectory.

We had a refrigerator in Dayton. We still called it "the icebox." It

---

[3] The printing plant for *McCalls*, a monthly women's magazine which lasted from 1873 until 2002, was a few blocks down the street.

had a tiny freezer compartment that contained a top shelf with a couple of metal ice cube trays, plus enough open space below it for either a pint or two of ice cream or a couple of packages of frozen vegetables — but not both. Frozen food was brand new at that time, at least to us. We also had our first dial telephone with a private telephone line because my dad, a priest, frequently had confidential conversations.

I entered grade one at nearby Jackson School in September 1947. The reader for this class was *Fun with Dick and Jane*, first published in 1946. It taught reading by word recognition, but my parents believed in teaching phonics. Consequently, I learned the best of both systems and became a strong reader.

My grade one teacher quickly discerned that I was near-sighted, and she notified my parents. They took me to an eye doctor who prescribed eyeglasses. After that, I wore glasses daily from first thing in the morning until bedtime. They rarely came off except for swimming or bathing. After I had cataract surgery around the age of seventy, I didn't need to wear glasses all of the time and kept losing them around the house.

We had inexpensive weekly movies on Fridays in the school gymnasium. There was at least a cartoon and a serial episode. *Flash Gordon* may have been one. My father did not allow me to attend the movies during Lent, but I did not understand why. We danced around a Maypole on May Day in grade one but, once again, I did not understand why. I quickly became the teacher's pet in grade two. My parents, disapproving of such favouritism, arranged for me to be moved to another class.

Other memories of living in Dayton were becoming an acolyte, confirmation, Grandpa Smith's wedding[4], my brother's birth[5], and my dog. Skippy was a beautiful mongrel, white with large black spots, part cocker spaniel and part English setter. I loved him dearly. My parents knew little about pet care. They never took Skippy to a veterinarian for shots. He came down with canine distemper during the winter of 1948 and was euthanized. I was heartbroken and have never been able to bond with another dog.

Dad needed an acolyte, specifically an altar server, for the early mass on Sundays at St. Margaret's. He quickly called me to duty. The instruction period was very brief. He created a series of discrete hand signals to tell when it was time to move the missal, bring him the bread and wine, and other necessary actions. Over the next six years in Dayton and Evanston, I would learn all the possible duties of an acolyte: server, torchbearer, crucifer, boat boy, and thurifer. Such liturgical functions were, at the time, limited to boys. It was not until the 1960s that some parts of the Church began slowly to realize that women and girls could do anything men and boys could do.

Soon after I became an acolyte, Dad began preparing me for confirmation. We had frequent instruction sessions in his home office where he taught me the catechism. He presented me to Henry Wise Hopson, Bishop of Southern Ohio, for confirmation in March 1948. The bishop initially refused to confirm me because at age seven, I was too young (the usual age being thirteen). He tested me to prove his

[4] I recount Grandpa Smith's wedding in Chapter 5: "My Paternal Grandparents."
[5] I tell of my brother's birth in Chapter 3: "My Mother."

point, but I had memorized the catechism so thoroughly that he could not find grounds to refuse.

We left Dayton for Evanston, Illinois, in February 1949.

-8-

Musical Beginnings
(1944-1956)

My earliest musical memories are of reaching above my head as a toddler to touch a piano keyboard and make a sound. I don't know where or when this happened as my parents did not own a piano. Was it the musical sound that attracted me, the ability to make a noise, or both? I don't know.

I have wanted to play the pipe organ for almost as long as I can remember. When I was in my teens, my mother told me that I fell in love with the sound of the organ at the age of four when Dad was ordained deacon in St. Paul's Cathedral, Detroit, in 1945. Decades later when I was dealing with his personal effects following his death, I learned that he was ordained deacon in St. Andrew's Memorial Church, not at the cathedral. So much for family mythology.

Dad consulted some knowledgeable person(s) who advised him that the ability to play the piano was essential to learning the organ. They also told my parents that organ lessons should wait until my legs were long enough to reach the pedalboard. This was predicted or assumed to be at about age thirteen.

In grade one, I started group piano lessons at Jackson Elementary School in Dayton, Ohio. We took turns playing the real piano while the rest of the class mimicked the proceedings on silent practice keyboards we each had. I have no idea how effective this system was. I do remember that I got sick and missed the year-end recital. I was scheduled to play *Rock-a-bye Baby* last in the programme, which indicated that I was either the most proficient student in the class or the teacher's pet.

WE MOVED TO Evanston, Illinois, in early 1949. I entered grade two at Foster School where music and art were a normal part of the curriculum. The teachers for these classes visited us at least once a week, and in between the classroom teacher helped us with our music and art lessons, in addition to the usual reading, writing, arithmetic, and geography. Music class was mainly singing but not necessarily vocal music. We learned some songs by rote and others by note. In other words, we learned some songs by repeating what the teacher sang, while we learned others by reading tonic sol-fa (in other words, do re mi) from the score. These rudiments have remained with me for life.

Elementary school music lessons planted the seed for a lifelong love of Mozart's *Symphony #39*. We sang descriptive words to the trio melody from the minuet movement. ("Hear the sound of the flute and clarinet, the flute and clarinet . . ."). My foster sister, Jean[1], planted another seed when she introduced me to César Franck's *Panis Angelicus*, part of her grade-six graduation ceremony. Such a religious song would no longer be allowed in today's secular curricula.

I began private piano lessons at the Evanston Conservatory soon after arriving in town. I remember very little of these. One piece that does stick in my memory is the *Prelude in C-sharp Minor* by Sergei Rachmaninoff. I thought I was playing the real thing until an older acquaintance explained that I was playing a simplified version in G minor. What a comedown.

I also played piano in the Foster School Orchestra. It was a horrid

[1] For details about Jean, see Chapter 9: "Life in Evanston."

little ensemble, comprising a few violins and perhaps a flute, clarinet and/or saxophone. Was there a trumpet? I doubt it. My role at the piano was to play *um-pah* or *um-pah-pah* bass-and-chord patterns to fill out the texture. The orchestra was so awful that more than seven decades later, I have nearly expunged it from memory. I now realize that this was my first continuo job. I learned how to go with the flow beneath the surface of the music, in short, how to make everyone else sound beautiful. I do not remember practising my orchestral parts. I suspect that the school orchestra also gave me early experience in sight-reading and perhaps even simple improvisation.

I broke my right forearm twice during grade four of elementary school: once in autumn, tripping over first base and again in the winter, falling down the stairs at home on Shrove Tuesday. The successive fractures were about an inch apart. Much later in life, a physician told me I was fortunate that these two fractures had not inhibited my digital dexterity.

DURING THE SUMMER of 1951, Charles Iles, my dad's parish organist, could not find a vacation substitute. I don't know whether replacement organists were in short supply, Mr. Iles waited too late, or St. Andrew's paid so poorly that no one was interested. I was pressed into service at the organ at the age of ten, three years earlier than expected. Mr. Iles gave me four weekly crash organ lessons in July on the parish's 1927 seven-stop Lyon & Healy mechanical action pipe organ. Dad, however, taught me the musical values that underpin me to this day. These included chanting texts in speech rhythm on one note before attempting a tune, and playing the chant tune from memory while visually following the words. He probably learned these techniques from Dr. Thomas Matthews, who directed Dad's musical training in seminary.

There was only one Sunday morning Eucharist with music during the summer. I successfully played the organ for the four Sundays of August, mostly without pedals. When the underpaid Mr. Iles returned, he negotiated a reduction in duties. After Labour Day, I assumed responsibility for the 9:15 family service that alternated Eucharist and Morning Prayer, while Mr. Iles continued directing the choir and playing the 11 o'clock high mass.

I began private organ lessons with Dr. Thomas Matthews at St. Luke's Church in September. Dad couldn't afford the usual fee, so Dr. Matthews gave him a special clergy rate of $2 per lesson. Dr. Matthews quickly discerned that my piano technique was inadequate. He recommended me to Mrs. Eva Jack who taught piano at her home not far from St. Luke's. She started me on scales, Hanon (60 exercises that focus on various aspects of piano technique), and Bach's two-part inventions. I studied with her weekly in the school year from late-1952 until the spring of 1956. Clementi, Mozart, Edward McDowell, and Debussy also entered my life under her guidance.

St. Luke's, an Anglo-Catholic parish, is an imposing gothic edifice. The church building is as large as the diocesan cathedral, perhaps larger, and certainly more beautiful. The main organ was a powerful four-manual electro-pneumatic Ernest M. Skinner organ (opus 327) built in 1922. While checking facts for this paragraph, I learned that more than a century after installation, this instrument is one of very few Ernest M. Skinner organs being preserved without significant tonal alteration. In other words, it is a veritable historical instrument. It even has a designated website.[2] Perhaps it is time for a visit (or pilgrimage) to St. Luke's, which I have not entered since 1956.

I would normally warm up on the main organ for perhaps thirty minutes before my weekday lesson began. Whenever a Saturday lesson was necessary, I would warm up on the organ in the Lady Chapel while another student's lesson was in progress at the main organ. I particularly liked the chapel organ. It had two manuals, possibly three. I specifically remember its mechanical action and gentle tone that I, a beginner, preferred to the powerful and much more complicated main organ.

I vividly remember that on Saturday mornings, the Blessed Sacrament was carried in procession from the chapel to the tabernacle on the high altar. At the sound of an approaching Sanctus bell, the organ lesson would stop to allow the procession to pass by and reach its destination. Did we kneel? Did we stand and perhaps genuflect? Did we cross ourselves? I can't remember posture, but I do remember a quiet moment of great reverence.

Dr. Matthew's started me on Sir John Stainer's organ method. Stainer's pedal technique was built on the principle of orienting oneself by finding the space between each group of black keys on the pedalboard. This is known today, rather derisively, as the kick-f-sharp method. Early lessons, once every two weeks, consisted of Stainer exercises (pedals, manual legato, and simple things for hands and feet together) and learning a new hymn each lesson. After perhaps a year, I was introduced to the *79 Chorales* of Marcel Dupré. I still use these as basic pedagogic materials. At least two of them (*In Dulci Jubilo* and

[2] http://www.opus327.org

Komm, Heiliger Geist, Herr Gott) are miniature masterpieces that I play at least annually juxtaposed with larger Bach and Buxtehude pieces built on the same chorale. The *Eight Little Preludes and Fugues*, attributed to Johann Sebastian Bach but perhaps written by one of his students, were added later during my five years with Dr. Matthews.

My daily routine consisted of thirty minutes piano practice at 6:30 each morning and thirty minutes organ practice each afternoon after school. I did not have even the tiniest inkling that I was approaching my future career path. I certainly received no encouragement from my peers. Words like "nerd" and "geek" were not yet in popular usage, but I was certainly labelled an egghead by the other kids. I don't mean to imply that I had no friends; it is nevertheless clear that my friendships were built on non-musical and non-intellectual interests.

Sometime later, perhaps in the fall of 1952, I also became thurifer for the 11 o'clock high mass at St. Andrew's. Dad meticulously taught me from *Ritual Notes*, and to this day I remember the correct number of swings to give to the celebrant, minor clergy, choir, other servers, and the congregation. It annoys me no end when I see thurifers, especially at major churches on television, get it wrong. Liturgical knowledge and experience are just as important parts of my professional toolbox as musical knowledge and experience.

THE ORCHESTRA WAS quite good when I entered Nichols Junior High for grades seven and eight. Orchestra was a class, just like math, English, social studies, or physical education. I am unsure if we met daily or every other day. Six pianists signed up when really none were needed. The conductor therefore auditioned us, and two were selected as the orchestral pianists. The winners were really the losers because they had little to do. The four losers, including me, were drafted to learn string bass. I took to this like a duck to water. Once again, my role was to support and make everyone else sound beautiful. The only orchestral repertoire I remember from Nichols is *On the Trail* from Ferde Grofé's *Grand Canyon Suite*, and Mozart's *Eine Kleine Nachtmusik*.

We had a full symphony orchestra at Evanston Township High School (ETHS).[3] Traugott Rohner, the conductor, was nationally known as the editor of *The Instrumentalist*, a monthly magazine. Orchestra was a credit class that met daily and the string players attended every day. The brass, woodwinds, and percussion (selected from the best players in the school band) attended every other day. The repertoire I remember included Carl Maria von Weber's *Invitation to the Dance*, the Second Symphony of Jan Sibelius, Johann Sebastian Bach's *Concerto for Four Keyboards*[4], as well as accompanying the massed choirs of the school and choir alumni in the audience for George Frideric Handel's *Hallelujah!* at the climax of the annual Christmas concert. As the school auditorium had not yet been built, we performed in the largest of the numerous gymnasia at ETHS. Beardsley Gymnasium seated over a thousand people in the bleachers and on the gym floor.

The first draft of this chapter completely overlooked the importance of public school music to my formation. I was awakened to this serious omission while watching a recent televised award show.

[3] https://en.wikipedia.org/wiki/Evanston_Township_High_School When I was a student there (1955-1956), the enrollment was about 1600.

[4] I auditioned unsuccessfully for one of the solo keyboard spots. The players who won the spots were likely seniors; I was only a freshman. At that time, my level of playing Bach keyboard music was only two and three-part inventions. The winners

More than one Juno-winning performer or technician paid tribute to his or her school music teachers for laying the foundations upon which later successes were built. I realized that I, too, owe as much to my public school music teachers as to my private ones. I am saddened to see music, art, and even physical education being removed from kindergarten through grade twelve curricula in Ontario and elsewhere in Canada and the United States.

I had numerous interests outside of music. One of my favourite television programmes was NBC's *Omnibus*, hosted by Alistair Cooke. The topics were wide-ranging. It is ironic that its most memorable influences on me turned out to be musical. A young, not-yet-well-known Leonard Bernstein (pronounced burn-stine) gave personable introductions to Beethoven, jazz, and other subjects. His *What is Jazz*, broadcast in October of 1955, opened my mind and ears to a whole new world. I was especially impressed by a young Dave Brubeck. I rushed out to buy a copy of his 1954 hit recording *Jazz Goes to College*. It was out of stock. Not wanting to wait for a special order, I purchased his second 1954 recording, *Dave Brubeck at Storyville*. Bernstein and Brubeck started me on a lifelong fascination with jazz and improvisation.

My family moved to Kansas City during the summer of 1956 and my musical training advanced to a new level.

were probably playing preludes and fugues from *The Well-Tempered Keyboard* and maybe even Bach suites. I had no idea then that this music, played on the piano, was for harpsichord. That discovery came much later.

-9-

Life in Evanston
(1949-1956)

We moved from Dayton, Ohio, to Evanston, Illinois, in February 1949. Dad had been appointed vicar of St. Andrew's Episcopal Church. I entered Foster Elementary School on Valentine's Day. My second-grade teacher carefully took me aside to explain why no Valentine cards were addressed to me. I could not understand why she would try to explain something so obvious. Did she think I was stupid? I failed to understand her intended kindness.

The students at Foster School were all black because our neighbourhood was black. Realtors effectively maintained de facto segregation throughout the Chicago area. Some towns, like Cicero, were all white: no black person could buy their way in, no matter how affluent they were.[1] In Evanston, black people lived in a particular area west and central in this 7.8 square mile town that was immediately north of Chicago on the shores of Lake Michigan. Other than our neighbourhood, it was a place for affluent Chicago executives and post-secondary students at Northwestern University and two seminaries.

I found Foster School easy, and quickly rose to the top of my class. I soon acquired a lot of privilege and was often excused from the classroom for in-school tasks or to serve my father at funerals. St. Andrew's rectory was next door to the church, separated only by a narrow sidewalk, and Foster School was only a block and a half away.

[1] Lorraine Hansberry's play and screenplay, *A Raisin in the Sun*, poignantly portrays a Chicago family's dilemma when deciding whether or not to move into a white neighbourhood. I saw the 1961 film version starring Sidney Poitier and Ruby Dee.

Toward the end of my time at Foster, achievement tests indicated that I was performing grade six work with the facility of a grade 11 student. This lack of challenge did me a great disservice because I was ill-prepared to face increasing academic difficulty as I moved on through life.

In grade six, I was one of two students who ran the projector for almost daily films in the auditorium, as scheduled by various kindergarten through grade six teachers.

SOON AFTER WE arrived in Evanston, Dad made contact with the Sisters of St. Mary (part of the Community of St. Mary, the oldest religious order in the Episcopal Church USA). They had a convent and retreat centre in Racine, Wisconsin, as well as a smaller home at the Church of the Atonement in Chicago. The sisters asked my parents to accept a foster child within six months of our arrival. Jean Anderson, a ward of the court whose parents were separated, came to spend two summer months with us in 1949. The match was successful, and she became a family member, staying with us until the end of the school year in 1955. Every month, Cook County paid my mother for Jean's clothing and food. She was six months older than I and a grade ahead in school. She entered grade four at Foster School in September. While living with us, she completed grade six at Foster, grade eight at Haven Junior High, and her first year at Evanston Township High School (ETHS).

Jean was joined by her elder sister Wilma in 1951. While living with us, Wilma completed Haven Junior High and her second year of ETHS. One summer, we had seven foster children: Jean, Wilma, Vicki (who was of high school age), and four young siblings (Danny, David, Kathleen, and Naomi). That's a total of ten kids around the table at mealtime. Mother was able to keep us all organized and ensure that each of us did our chores. I think Jean and Wilma likely escaped for a few weeks of summer camp. The inclusion of foster children in our family ended in the summer of 1955 because my mother faced serious health challenges that required major surgery.

CHICAGO AND NEW YORK CITY were leaders in the early days of television broadcasting. Most of my classmates at Foster School had televisions in their homes. We didn't until 1952. Our first set had a tiny circular black-and-white screen, six or seven inches in diameter. It was modest, but we thought it a significant improvement over radio. Many of the early television shows were simulcast radio programmes. (Most were telecast live, as recording technology was still somewhat primitive, and a recorded show was visually inferior.) I think of Arthur Godfrey in particular. He had a weekly evening show called *Arthur Godfrey and His Friends*; a daily morning show, *Arthur Godfrey Time*; and another weekly show, *Arthur Godfrey's Talent Scouts*. These were all simulcast live. Godfrey avoided using written scripts, preferring to improvise.

Professional entertainers were featured in the talent scout show, with first prize consisting of an engagement to perform on Arthur Godfrey's daily programme for an entire Monday-Friday week. A few of these winners became regulars. Many performers were introduced to a much wider public by appearing on Godfrey's various shows. To name just four: Tony Bennett, Rosemary Clooney, Lenny Bruce, and Patsy Cline. Two who auditioned and were surprisingly rejected by Godfrey later became famous: Elvis Presley and The Four Freshmen.

Sponsorship distinguished early broadcasting and telecasting from the form of advertising we know today, with one company sponsoring an entire programme. Godfrey's sponsor was Lipton Tea. I learned the word "steep" from him.

Your Hit Parade, sponsored by Lucky Strike cigarettes, was also popular with my family. It counted down the top seven popular songs of the week, recreated by the show's own orchestra and four regular singers. This is how I first heard Gisele MacKenzie, who sang on *Your Hit Parade* from 1953 until 1956, though it was never mentioned that she was a French-Canadian from Winnipeg.[2]

TELEVISION GAVE ME Chicago Cubs baseball. Their home games were telecast daily, and I watched as often as I could. Dad once took me to Wrigley Field for a doubleheader on Memorial Day. The Cubs were playing the St. Louis Cardinals. It poured rain somewhere around the sixth or seventh inning of the first game, but at least the Cubs officially won. I was able to see Stan Musial, Red Schoendienst, Ralph Kiner, Ernie Banks, and Gene Baker all in a single afternoon. It was magic for me.

We never returned to Wrigley Field. The Cubs only played day games as there were no lights on the field in those days, and Dad was unwilling to take a day off work for baseball. He did obtain a discount clergy pass for White Sox games in Comisky Park. We attended several

[2] I fact-checked my television memories against various Wikipedia articles. It was very common until relatively recently to avoid identifying Canadians as such. I think particularly of Lorne Greene, the popular star of Bonanza, whose career began at the CBC.

of their night games, but I never became a White Sox fan.

I have returned to Wrigley Field several times as an adult and loved it. I also attended a White Sox vs Toronto Blue Jays game just after the Sox moved from old Comisky Park to their present stadium. It seemed strange that the faint odour of the stockyards was no longer noticeable.

☺ I have also attended games at Riverfront Stadium in Cincinnati, Shea Stadium in Queens, Fenway Park in Boston, old Tiger Stadium and Comerica Park in Detroit, and Camden Yards in Baltimore. Over the years, my allegiance has quietly shifted to the Toronto Blue Jays. I have attended numerous Jays' games since 1978 in old Exhibition Stadium, and, more recently, in Skydome (now called the Rogers Centre).

THE CORONATION OF Queen Elizabeth II was the climax of memories that began in 1951. I was then ten years old and delivered the Chicago Herald American newspaper. My first royal memory was of news headlines announcing that King George VI was going for surgery with a 50-50 chance of survival. He survived well enough to leave the hospital, and I assumed all was well. It was a big surprise to me when he died in February 1952. Dad instructed me that Princess Elizabeth now became Queen. He also taught me that Elizabeth, the Queen Consort and widow of George VI, now became the Queen Mother, and that Queen Mother Mary, the widow of George V, became Dowager Queen. I never questioned how or why Dad knew such things. He was smart, and I probably assumed all smart people would also know. Queen Mary had instructed that the coronation not be postponed if she died before it occurred. She did die, and her wishes were honoured.

When coronation day arrived on 2 June 1953, we rose early and turned on our recently acquired black and white television. In 1953, there were neither artificial communications satellites in space nor transatlantic television cable, so we could not see what was happening in Westminster Abbey. The image on the NBC telecast was of an artist in New York City drawing on a flip chart with a black writing tool. The artist listened to the BBC shortwave broadcast and sketched his impression of what was happening in the ceremony.

The US Air Force and the Royal Canadian Air Force later raced each other across the Atlantic with kinescopes of the ceremony. The Canadians won, partially because London is closer to Newfoundland than New York City. The recorded ceremony, billed as a live telecast because it happened on the same day, was shown in each country in the early evening.

Rosie, my life partner from 2009 until 2020, told me that only a few British people owned televisions in 1953. Those who did invited their neighbours to gather and watch with them. The coronation was the psychological end to wartime austerity and rationing. I had no inkling at the age of twelve that I would become a Canadian citizen in 1971 and swear allegiance to Queen Elizabeth II and to all her rightful heirs and successors.

ST. ANDREW'S ALMOST always had seminarians from Seabury-Western interning with my dad. Back then, communicants fasted from midnight until after receiving the sacrament. A highlight each Sunday afternoon after high mass was going home to the rectory next door where my mother had a large breakfast waiting for us. I was the only child at the table and felt very important. The seminarians raved about the weekly breakfasts, and I was proud of my mother's culinary skills.

Two seminarians I remember were William DuBois (pronounced Do-BOZE), and Congreve Quinby. Both subsequently had long careers in the Episcopal Church. As they were each ten or more years older than I was, I'd be surprised and delighted if either of them were still alive. Quinby ("Call me Con, like concrete, solid man.") was a big fan of Kellogg's Sugar Frosted Flakes, then a new product.

Another person I remember was our mailman, Thomas Gibbs. We would call him a letter carrier today, but no woman was allowed to deliver mail back then. He was also my Scoutmaster when I joined Boy Scouts at the age of eleven. He had a keen mind and a degree from Amherst but, as a black man, the best job he could find was to deliver mail. Dad had a significant role in helping Tom discover his vocation to the priesthood, and he enrolled in Episcopal Theological School in Cambridge, Massachusetts. After ordination, he spent most of his career in the U.S. Virgin Islands.

As mentioned above, I delivered the Chicago Herald American daily after school, Saturday afternoons, and Sunday mornings for one or two years. When I entered junior high in 1953, I changed jobs to deliver the Evanston Review, a weekly, on Thursday mornings before school. I had to collect payment from the customers, weekly for the Herald American and monthly for the Evanston Review. I gave each customer a greeting card just before Christmas, and was — more often than not — given a cash gift. These totalled at least $100, and toward the end reached $200. I accumulated money in my savings account until I could make a major parentally-approved purchase, such as photographic equipment.

THERE WERE NUMEROUS neighbourhood elementary schools in Evanston, two junior high schools (grades 7 and 8) and one high school. Students chose which junior high to attend. Most students in my neighbourhood opted to go north to Haven because it was closer. I, as is my wont, chose not to follow the crowd. I went to Nichols Junior High, and still have great affection for it. The building was modelled after the Doge's Palace in Venice. The campanile (bell tower) of St. Mark's Cathedral graced one corner of the building, and the school yearbook was appropriately called *The Gondolier.*

Two teachers stand out in my memory. Gertrude Peters was my homeroom and social studies teacher, as well as faculty advisor to the Service Club. She married between my two years at Nichols and became Mrs. Schaube. She has been a strong influence throughout my life. On the positive side, she taught organization and self-discipline. I remember she disapproved that I read mostly non-fiction, including history books. She wanted me to enrich my literary experience with more romance, by which she meant fiction. When she said this in front of the class, it caused many smirks and snickers because they misunderstood her to mean love stories. I was embarrassed. On the negative side, she gave me, or perhaps only enhanced, a pursuit of perfection. Perfectionism can be a gift that encourages one to reach beyond one's grasp. On the other hand, it can lead to a sense of guilt because one never attains the goal. It took me decades to silence Mrs. Schaube sitting on my shoulder, telling me my priorities were in the wrong order.

Each homeroom at Nichols elected two representatives to the Student Council and two to the Service Club, with each group meeting weekly. The Student Council focused on the social life of the school, for example, dance lessons and school dances. The Service Club's focus was charitable. We were, among other things, the liaison with an overseas child the school sponsored through Foster Parents Plan, now known as Plan International. We corresponded with our child and communicated pertinent information to the various classes within the school. We were also involved with the Red Cross, the March of Dimes and other charities. I was elected President of the Service Club in grade eight.

Math instructor Karl Wildermuth was the other teacher whose influence has stayed with me. He was so effective that I believed I loved math. I even thought electrical engineering should be my chosen career path. I learned the basic workings of the stock market and investing from him; the duodecimal counting system (which I am glad was never adopted); and the metric system. When I went to France four years later, I was well-prepared to live in a metric country. I was happy when Canada began metric conversion in the late sixties. Sadly, Canada stopped metrication about halfway through the process.

At Nichols, we had elective classes or activities at noon hour while the other half of the school ate lunch. The only elective classes I remember are Spanish and the photography club where I learned about different kinds of cameras and film. I also learned darkroom skills such as mixing chemicals, developing film, and making prints. My Uncle Bruz in Detroit helped me enhance my skills in his home darkroom which was better equipped than the one at school. Physical education was, by the way, mandatory for all twelve years of public school in Evanston.

We studied the US Constitution and the Illinois State Constitution in detail in grade eight. We were required to pass an exam on these two documents for admission to high school. In preparation for that test, my parents took the family on a road trip to Washington, DC, in the summer between grades seven and eight to increase my knowledge. We stayed with Dad's friend, Canon John M. Burgess, later Bishop of Massachusetts, at the Washington National Cathedral. The cathedral, which at the time lacked a nave, was the biggest church building I had ever seen. While in the city, we visited the White House, Capitol, Washington Monument, Lincoln Memorial, and Tomb of the Unknown Soldier in Arlington National Cemetery. I can't say that the trip helped me pass the exam, but it was a memorable experience for which I shall always be thankful.

I graduated from Nichols in June 1955. The only detail I remember from the ceremony is the Boys Glee Club, under the direction of Charles Jenks, singing Randall Thomson's soaring setting of Thomas Jefferson's words: *The God who gave us life, gave us liberty.* It still rings in my mind from time to time. I admire a great deal of Thomas Jefferson's legacy despite the recent revelations of his flaws and clay feet; the logical self-contradictions which allowed him to own slaves and even father a second family with Sally Hemings, an enslaved woman.

EVANSTON TOWNSHIP HIGH SCHOOL (ETHS) was four blocks from home. It was widely and locally known to be one of the top public secondary schools in the nation. On rare occasions we grudgingly accepted New Trier High School in nearby Winnetka as our equal. I took four weeks of orientation at summer school between grades eight and nine to prepare for the high school challenge. We learned the layout of the large building complex. I took courses in public speaking (including extemporaneous speaking, parliamentary procedure, and debate); theatre (I played Mr. Di Pinna in George S. Kaufman and Moss Hart's *You Can't Take It With You*); and English (including increasing vocabulary and reading speed). I was, as usual, the only black student among several hundred taking summer school orientation. The fashionable colours that summer were pink and charcoal. I still like that colour combination, even though the fashion world has never repeated it.

I entered ETHS in the fall brimming with confidence thanks to knowing my way around. That year there were ten homerooms of about 160 students in each. I was placed in homeroom 364, which included both freshmen and sophomores. Mr. Rasmussen, our homeroom teacher, commanded attention by speaking very clearly and quietly. It was there that we received announcements, learned the length of the variable class periods (or even their occasional omission for a school-wide assembly or pep rally) and other important information.

There were seven periods in the day. These included five classes, mandatory physical education, and a period divided between study hall and lunchtime. School started at 8:30 a.m. and finished at 3:05 p.m. My schedule included Core (a nickname for a two-period combined studies class of English, civics, and social studies), French, algebra, orchestra, and phys ed. My parents were away in Honolulu, my dad being a deputy (a delegate who is not a bishop) at the General Convention of the Episcopal Church. Aunt Sis, my mother's sister, was in charge during their absence. I therefore took advantage of the situation and joined the freshman cross-country team which practiced after school. Interscholastic athletes were excused from phys ed class and given a full period study hall. Consequently, I had enough time to complete all my homework before I left the building. I enjoyed cross-country. I would shower afterward and rush home to practice the organ before dinner. Each week, we would compete at home or away against one or more of the area high school teams: Oak Park, New Trier, Niles, Maine, Highland Park, and others.

On my parents' return, I was reprimanded for joining an extra-curricular sports team, but my grades were good enough for them to allow me to continue. At the end of the cross-country season, I ran freshman indoor track. We had a field house with a ten-lap-to-the-mile dirt track. (In the spring, we moved outdoors to a quarter-mile cinder track.) Freshmen were not allowed to run the mile so I ran the half mile. Field events (high jump, long jump, pole vault, and shotput) took place in the centre of the track. That winter I won the only race in my life. We were away at another school. My running strategy was to save a bit of energy for the end. I remember coming around the final turn of my five laps with all the kick I could muster, trying to gain on whoever was in front of me. I was utterly surprised to find no one there. I won. What a wonderful feeling that was. I was a minor hero among my classmates the next morning and was particularly pleased when girls complimented me. It never happened again, but I will always remember the thrill of winning.

I WAS ALSO involved in the church youth group. On occasion, we met with youth groups from other Episcopal parishes in the diocese. The other groups were not necessarily from black parishes. An early evening get-together usually included discussion, a meal, and dancing. At one such meeting with youth from St. Edmund's, a black parish in

Chicago, I met Harriet Hutt, my first serious girlfriend.

My parents thought that dating should wait until the age of sixteen, but I was permitted to ask her out in January 1956, even though I was barely fifteen. Dating her was inconvenient as she lived twenty-six miles away on the south side of Chicago. Phoning her was a toll call. As we only had extensions of the St. Andrew's Church phone in the rectory, my father insisted that I go around the corner to the pay phone in the variety store and pay for my own calls. Getting to her house to pick her up for a date involved a bus or elevated train ride to the city limits (Howard Street), and then a combined elevated train (known as the L) and subway ride to 63rd and South Park on Chicago's south side.[3] Returning to downtown Chicago, popularly known as The Loop, involved another train ride. Our first date was to see the newly-released Todd-AO film[4], *Oklahoma!* starring Gordon MacRae and Shirley MacLaine.

The youth of the Diocese of Chicago held a formal event called the May Ball each spring. I wore a pink dinner jacket, formal black trousers, white shirt, black bow tie and cummerbund, rented of course. I was St. Andrew's parish candidate for King of the Ball. I was bitterly disappointed that I was obliged to escort the parish's candidate for Queen and could not take Harriet.

I suspect my dates with Harriet were occasional rather than frequent. I remember only two of them in any detail, the first and the last. I took her to a Stouffer's restaurant in the Loop for our final date. I also remember the kisses we shared. I had no previous experience with

[3] South Park is now Martin Luther King Drive. The intersection of 63rd and South Park lives on in the lyrics of some popular songs.

[4] *Oklahoma!* was the first film to use Todd-AO, a wide-screen film technique.

which to compare them, so I thought them sublime.

In June of 1956, we moved to Kansas City, Missouri. I was unhappy to leave Evanston, ETHS, and Harriet behind.

-10-

High School Years in Kansas City
(1956-1959)

My family arrived in Kansas City by automobile in the early summer of 1956. Our car was a black 1950 Plymouth four-door sedan, purchased new in Evanston to replace the used 1936 Chevy two-door which had been our family car since Keokuk. My mother drove the car in Keokuk, but I do not recall her ever driving again after my dad returned from seminary in 1946.

We were relocating so that Dad could become rector of St. Augustine's Episcopal Church in Kansas City, Missouri. Kansas City was transitioning from being rigidly segregated to being not so segregated. The public schools had integrated at the beginning of the 1955-1956 school year. New neighbourhoods opened to black people as the white population fled south in the city and into nearby towns around the city's edge.

As usual, we stayed in temporary accommodation while the newly-purchased rectory was renovated. Our home for the summer and into the early fall was a rented house near 27th Street and Brooklyn Avenue.

We lived just a few blocks from Municipal Stadium, home of the Kansas City Athletics, an American League baseball club. The 'As' are one of the oldest franchises in major league baseball. They date under various names from about 1860. They were the Philadelphia Athletics before moving to Kansas City in 1955. They moved to California in 1968 to become the Oakland Athletics, where they remain. The team had limited support from the black population because they had only one black player, even though this was nine years after Jackie Robinson had broken the baseball colour barrier with the Brooklyn Dodgers. That support was further eroded when the black player was traded to another team. I had been a loyal Chicago Cubs fan when we lived in Evanston, but I never became interested in the Kansas City team, perhaps because my focus was solidly turning to music.[1]

Another feature of the neighbourhood was the original Gates Bar-B-Q, which was my introduction to barbecued meat. My parents even had them barbecue a Thanksgiving turkey for us that first year. I have spent very little time in Kansas City since 1959, but I made sure to treat Rosie and myself to Gates' ribs, chicken, and baked beans when we visited in 2013.

The patron of St. Augustine's Church was St. Augustine (pronounced AW-gus-teen) of Hippo. This pronunciation distinguishes him from St. Augustine of Canterbury, pronounced a-GUS-tin. The parish had relocated to a large house, some called it a mansion, on Benton Blvd. near Lockridge, which served as church, church office, and parish hall. Dad's predecessor also lived there. The rest of the block, fronting on Benton Blvd and vacant from the house to the corner of 28th Street, was where the congregation planned to build a new church. They called Dad to lead them through the design and construction of a new edifice. The parish purchased a rectory for us, about a block and a half away, on 28th Street near Indiana.

I ENTERED CENTRAL HIGH SCHOOL in the fall of 1956. *Brown v. Board of Education* — the U.S. Supreme Court decision declaring public school segregation unconstitutional — had only been passed

[1] My musical activities are detailed in Chapter 11: "A Young Musician in Kansas City."

down in May of 1954. Kansas City public schools integrated in the fall of 1955. Our temporary home was located within the Lincoln High School district, which was the former blacks-only high school. It was at least a thirty-minute walk to Central High. Edgar Lynk, a classmate and parishioner, lived nearby so we walked together. After my family moved into St. Augustine's rectory, which was within the Central High School district, Edgar would walk the first half alone, and I would join him for the final fifteen minutes.

Central High seemed an awful comedown after Evanston Township High School, but I made the most of it. The building seemed to me to be old and ill-equipped by comparison. I continued my English, mathematics, history, and French studies to qualify for graduation and eventual college or university entrance.

I continued to run cross-country in the fall and track in the spring. As Central had no field house, there was no winter track competition. Kansas City winters are short compared to those in Illinois; we continued to train on a small indoor oval. It had steeply-banked curves at balcony level above the boys' gymnasium, and twenty or so laps around the track equalled a mile. I was enthusiastically welcomed by the other team members, but never lived up to their or my expectations. They had two champion runners, a miler named Wayne Studyvan and a quarter-miler named Sterling Burgette.

In retrospect, continuing my French studies was the most important thing I did at Central. I entered a second-year class when I arrived, and was taught by Agnes Engel who also taught German. She spoke French with a horrid American accent, but was a thorough pedagogue of grammar, vocabulary, reading, and conversation. The next year, no one but me took third-year French, so I had private tuition at the side of the second-year class. They had a full fifty-minute lesson followed by a twenty-five-minute study hall before lunch, during which I had Miss Engel's undivided attention. The main thing I remember about that third-year class was reading *Carmen* by Prosper Mérimée. This novella became the basis of Bizet's opera of the same name.

Miss Engel enthusiastically supported the American Field Service (AFS) student exchange programme. She encouraged her third-year students to apply for placement, and two of us did. Thanks to her, I spent five life-changing months in France.[2] I remember becoming friends with John Jackson from England, the 1956-1957 exchange student at Central. We had some fascinating and intense discussions during the Suez Crisis. I strangely have no recollection of the 1957-1958 exchange student. This memory gap puzzles me.

I ARRIVED BACK in Kansas City from France in early February 1959 and re-entered Central High in the middle of my senior year. The school administration figured out some way to evaluate my grades from the *Lycée de Lillebonne* to give me credit toward graduation. One graduation credit was lacking: first semester American history. I consequently boarded a city bus each morning to attend that class at Kansas City Junior College while attending the second semester class at Central. Entering second semester chemistry was challenging because I knew French rather than English vocabulary for lab utensils. I also took second semester English literature.

[2] My time in France is detailed in Chapters 12 and 13: "An Exchange Student in France" and "A Young Musician in France."

Central's exchange student from Guatemala kept her distance, I will never know why. Perhaps she felt that the fanfare surrounding my return was stealing attention away from her, or perhaps she looked down on a Negro boy. Black and white students attended the same school and behaved civilly toward each other, but there was no social mingling. The white kids never invited blacks to their parties. The so-called literary societies that met after school, sort of pseudo fraternities and sororities, never invited a black member during my three years at Central. They never admitted any black students in the few years after my graduation, and were subsequently abolished.

I was, however, included in the group activities of the AFS exchange students attending other schools in the area. These were enjoyable, even inspiring. I developed a crush on a girl from England, Anne Seller, but we could get no closer than occasional telephone conversations. We both knew and discussed the uncomfortable fact that her host family would never allow interracial dating.

I was admitted to Trinity College, Hartford, in March pending satisfactory final grades and College Board achievement test results. I graduated on schedule in June, 34th in a class of 360 students. That summer, I worked selling refreshments at Starlight Theater in Swope Park before heading east for college in late August.

A Young Musician in Kansas City
(1956-1959)

I was fifteen when my family moved to Kansas City, Missouri, in the summer of 1956. It was, for me, a reluctant move. In my mind, I was leaving behind the finest high school in the USA and a girlfriend. Need I say more?

That September, I enrolled in the Kansas City Conservatory (a division of Kansas City University) for piano study and also privately for organ lessons with Edna Scotten Billings, music director at Grace and Holy Trinity Cathedral. The glass ceiling was nearly impenetrable but she was one of very few female cathedral organists in the United States. Mrs. Billings was also Organist and Music Director at Temple B'nai Jehudah.

I entered my sophomore year at Central High in its second year of racial integration. The school orchestra was pathetic after the symphony orchestra of Evanston Township High. The only nice thing about it was that I took possession of a brand new string bass which stayed with me for the next three years. I loved that instrument and enjoyed hearing it mature over time. Sadly, vandals destroyed it the summer after my graduation. I was the only person ever to play it.

Vern Sinclair, the music teacher, quickly realized that there was no future for me in the orchestra and suggested that I switch to the band. He surprised me; I had never before known that most concert band pieces included a string bass part. I played string bass until graduation in 1959. I learned to play E-flat Sousaphone the following fall during the marching band season, and this flexibility stood me well when the concert band was playing a march or other music that didn't have a specific string bass part.

The highlight of my time in the band was conducting *Chaconne* from Gustav Holst's *First Suite in E-flat for Military Band*[1] at our 1958 spring concert.

MY STUDIES AT the conservatory from 1956-1959 expanded to include theory classes, sight singing, and orchestral string bass at various times. The conservatory string orchestra was conducted by Eugene Stoia. Vivid memories include playing Bach's *Violin Concerto in A Minor* with Maestro Stoia as soloist, and Bach's *Brandenburg Concerto #3*. I played bass in the pit orchestra for three performances of Gilbert and Sullivan's *Iolanthe*. The Lord Chancellor's nightmare song, *Love, Unrequited, Robs Me of My Rest*, has been a lifelong earworm.

During the spring of 1958, I auditioned for the Youth Orchestra of the Heart of America. This was a full symphony orchestra of players drawn from a fifty-mile radius around Kansas City. I won the position of principal string bass. My pal, Gerald McWorter, played principal bassoon. On the bus ride home we often congratulated ourselves for making everyone else sound beautiful. I never played a concert with the orchestra because I left for France later that summer.

ORGAN LESSONS and organ playing were, of course, the primary focus of my musical education. Edna Scotten Billings lit a fire under me that has never been extinguished. Once, when she asked me about my professional aspirations, I said I planned to be an engineer. She replied

[1] First Suite in E-flat: Chaconne - YouTube

that she thought not. She was sure that organ was my vocational path.

I received no encouragement toward a professional music career from my high school teachers. Mrs. Billings saw who I was and set me on a path to realize my potential. I quickly advanced from Dupré's *79 Chorales* and Bach's *Eight Little Preludes and Fugues* to Bach's major preludes and fugues and the wonders of French music. I soon added to my repertoire *Prelude-Toccata* by Gabriel Pierné, *Sortie de Messe Basse* by Louis Vierne, *Noël Parisien* by Charles Quef, and the *Toccata from Suite Gothique* by Léon Boëllmann. Other repertoire included *Communion* and *Chorale Prelude on Greensleeves* by Richard Purvis, *Fifty Elevations for Organ* by Dom Paul Benoit, *Bell Benedictus* by Powell Weaver, *The Bells of Ste-Anne de Beaupré* by Alexander Russell, and *Carillon* by Leo Sowerby.

I do not like organ chimes. I almost never play them and do not include them in any organ I design. My mother didn't much like organ music, but she loved to hear the chimes. I therefore included one piece for chimes in every recital I played in her presence.

I consider 1927 to be the nadir of North American organ building. Ernest M. Skinner may have been an exception. Although Grace and Holy Trinity Cathedral had a three-manual 1927 Austin Organ, I nevertheless learned a great deal playing it because I had an inspiring teacher. Mrs. Billings taught me an incredible amount about music in general, and many of the skills necessary to make a less-than-ideal instrument sound as good as possible.

Austin Organs had a unique feature: the Universal Air Chest.[2] The pipes of each division sit atop a wind chest. The Universal Air Chest, unlike other companies' wind chests, was about six feet from floor to ceiling. One can therefore enter it through an airlock and stand inside

[2] http://www.austinorgans.com/aoiuniairchest.html

while someone is playing. The observer can then watch the key action under each rank (or set) of pipes, as well as the stop action which selects which ranks of pipes make a sound and which are silent. The wind pressure inside an organ chest is much lighter than most people imagine. I was standing inside the guts of an organ, watching it work. I was also encouraged to climb ladders to make my way gingerly among the pipes. Doing so was dirty work because most organs had accumulated years of coal dust which had not yet been removed after the churches converted to oil or gas furnaces.

My first organ recital was in December 1956 on the nasty-sounding Baldwin electronic at St. Augustine's Church, my dad's parish. Mrs. Billings was so pleased that she decided I should present a recital at the cathedral in the spring. I played spring recitals there in 1957 and 1958. In the spring of 1959, after my return from France, I played a scholarship recital on the McManus organ at St. Paul's Episcopal Church, Kansas City, Kansas, to raise money for college.

I occasionally substituted for the organist at St. Augustine's. I also substituted in other places: month-long summer jobs in 1957 and 1958 at Trinity Church, Independence (Bess Truman's parish); one summer month at Church of the Epiphany in Grandview; and occasional Sunday services at Temple B'nai Jehudah while Mrs. Billings was busy at the cathedral. I also played a couple of weddings, and a month of Friday evening Shabbat services one summer at the synagogue.

THE KANSAS CITY chapter of the American Guild of Organists (AGO) sponsored four major organ recitals annually. Some of the local churches also sponsored recitals. I remember hearing E. Power Biggs,

Catherine Crozier, Mildred Andrews, Marilyn Mason, Oswald Ragatz, Fernando Germani and others during my time in Kansas City. I was elected the first President of the newly-formed Junior Chapter of the Kansas City AGO for 1957-1958, and attended my first AGO National Convention in Houston, Texas, in June 1958. There I heard Leo Sowerby preach at the opening Evensong in Christ Church Cathedral. I attended numerous organ recitals during the week and enjoyed perusing music, books, recordings, and instruments in the convention exhibit area. I especially remember the pleasure of playing several harpsichords, an instrument I had only previously experienced on recordings, and repeatedly returned to the display area to play them.

The week's climax was Virgil Fox playing his solo organ transcription of Joseph Jongen's *Symphonie Concertante*. I met Alec Wyton, Organist & Master of the Choristers at the Cathedral of St. John the Divine in New York City, and Joseph Blanton, author of *The Organ in Church Design*.

I READ VORACIOUSLY about organs and organ building, starting with *The Contemporary American Organ* by William H. Barnes. It was a thrill to encounter the author's admiring mention of Thomas Matthews, my first organ teacher. I created organ specifications on paper and shared them with Mrs. Billings, fellow organ students, and a few professional organists. In the fall of 1957, while awaiting the beginning of an organ recital by E. Power Biggs at St. Paul's Church in Kansas City, Kansas, I discovered I was sitting next to Charles McManus, the builder of the organ about to be played. I proudly shared a recent organ specification I had written on paper. He studied it briefly and said, "You've been reading Audsley". Right he was. I had been reading *The Art of Organ Building* by George Ashdown Audsley. He then explained why Audsley's thinking was considered outdated in 1957. Thus began a long friendship with Charles McManus, my earliest organ design mentor.

I discovered the wonders of the phonograph record collection at the Kansas City Public Library. There, I borrowed recordings by organists E. Power Biggs, Robert Noehren, Marilyn Mason, Alec Wyton, Catherine Crozier, Richard Elsasser, Mildred Andrews, and many others. I also found early music recordings by harpsichordist Wanda Landowska, the New York Pro Musica under Noah Greenberg, and the Alfred Deller Consort. Countertenors Russell Oberlin and Alfred Deller opened my ears to a sound I never knew existed. I was exposed to organ composers such as Virgil Thompson, Olivier Messiaen, and Leo Sowerby.

Long-playing records also exposed me to a wide variety of styles in organ building. I made a pilgrimage by bus from a family vacation in Detroit to Grace Episcopal Church in Sandusky, Ohio, to play a mechanical action organ by Schlicker. I had heard it on a recording by Robert Noehren, which introduced me to repertoire such as *Vom Himmel hoch* by Johann Pachelbel. I devoured G. Donald Harrison's recording, *The American Classic Organ*, the first volume of Aeolian-Skinner's *The King of Instruments* series. Through the magic of the long-playing record, I heard organs at the Cathedral of St. John the Divine in New York City, the First Presbyterian Church in Kilgore, Texas, and Boston Symphony Hall. The latter was a recording by Pierre Cochereau, titular organist of Notre-Dame Cathedral in Paris, where he improvised a four-movement organ symphony. Cochereau's recording and my exposure to jazz fueled my desire to improvise.

Meanwhile, I was encountering recorded symphonies by Beethoven, Mozart, Dvorak, Schubert and others through the Columbia Record Club and personal friends. Bartok's *Sonata for Two Pianos and Percussion*, Mozart's *Epistle Sonatas*, Brahms' Double Concerto, Brahms' *Piano Concerto #1*, and Vivaldi's *Winter* are particularly vivid memories.

Mrs. Billings arranged complimentary tickets for me to attend downtown Kansas City Music Hall concerts by the Kansas City Philharmonic Orchestra, conducted by Hans Schwieger. I heard Hector Berlioz' *Symphonie Fantastique* and Beethoven's Piano Concerto #4 with a young Daniel Barenboim as soloist. Although I can't remember what he played, I also heard an even younger André Watts.

The Philharmonic also presented a series of contemporary *Connoisseur Concerts* at Temple B'nai Jehudah. The smaller venue was chosen because the repertoire was too adventurous for the traditional symphony audience. I remember hearing *Music for Strings, Percussion and Celesta* by Béla Bartók, *Mysterious Mountain* by Alan Hovhaness, *Rhapsodic Variations for Tape Recorder and Orchestra* by Otto Luening and Serge Ussachevshi, and many other pieces.

LET'S NOT OVERLOOK jazz and theatre. As its theme, a local evening jazz radio show played *Django* by Cal Tjader. I attended a series of jazz concerts at the Kansas City Conservatory. I heard Kansas City pianist Betty Miller, bassist Paul Chambers, and numerous others there.

I listened to recordings by Dave Brubeck, Louis Armstrong, Miles Davis, George Shearing, Gerry Mulligan, the Modern Jazz Quartet, and Betty Miller.

I also heard many jazz musicians in person: Miles Davis, George Shearing, Gerry Mulligan (I don't recall whether with Chet Baker or Bob Brookmeyer) and numerous others at the Kansas City Music Hall. I was there the first night that Joe Morello joined the Dave Brubeck Quartet. I remember once standing in the wings with my pal Gerald McWorter, the kind of thing impossible in today's security-conscious society, discussing who was the best trumpet player. The vibraphone player from the George Shearing Quintet overheard the conversation and interrupted us. "There is no such thing as the best," said he. "Each person has something unique to contribute." This is a lesson I will never forget. Yes, we may have favourites but, in art, there is no such thing as the best.

During summer evenings from 1958 through 1960, I sold refreshments at the outdoor Starlight Theatre in Swope Park. Over three summers, I worked my way up from selling popcorn, hot dogs, and soft drinks in the seats before the show and during intermission, to working from a refreshment stand the following year, to running my own stand in 1960. Broadway musicals played there for seven nights, sometimes fourteen. I was able to experience *Oklahoma!, Carousel, Showboat, Annie Get Your Gun, Li'l Abner, Carousel, West Side Story,* and many other shows.

I left Kansas City for Trinity College, Hartford, Connecticut, in late August 1959. I returned in the summer of 1960, between my first and second years, and again worked at Starlight Theatre. I schmoozed after the shows with chorus members I knew from the Kansas City Conservatory, and even a few stars such as Gordon and Sheila MacRae, until I was told in no uncertain terms that concession staff were not permitted to mingle with performers.

-12-

An Exchange Student in France
(1958-1959)

I was unhappy to move to Kansas City, Missouri, in 1956. It however turned out that two of my life's most important opportunities happened there: to study with an organ teacher who inspired me and to apply for placement as a foreign exchange student.

Central High School participated in the American Field Service (AFS) exchange programme. The motto of AFS was "Walk together, talk together, all ye peoples of the earth. Then and only then shall ye have peace."[1] A student from another country lived with one of our families, and attended classes with us. In return, our third-year students were eligible to apply for summer placements with host families abroad. Foreign students attended American schools for a full academic year, but American students only attended a summer programme because it was believed that foreign schools, especially those in Europe, were too rigorous for us.

Two of us applied during the 1957-1958 academic year. The application was long and detailed, part done by me, part by my parents, and part by the school. A new possibility was offered: one could apply for the usual summer programme or a new five-month school programme. I checked both boxes even though I preferred the longer and more challenging school option.

The only section of the application I remember was an essay question asking how and where I would spend the last twenty-four hours of my life. It was probably posed in a more complicated form

[1] Sanskrit proverb.

than that. I only remember answering that I would spend the day in Paris. It included visits to Notre-Dame Cathedral and the Louvre. Not yet having any concept of the immensity of the Louvre, I thought I could see much or most of it in one afternoon. I mentioned the Mona Lisa and Venus de Milo; I probably didn't know anything else in the collection by name.[2] That's all I can recall of the essay except that the day ended watching the sunset from a hill overlooking the city. Looking back as an old man, I am intrigued that my memories seem to indicate a day of solitude. Did the question presuppose that I was the last person alive on earth?

The other applicant was John Hunkelor from Independence, Missouri. The AFS office in New York City found that our applications were equally strong, and apologized that they could find no way to choose between us other than our grade average. John's grades were slightly higher than mine and he was selected. He was assigned to spend the summer with a family in Stuttgart, Germany.

When John was chosen in late winter or early spring, my parents and I assumed the matter ended there. As I remember, the $500 participation fee put aside for the trip was reallocated toward buying a replacement family car.

Behind the scenes, and unbeknownst to me (but with my parents' permission) Agnes Engel, the German and French teacher from Central was championing my cause. Miss Engel, who believed that Adolf Hitler

---

[2] I finally saw both during the summer of 2018. *Venus de Milo* is beautifully displayed and accessible. The room in which *Mona Lisa* is displayed is perhaps the most popular one in the Louvre. One has to suffer more than two hundred people between you and the not-very-large painting. Many visitors, if not most of them, seem more interested in having their own photo taken to prove that they have been there, rather than viewing the painting itself.

had done many good things for Germany[3], got in touch with the New York City headquarters of AFS and presented a strong case on my behalf. I am puzzled to this day that someone who could explain "the Jewish problem" as if German Jews were not real Germans could champion the cause of a Negro student.

In May or June, AFS notified us that I had been placed in their School Programme: five months in Europe. France may or may not have been specifically mentioned in this early notification. My parents declined the invitation because we no longer had the required $500 placement fee. AFS replied by waiving the placement fee if we could figure out how to get me to New York and provide the allowed $5 per week spending money. We accepted. I emptied my savings account, and my mother organized a bon voyage party which raised the necessary funds and a bit extra to buy clothing. I particularly remember a light grey wool suit which also included an extra pair of navy blue pants.

I TRAVELLED BY Greyhound bus from Kansas City to New York City. The seventy-six school programme students gathered there in mid-August for two or three days of orientation at the old 29th Street East headquarters of the American Field Service. Most girls stayed overnight at the Martha Washington Hotel, while the boys stayed at the Sloane House. They were both basic YWCA/YMCA accommodations. Perhaps some of the more affluent students stayed in better places. I avoided expenses by staying with my godfather, Eddie Pitt, who lived in Queens. I must have arrived in New York City several days early. I took an all-day bus excursion to Waterbury, Connecticut, to play the McManus organ at

[3] I do not in any way wish to imply that Miss Engle supported Hitler's extermination policies.

St. John's Episcopal Church, an instrument upon which I would make my first long-playing recording seven years later.

Our orientation instructors told us Americans appeared rich and obnoxious to most non-Americans. We were instructed to be on our best behaviour at all times. The highlight of our orientation was meeting Stephen Galatti, the Director General of AFS, a man of legendary stature in my mind.

All seventy-six students and one or two AFS staff departed Idlewild Airport (later renamed John F. Kennedy Airport) in the evening of August 18th on a chartered DC-6 bound for Brussels. The plane was supposed to refuel in Gander, Newfoundland, but the weather was rough, and we continued instead to Shannon, Ireland.

I remember little of Shannon Airport except that the sun was shining, the temperature was mild, it seemed very quiet, and we were all tired after flying through the night.

We continued to Brussels International Airport. AFS representatives met us there and separated us into groups to continue toward our various destinations: Norway, Sweden, Italy, Germany, France and Spain. The groups going to France and Spain boarded a chartered bus for the train station, where an afternoon meal was ordered for us by our AFS chaperone. After dinner, we took a train to the Gare du Nord in Paris, arriving well after dark. We were then herded into taxis and driven across Paris to the *Cité Universitaire*, a student accommodation complex on the city's southern edge. I vividly remember passing the floodlit Notre-Dame Cathedral on the *Ile de la Cité*.

At *Cité Universitaire*, we stayed at the *Fondation des Etats-Unis*. We probably had some more orientation sessions there. I recall being very fond of Danielle Nytré[4], the Paris representative of AFS. I also remember that the food was very good, seemed very French to me, and included a single-serving bottle of wine. A delicious dessert called *Petit Suisse* was particularly memorable: a small cylinder of creamy cheese served on a plate with a little mound of granulated sugar. One stirred some or all of the sugar into the cheese and ate it with a spoon. One of the boys from Utah had a particularly sweet tooth and wanted more sugar. He had never before seen a salt cellar and mistakenly dumped a pile of salt onto his *Petit Suisse*, thereby rendering it unpalatable.

Some time during our first day in Paris, the students bound for Spain headed toward their new homes. After the midday meal, some of us who remained boarded the métro and headed to the city centre. We wandered around the Tuileries Gardens, then headed past Place de la Concorde, either up the Champs-Elysées or along the Seine to the Alexandre III Bridge, and across to the boulevard Saint-Germain in the Latin Quarter. We took another walk after supper, but my little diary doesn't say where.

ON THE MORNING of our second day, I said goodbye to the remaining AFS students. I ventured off on my own to visit Notre-Dame Cathedral.[5] Then after the midday meal I was picked up by a chauffeur-driven Citroën DS-19 and taken to my new home for the next five months, *Le Château de Lillebonne*. 1958 was before today's superhighways, and the three-hour drive through the countryside along the Seine was

[4] I attended her wedding in Paris later in the fall. She and her husband took up residence in Casablanca. I never saw her again. Jewish weddings normally occur on Sundays. I was, therefore, able to schedule my first visit to the tribune of Notre-Dame earlier that day to meet Pierre Cochereau.

[5] See Chapter 13: A Young Musician in France, for details.

mesmerizing. After we passed through Rouen, the chauffeur stopped on a hillside to show me a gorgeous panorama of the city and Seine River Valley. Rouen is beautiful and it's an important port. Ships enter the winding river from the English Channel at Le Havre and sail 202 nautical miles (374 km) upstream to unload. The driving distance is only about 90 km. Pedestrians and vehicles could cross by ferry at numerous places, such as at Duclair and Caudebec-en-Caux. While there are now three high-level bridges crossing the Seine between Rouen and Le Havre, none of them existed back then. The first of the three, the majestic suspension bridge at Tancarville, completed in 1959, was still under construction.

The American Field Service placed me with the family of Charles and Eva Bost in Lillebonne, Seine-Maritime. Seine-Maritime is a *département* in the ancient province of Normandy. Lillebonne is a small town, a few kilometres from the Seine River, about halfway between Rouen and Le Havre. The Bosts were an aristocratic Protestant family with deep roots. Their house[6] was on a hilltop overlooking the town, and the property had a long history. It was there that William the Bastard, Duke of Normandy, gathered his barons in 1064 to begin planning an invasion of England. After the Norman Conquest two years later, he became known as William the Conqueror. The property was also used by Phillip Augustus, Duke of Normandy and King of France (but not King of England) a few generations later.

The Bost family home was a large hilltop structure built of brick in the mid-19th century by the Harcourt family, ancestors of Madame Bost. The castle of William the Conqueror, which by then had fallen

---

[6] The family always called it *la maison* (the house). I suspect that calling home *le château* would have been considered pretentious.

into ruin, was razed to make room for it. I don't really think in acres or hectares, but the property certainly exceeded several city blocks in area, and included a substantial front lawn and woods. It was surrounded by a stone wall, and included a ruin (most of one side of an octagonal war tower), built during the era of Phillip Augustus. There was a 16th century tower, *Le Donjon*, surrounded by a moat that no longer had any water. The simple wooden bridge stretching over it was probably built in the 20th century. A third small tower was probably a 19th-century copy constructed as a tool shed. A white pony named Baldi lived in it. There were also several peacocks.

As an American teenager, I had no concept of aristocracy. This was not explained to me until I visited Lillebonne again in 1980 with my Scottish wife, Thalia. I understood that some people were rich, some were poor, and most were in between. Monsieur Bost and his family lived in a castle, and he worked as a chemical engineer for Esso-Standard. He certainly wasn't poor. He wasn't rich either as he had tenants living in apartments in the basement and on the third floor.

It was normal, or so I believed, for AFS students to refer to their hosts in parental terms. Monsieur and Madame Bost initially found it awkward that I called them *Papa* and *Maman*. Perhaps I should have waited for an invitation, but I didn't. They however got used to the idea, and I addressed them as *Papa* and *Maman* for the rest of their lives. When I walked in town with Papa, men would tip their hats, and everyone would address him politely. I really should say that they addressed him deferentially, but at seventeen I had no concept of deference. He was, in fact, Lord of the Manor, *Le Seigneur de Lillebonne*.[7]

---

[7] Monsieur Bost wrote a book about his predecessors called *Les Seigneurs de Lillebonne*. I own a copy and sadly have never made time to read it.

I did not understand this until decades later.

There were three Bost children. Brigitte, the elder daughter, was about my age. She was an AFS exchange student who had already left to spend the academic year attending high school and living with a family in Milwaukee, Wisconsin. Jérôme was about twenty-two months younger than I. Jeanne, usually called Jeannette, was twelve. Monsieur Bost's mother, Grand-mère, had her own apartment on the main floor of the house.

Jérôme was my almost constant companion for the next five months. He taught me more French than I ever learned in school. Our first few minutes together were, however, less than auspicious. My accent, after three years of high school French, was still very American. I vividly remember him saying, «*Tu parles français comme une vache espagnole.*»[8]　Despite this rocky beginning, he quickly became a real brother to me and remains so to this day.

The school year began in a few days. I was placed in Jérôme's class at the Lycée de Lillebonne. The students were a year younger than I, but I was glad to be with Jérôme rather than a room full of total strangers. We attended school four-and-a-half days each week: Monday, Tuesday, Thursday, Friday, and Saturday morning. We were in the modern as opposed to the classical stream where Greek and Latin were taught. Our classes included physics, chemistry, English (as a foreign language), 16th and 17th-century French literature, French history, math (algebra and geometry), and drawing.

I only remember random details of school. Math was process rather than goal-oriented, presented in a totally different perspective from

_____

[8] "You speak French like a Spanish cow."

what I was used to. In the USA, the correct answer was virtually all that counted. In France, the steps toward the answer were examined in detail. A student could therefore get significant points for the correct procedure despite arriving at an incorrect answer. Physics was no problem because I had taken it the previous year in high school. I don't remember chemistry being difficult until I returned to Kansas City where I had to learn a new English vocabulary for the tools and concepts initially learned in French. French history must have included the late 18th and early 19th centuries. The name that rings in my memory is Talleyrand. The French literature classes were my favourite. We read poetry, prose, and plays by Joachim du Bellay, Pierre de Ronsard, Pierre de Corneille and possibly Molière. We also memorized texts for recitation. Literary memorization had long been discarded by American schools and presented me with a new challenge. My first memory assignment was a sonnet by du Bellay.[9] I can still recite it more than sixty years later. In 1977, I set the sonnet to music for choir, harpsichord, flute, and viola da gamba.

Family life with the Bosts was very comfortable for me. As Brigitte was in Milwaukee, I stayed in her bedroom on the second floor in the right turret as seen from the front lawn. It had three large windows which from left to right, overlooked the *donjon*, the octagonal tower, and a large vista of front lawn continuing out over the town. Thalia and I slept there when I returned in 1980 with my family. Brigitte's pastel drawing of that bedroom is one of my most precious art objects. She gave it to me in 1997.

[9] Joachim du Bellay (1522–1560), 'Sonnet XXXI' from *Les Regrets*. It is sometimes called 'Mal de pays'. It begins with the words «*Heureux qui comme Ulysse, a fait un beau voyage . . .*» The author, returning home full of experience and knowledge, prefers his poor village in Anjou to the magnificence of Rome.

One part of family life was new to me, and I liked it. The first time that you saw any family member each day, you greeted each other by name (for example, *"Bonjour, Papa"*) and exchanged a kiss on each cheek.[10] It didn't matter whether this was first thing in the morning or later in the day. A similar exchange took place each evening before retiring. Close friends were greeted similarly. Even when walking into a shop to do business, saying, *"Bonjour, monsieur"* or *"Bonjour, madame"* before asking for what you want was customary. To begin with "May I have four croissants?" without a greeting was, and still is, extremely rude and might be greeted with a stony glare. By the way, a young woman working in a store was always addressed as *"Madame."* A stranger was never addressed as *"Mademoiselle."*

Each morning, Jérôme and I would descend to a side table in the dining room for *le petit déjeuner*, a continental breakfast of bread fresh from the bakery, butter, jam, and *café au lait*. Sometimes we had hot chocolate instead of coffee. Papa had already left for work by then. I don't remember Jeanette at breakfast. Perhaps she, being younger, started school later than we did. Then off to school, just across the street outside the main gate, for the morning.

School dismissed for two full hours for *déjeuner*, the day's main meal. All six of us, including Grand-mère, gathered in the living room until summoned to table by Annie, the maid. In my opinion, these were the halcyon days of the Château de Lillebonne. Annie started working for the family a few days after my arrival and remained until she married a year or two later. She lived in a small apartment on the second floor and was the last full-time maid employed by the family. Full-time domestic

[10] I have since learned that the number of kisses varies among two, three, or four depending on the region of the country. In Normandy, two was the norm.

servants were becoming a thing of the past. After her, I am told, the part-time staff never achieved Annie's culinary standards.[11]

Déjeuner consisted of no fewer than five courses: meat or fish, vegetables served before the meat was finished, green salad with oil and vinegar dressing, assorted cheeses, and a selection of fresh fruits. There might, on occasion, have been an appetizer before the main course. There was always a loaf of delicious crusty bread on the table which Papa sliced for us on request. Butter was not normally set for dinner or supper. Papa also served the wine upon request, which was almost always a simple Algerian red table wine. Jeannette, being only twelve, diluted hers with equal water. On occasion, we had Normandy cider, and on special occasions a bottle of Beaujolais. After déjeuner, we would gather in the living room for a demitasse of black coffee with an optional lump of sugar.

After school, Jérôme and I would return home for tea. This was served at the small table where we had taken breakfast. Tea was accompanied by bread, butter, jam, or pastries such as apple tarts, mille-feuilles or éclairs. Afterward we would head upstairs to our respective bedrooms to do homework.

Diner, the evening meal, was served around 8:00 or 8:30 in the evening. It was lighter than déjeuner. It usually began with soup. The main course might be meat and vegetables, but I also remember the occasional plate of bacon and eggs and especially Annie's sensational *quiche lorraine*. I have never again tasted any that equals hers.[12] Then

[11] In May of 2015, Jeannette and her husband Dominique hosted a delightful family supper at their apartment in the Marais district of Paris. Jérôme, Brigitte, Rosie and I howled with laughter at Jeannette's imitation of Annie, shyly peeking around the door frame and announcing that dinner is served.

[12] Rosie and I stayed in Nancy, capital of Lorraine, for three days in 2018. I ate quiche

followed the salad, the cheeses, and either fresh fruit or a special dessert. I was particularly fond of *pain perdu*, which North Americans would call French toast. It is a breakfast food here but a dessert in France. It was originally a way of saving old bread from being discarded. Slices of bread were dipped in a mixture of egg and milk, sautéed in butter, then sprinkled with powdered sugar. It was served at the table with a pitcher of warmed and sweetened red wine sauce.

Foods I met for the first time at the Bost family table include *quiche lorraine*, *boudin noir* (a soft sausage made with pork blood), fresh homemade soups (especially cream of broccoli), *pot au feu* (a hearty soup or stew), macaroni salad, fresh whole fish, crayfish, oysters on the half shell, camembert and other cheeses, fresh honey, mandarin oranges, pain perdu, croissants, coffee eclairs and Normandy cider to name just a few. Many of these things, or imitations thereof, are now readily available in North American restaurants and supermarkets but were certainly not normal fare for a black teenager from Kansas City in 1958. Even roast chicken, as opposed to fried, was new to me.

A school friend and neighbour, Didier Lemaistre, and his mother invited me over for supper, just the three of us, a few days before I returned to the USA. Madame Lemaistre introduced me to traditional *fondue suisse*. She then served fresh sliced strawberries and pineapple for dessert. I still count this as one of the most memorable meals of my life. Didier and I lost touch with each other after I left France. We reconnected on Facebook in May of 2016. I'm happy that I could share

lorraine every day and loved it. Annie's was, however, unique. It had a thin crust and was flat like a pizza. I discussed this with a couple of different pâtissiers in Nancy. They said that authentic quiche lorraine was deeper, perhaps 2cm, with a crust below and surrounding the filling. Interesting to learn, but it does not dull my memory of Annie's quiche.

the story of this special time with him a month or so before he sadly died in 2018.

Basic European table manners were fairly easy. At a young age, I had learned from a visiting Maltese missionary to hold my fork, tines down, in my left hand and my knife in my right. Fingers were very seldom used in France except for some fruits, and bread, a slice of which was placed on the tablecloth beside your plate. Some of the other details were however challenging, such as navigating a whole fresh trout, backbone and all. Elbows were never allowed on the table. I forgot this often and had to be gently reminded by Jérôme.

LIVING IN FRANCE changed my whole outlook on life. It inspired me to learn to cook for myself, my family, and for company. Some things, however, are never as good in North America as in France. It is nearly impossible to explain why. Try as they may, North American bakeries and patisseries can only come close but never duplicate French bread or croissants. Some people have posited that the microbes in the air are different here and that the natural yeast in bread and croissants must therefore be different as a result. Eclairs are not even a near miss. Our fruits and vegetables are usually bigger than their French counterparts but almost always lack some flavour. Perhaps terroir (soil, climate, and topography) is everything.[13]

[13] We have many wonderful foods here in North America, and I suspect that many travelling here will find things they love and cannot duplicate back home. This is the best argument for food lovers to travel. Quite frankly, I have difficulty with travellers trying to eat their own familiar cuisine. I am proud to say that I have never frequented a North American restaurant while travelling in France or the United Kingdom. I have however experienced French cuisine in Oxford, Indian cuisine in London, and Vietnamese cuisine in Paris.

There was neither television nor refrigerator in the house until many years later. Papa did not allow them. Jérôme had a phonograph in his bedroom, and we often shared music together. He introduced me to Borodin's *Polovtsian Dances* from Prince Igor, Ernest Bloch's *Concerto Grosso #1*, Georges Brassens, Charles Aznavour, and Juliette Greco. I introduced him to Miles Davis' 1957 recording *Round Midnight* and the Playboy 1957 Jazz Poll Winners, which included Dave Brubeck, Gerry Mulligan, Stan Getz, Chet Baker, and Bob Brookmeyer. Pierre Cochereau, titular organist of Notre-Dame de Paris, improvising on the Boston Symphony Hall organ was another important recording I shared with him.

We would occasionally go out to attend a concert or see a movie. These were classic French films rather than the latest release. I saw several directed by Jean Renoir, son of the impressionist painter, Auguste Renoir. A bonus was that Monsieur Bost had two brothers, Pierre and Jacques, who appeared in some of the films I saw. I was also introduced to surrealism, a totally new genre for me. I particularly remember *Un Chien Andalou* (An Andalusian Dog), a 1929 short silent directorial collaboration of Luis Buñuel and Salvador Dali. I've seen it several times as an adult but have never learned to like it. I have however grown to appreciate other films by Luis Buñuel and some of Salvador Dali's paintings.

Concerts were all classical small-ensemble performances. Some were professional evening events, others were afternoon Jeunesse Musicales concerts aimed at student audiences.

I managed two solo excursions to Paris. The first was for Danielle Nytré's wedding in the fall. When in Paris, I stayed with Guy Selz, his wife, Françoise (Papa's sister), and their family. My ear found their address very exotic: 11bis (onze bis) rue Géricault. Monsieur Selz was Secretary General of Elle Magazine. He was an engaging raconteur and I enjoyed listening to his stories. While Guy Selz addressed his children familiarly, he always addressed his wife formally as *vous*, never the familiar *tu*, very unusual for a married couple. (He had a large, and I am told distinguished, collection of printed pornography. I was too young to appreciate it then. I probably disapproved.)

My second trip to Paris was in January, shortly before I left France. I visited the Rodin Museum and attended a performance of Mozart's *The Magic Flute* at the Paris Opera. The highlight for me was a train trip on January 6th to the Cathedral at Chartres. It was an unforgettable day examining the amazing sculpture and luminous stained glass, even though I was disappointed there was no high mass to celebrate the Feast of the Epiphany.

NORMANDY'S CLIMATE IS moderated by the English Channel. Snow was therefore fairly rare by comparison to my youthful midwestern experience. To my delight, Lillebonne received a beautiful blanket of snow a few days before my departure on January 15th. When that sad day arrived, a chauffeur again picked me up. This time, he took me to Le Havre where the last group of us joined the other AFS students who had already embarked aboard the SS Seven Seas at Rotterdam.

We sailed just after dark and stopped at Southampton later in the evening to pick up more passengers before heading to Halifax and New York. An AFS staff member was on board to debrief us during the voyage home. The Seven Seas was fairly old, small and slow, and the North Atlantic crossing very stormy. The scheduled ten-day trip actually took eleven.

When we arrived in Halifax, I had to ask which country we were in because I had never heard of it. Then I asked what province. We had a few hours of shore leave, and many of us ran out in search of hamburgers and malted milkshakes. I was surprised to learn that some maritime residents took the ship from Halifax to New York because it was more pleasant and perhaps more direct than the rail journey.

We arrived in New York on January 26th. I started the bus journey home, stopping in Evanston, Illinois, to visit friends and my old high school. I also took a day trip on the old North Shore train on January 29th, my birthday, to Milwaukee to meet my French sister, Brigitte. That evening, four of us attended a dress rehearsal of the Milwaukee Symphony to hear Van Cliburn perform Tchaikovsky's First Piano Concerto.[14]

After Evanston, I boarded a Greyhound bus for home. I looked forward to seeing my family. In Kansas City, Dad and Mother were waiting for me at the second-floor arrivals platform as the bus pulled in. Hugs and kisses were exchanged. I particularly remember surprising my Dad with a kiss on both cheeks. We had stopped kissing years before as it was the grown-up thing back then for American fathers and sons to shake hands. My attitude toward kissing had changed in France. A handshake now seemed cold.

[14] Cliburn was still flying high after his surprise victory at the first International Tchaikovsky Competition in Moscow the previous April. The four of us who attended were Brigitte, her American sister, Sandra Bartels (one of the seventy-six AFSers who had just returned on the Seven Seas), and me.

Dad took my luggage and told me that the car was parked downstairs. He stepped back as we reached the top of the escalator. I was nearly knocked over by the roar of a hundred or more cheering students from Central High, my sister and brother, numerous personal and family friends, a few parishioners from Dad's church, and the local French consul. What an unforgettable moment. The press was there too. An article and a large photo appeared in the next issue of the Kansas City Star.

Before leaving New York the previous August, we had been carefully briefed to prepare for new experiences. Little, however, prepared me for the culture shock of returning home. The Bost family and France had changed me. I now saw the world through new eyes.

-13-

A Young Musician in France
(1958-1959)

In July of 1958, my parents and I received word that I had received a scholarship as an exchange student to France.[1]

My first solo excursion after arriving in Paris was to Notre-Dame Cathedral on August 21st. Notre-Dame is normally full of tourists. I wandered around a bit before I heard faint music in the distance and walked toward it, away from the footfalls and conversation. I found a requiem mass in progress in one of the apse chapels. The music was supplied by a harmonium. It sounded so beautiful in the distance that my desire to hear the gallery organ, standing in its magnificent case in the west gallery, was set ablaze. I then paid a few francs to climb a tower to the roof where I could view the gargoyles.

Shortly after arriving in Lillebonne to live with my host family and attend school, I was granted practice privileges at the local parish church, Notre-Dame de Lillebonne. Lillebonne is a small town in Normandy about halfway between Rouen and Le Havre. The 16th-century Gothic church is beautiful, but the organ was a small two-manual instrument that badly needed tuning. I spent very little time there. The local Protestant temple had a harmonium. It may have been better than I thought, but I had not yet realized that a French harmonium was much more musical than an American pump organ. I soon set out for Caudebec-en-Caux, about fifteen kilometres toward Rouen. The beautiful 15th-century flamboyant Gothic church there, also

[1] For personal details, see Chapter 12: "An Exchange Student in France."

called Notre-Dame, became my musical home for the next several months.

The gallery organ at Notre-Dame de Caudebec-en-Caux was an old instrument in the process of being rebuilt. The work in 1958 was not very successful, and the organ had to be rescued later by major restorations in 1972 and 2005.[2] It was however good enough for me and was my first real French organ. I played many Sunday morning masses in Caudebec, getting there by riding on a motor-assisted bicycle. More than six decades later, I still play from a couple of scores that were water stained while riding to mass in the rain.

My second French organ was in the Abbey Church of Saint-Ouen in Rouen, which I had first encountered in a book. More specifically, I saw a photograph of its 1630 organ case[3] in a chapter about French Renaissance cases in *The Organ in Church Design*. The book, a tome for architects, was one of the hottest items in the 1958 organ world. Years later, I heard that organists purchased many more copies than did architects. This is unsubstantiated, but I suspect true.

The author, Joseph E. Blanton, used St-Ouen as an example.[4] I met Joe Blanton in Houston, Texas, in June 1958 at the National Convention

[2] http://musiqueorguequebec.ca/orgues/france/caudebecnd.html
Read this, and other musiqueorguequebec links in French if you are able. The English translations are merely adequate.

[3] Blanton, Joseph Edwin; *The Organ in Church Design*, Venture Press, Albany Texas, 1957. Figure 279, page 249.

[4] One of the challenges of writing is the fickleness of human memory. I remember an impressive full page black-and-white photo on a left-hand page. The actual photo is about one-twelfth of a right-hand page, yet it somehow caused me to make a life-changing decision. While fact-checking for the previous footnote, I discovered a photo of the 1620 organ case at Caudebec-en-Caux (fig. 277) which I had never before noticed.

of the American Guild of Organists. If I remember correctly, he was one of the featured speakers. I eventually purchased and still own an autographed copy of his book, together with its supplement, *The Revival of the Organ Case.*

Before leaving Kansas City for France, I knew my destination was Lillebonne. I don't know when I realized it was only a few kilometres from Rouen. Shortly after my arrival, I fearlessly and shamelessly wrote to the titular organist and requested permission to visit. I had no clue that this organ case housed one of the world's greatest organs.

When you visit an organ in North America, you are usually welcomed into an otherwise empty church by the organist or other staff person who shows you where the instrument's key and light switches are, perhaps answers a few questions, and then leaves you to your own devices. In France at that time you were welcomed to the organ gallery on Sunday morning during mass. Holding a conversation during the liturgy seemed irreverent to this seventeen-year-old priest's kid. But that's how it was done.

I arrived in Rouen on Sunday morning September 28th by intercity bus and walked to St-Ouen. I met Maurice Gouellin, the titular organist, at the door to the organ gallery. Such doors, usually at the back of the nave, are locked; one gains access only with a key which is often centuries-old and made of iron. Once inside, one climbs a spiral staircase, usually stone, to the organ gallery. To my utter surprise, I discovered that the French Renaissance organ case housed, not a Renaissance organ, but a Cavaillé-Coll.[5] I was thrilled. Aristide Cavaillé-Coll was the primary creator of the French symphonic organ. His organs enabled and inspired a whole new approach to composition and

[5] http://musiqueorguequebec.ca/orgues/france/rouenso.html

improvisation. They were the instruments at which presided César Franck, Charles-Marie Widor, Camille Saint-Saens, Louis Vierne, Marcel Dupré, and many others too numerous to name.

After mass, Monsieur Gouellin showed me how to operate the ventils and invited me to play. I was excited to hear the organ played, but even more thrilled to play it myself. To my utter surprise, he then invited me to return in two weeks to take his place while he was out of town adjudicating. I did not then realize that Maurice Gouellin and the organ of St-Ouen were presenting me with a life-changing opportunity.

I returned on Sunday, October 12th with my French brother Jérôme, Linda Lancione (an exchange student from California), and her French sister.[6] We lingered after mass, and I continued to play for perhaps thirty minutes until the sacristan shouted from the nave floor that it was time to close and lock the building.[7]

Even after this incredible experience, I still had no clue that this was one of the greatest historic organs in the world. I am the envy of several of my colleagues today because I played mass there. It is no longer a functioning church but a heritage site and concert venue.

[6] Music played at St-Ouen on 12 October 1958: Prelude: Bach *Little Prelude and Fugue in B-flat Major*; Offertoire: Searle Wright *Chorale Prelude on Brother James' Air*; Communion: Léon Boëllmann *Prière à Nôtre-Dame*; Sortie: my own semi-improvised variations on *Lobe den Herren*.

[7] I recently discovered a newspaper clipping in my 1958 diary. On that same afternoon, Marcel Dupré was playing Vespers at the Church of Ste-Vivian in celebration of the 60th anniversary of his appointment there as titular organist at the age of twelve. This was also the dedication of a new organ by Jacquot-Laverne de Rambervilliers to replace the one destroyed during the war. I, however, spent the afternoon with my friends. I later heard Dupré play a recital on the new organ but cannot remember when it occurred. I recall writing an arrogantly critical review of the recital. I submitted it to *The American Organist* magazine. I am eternally grateful that the editors did not publish it.

Charles-Marie Widor, who composed and premiered his *Symphonie Gothique* here for the organ's dedication in 1890, said of this organ, "It is a work of art worthy of Michelangelo."

Albert Dupré was the titular organist of St-Ouen at the time. His four-year-old son Marcel, who was deemed too young to attend, escaped from his nanny (who was walking him in a nearby park), climbed the gallery steps and listened unobtrusively from a dark place where he could hear everything.[8]

On one of my visits to Caudebec I met Monsieur Jean Yon (a printer from Rouen, organ enthusiast, and friend of Marcel Dupré) who was very kind to me. When he discovered my interest in improvisation, he recommended that I study with Marcel Lanquetuit, titular organist of the cathedral in Rouen[9], who was the first organ student of Marcel Dupré and a lifelong friend.

All Saints Day, November 1st, is a holiday in France: no school. I took the bus to Rouen, attending Terce (which included a solemn Te Deum) and a pontifical mass at the Cathédrale Notre-Dame de Rouen, to meet Marcel Lanquetuit.[10] We agreed to meet at his home on Wednesday mornings for the rest of the year. As AFS exchange students were on a very strict personal budget of five dollars per week, he deferred my tuition fees until after I returned to Kansas City in January. I don't remember how much he charged me for each lesson, but the money order I sent him on my return to the United States was certainly less than a hundred dollars. The instrument at his home was a two-

---

[8] Dupré, Marcel; *Recollections*, English translation published by Belwin-Mills Publishing Corp, Melville, New York. © 1972, 1975 Éditions Bournemann, Paris. pp 8-9.

[9] https://en.wikipedia.org/wiki/Marcel_Lanquetuit

[10] Many churches and most cathedrals in France are dedicated to Our Lady, the Blessed Virgin Mary. Rouen Cathedral is the fourth such edifice mentioned above.

manual-and-pedal harmonium with an electrical wind pump.[11] My lessons consisted of rigorous exercises in harmonizing scales and simple melodies at the keyboard, followed by simple improvisations. The instruction book was *Exercices préparatoires à l'improvisation libre* by Marcel Dupré.

I played a semi-private recital at Rouen Cathedral on 3 January 1959. The programme consisted of music I had learned before coming to France.[12]

The historic gallery organ at Rouen Cathedral was blown off the west wall on 30 May 1944 when an Allied bomb exploded in the north tower. The organ crashed to the nave floor and nothing could be salvaged. Marcel Dupré donated an eleven-stop organ which Cavaillé-Coll had built for his father's music room in 1896.[13] It served as the only organ in the cathedral until the current gallery instrument was finished and dedicated in 1956. The new organ was designed by Marcel Dupré and built by Jacquot-Laverne de Rambervilliers.[14] It included state-of-the-art electro-pneumatic key, stop, and combination actions. Now, nearly seven decades later, it needs a thorough rebuild, and sufficient

---

[11] The turbine which compresses air for a pipe organ is normally called a blower. Harmonium reeds are powered by sucking, rather than blowing, the air. It is therefore a vacuum rather than a blower. I avoided calling it that in the main text to avoid confusion with a vacuum cleaner.

[12] Recital played at Rouen Cathedral on 3 January 1959: Ralph Vaughan Williams, Chorale Preludes on *Rhosymedre* and *Hyfrydol*; Bach Fugue in D major (BWV 532); Searle Wright, Chorale Preludes on Brother James' *Air and Greensleeves*; Richard Purvis, Chorale Prelude on *Greensleeves*; RBS, semi-improvised variations on *Lobe den Herren*; Pietro Yon, *Gesù Bambino*; Leon Boëllmann, Toccata from *Suite Gothique*.

[13] http://musiqueorguequebec.ca/orgues/france/rouennd.html

[14] Ibid

money does not seem to be available. I contributed €100 in 2015, but they need hundreds of thousands.

In early January 1959, shortly before my return to the United States, I made a week-long excursion to Paris.[15] During that time I visited Pierre Cochereau in the gallery at the cathedral and Marcel Dupré in the gallery of St-Sulpice. This was my second visit to the tribune of Notre-Dame. I had earlier visited there in October when I came to Paris for Danielle Nytrée's wedding. Monsieur Cochereau shared his goal of replacing the mechanical action and Barker levers at Notre-Dame with modern electro-pneumatic action and a modern console. I was horrified and, I hope tactfully, told him so. Needless to say, the opinion of this brash American teenager carried no influence at all.

I returned to Notre-Dame in 1973 to play a public recital on the rebuilt organ and console.[16] It was — new action and console notwithstanding — one of the greatest thrills of my life. The organ was rebuilt again in 2012 with yet another new console. On 15 April 2019 the cathedral suffered a catastrophic fire, but fortunately the organ suffered no structural damage. The smoke and soot ,though, require it to be completely dismantled, cleaned, revoiced, and reassembled. No one knows how much the acoustics of the building, a key component of organ sound, will be affected. Completion of the architectural and organ work is scheduled for 2025.

My visit to Marcel Dupré was likewise an important moment in my young life. I had, of course, written in advance to request permission to visit. As mentioned earlier, French organists received guests in the gallery during mass. Monsieur Dupré, one of the most famous organists

[15] Details in the chapter called "France 1958-1959."

[16] http://musiqueorguequebec.ca/orgues/france/ndamep.html

in the world, attracted a couple of dozen admirers to the rather small gallery at St-Sulpice.[17] I was warned of this by Marcel Lanquetuit and advised to present myself to Mme Dupré. This I did. She quietly told her husband that I was the expected student of *le petit Marcel* and he immediately invited me to sit to his left on the organ bench. I cannot remember any conversation between us. I do remember well that he played a simple piece from his *79 Chorales* during communion. It was a piece I knew. One of the sycophants in the gallery asked, in French of course, "O master, what was that?" Dupré replied modestly, "Something that I wrote for kids."[18]

I departed France on 15 January 1959.

---

[17] http://musiqueorguequebec.ca/orgues/france/ssulpice.html
[18] «Ô maître, que-ce que c'est? » « Quelque chose que j'ai écrite pour les gosses. »

A Young Musician at Trinity College, Hartford
(1959-1964)

I didn't choose Trinity College. The Holy Spirit chose it for me.

I was born in Michigan, as was my mother. From a young age, we both assumed I would attend the University of Michigan. This was later reinforced by the presence of both Robert Noehren and Marilyn Mason in the organ department of the School of Music. Both had exerted a positive influence on me during my Kansas City years: he from long-playing records borrowed from the public library; she from personal recital visits to Kansas City, as well as recordings. I admired his scholarship; I esteemed her virtuosity and advocacy of contemporary American organ composers.

I applied to the University of Michigan from France in the fall of 1958. This was decades before the internet so all such things were done on paper and sent by mail. I sat the Scholastic Aptitude Test in Paris in early December. On the way home in late January, I stopped in Ann Arbor for my admissions interview. There I received both good and bad news. The good news was that I had been admitted; the bad news was that Michigan Governor G. Mennen "Soapy" Williams had created a budget crisis. There were no scholarships for out-of-state university students that year. That afternoon, I had a lovely visit with Marilyn Mason at her home and an early evening dinner on campus with both of my grandfathers.

In addition to Michigan, I had successfully applied to Yale where there were special scholarships for Kansas City men. Dad also learned that there were scholarships at Trinity College, Hartford, for clergy sons, for which he obtained permission for me to make a late application after my return from France. My reaction to this was, "Trinity, shminity." I'd never heard of the place and was not in the least interested. I nevertheless filled out the application to keep the peace.

A local alumni representative visited my home soon thereafter to conduct an admissions interview. I learned from him that the Chair of the Music Department and College Organist, Clarence Watters, had been a distinguished student of Marcel Dupré in Paris. That changed everything: Trinity suddenly became my first choice.

I was quickly admitted with a scholarship that paid for about 75% of all expenses. The remainder was covered by a student loan (repayable after graduation) and an on-campus job. I only needed to take care of transportation costs and pocket money. I immediately notified Yale that I would not be attending and withdrew my scholarship application there.

I soon ordered a Clarence Watters recording at the local music store. I received a short letter from Professor Watters that summer welcoming me to Trinity and offering me a position as one of his two chapel assistants. The job, which paid around $100 per semester, was to play for the weekday Morning Prayer services in the crypt chapel. The unit pipe organ[1] there was designed by G. Donald Harrison. It was small but sufficient for practice or leading hymns and canticles in the warm, intimate, and reverberant crypt-chapel acoustics.

I travelled from Kansas City to Hartford by Greyhound bus, with changes in Chicago and New York City. I probably stopped in New

[1] A unit organ is one where the electrical action is wired so that some or all of the ranks may be used at several pitches, often on more than one manual. This creates the illusion that the organ is larger than it is, while lowering the cost by requiring fewer

York City for a visit with my godfather, Eddie Pitt, who lived in the Hollis section of Queens. I recall attending Sunday morning solemn high mass at the Church of St. Mary the Virgin (affectionately known as Smoky Mary's) on 46th Street in Manhattan, and Sunday Evensong at the Cathedral of St. John the Divine. I particularly remember Larry King, then assistant cathedral organist, playing the *Passacaglia* from Leo Sowerby's *Symphony in G Minor*. I learned a useful trick from him when playing a large piece in extremely reverberant acoustics: start at a normal tempo, then slow down a bit to keep the building from muddying the texture. Little did I know that more than a decade later Larry King would become a trusted friend and colleague when he and Dad served together at Trinity Church, Wall Street.

I arrived in Hartford in the latter part of the afternoon on Labour Day, 7 September 1959. I took the Broad Street bus from downtown to the college. The bus ride was uneventful, but the walk across campus carrying my suitcase and heavy portable phonograph was an ordeal. A taxi would have been sensible, but taxis were not part of my vocabulary as a rectory kid.

I SHARED a choice dormitory room on the third floor of Cook A. It was, at that time, one of the nicest dorms on campus. There was a window just outside our door which overlooked Hamlin dining hall. From there, we could see whether the line to food service at the steam table was long or short. My roommate was Ray Drate from Brooklyn.

ranks of pipes. It is useful for practice and for playing simple music, but fails when playing larger organ literature. For example, on a unit organ it is possible to need the same pipe simultaneously in two or three different places. On a normal organ, these notes would be played on two or three independent ranks of pipes, therefore producing two or three discrete sounds.

We were probably placed together because we each had serious musical interests, albeit from different parts of the universe. His great loves were opera and Broadway theatre, while mine were church music and jazz. He was a mathematical genius and an academic perfectionist.

Ray was of Russian Jewish ancestry. He told me that his family name was Dratevka, but that the immigration officer at Ellis Island Americanized it to Drate. As Dratevka is the feminine form of his surname, I suspect that he learned this bit of family mythology from his grandmother. His grandfather's surname would probably have been Dratevky or Dratevki.

As a young person raised in the Episcopal Church, and occasional organist at Temple B'nai Jehudah, a reform synagogue in Kansas City, I was only aware of Judaism as a faith community. I thought that being Jewish only implied certain beliefs about God. Ray himself was agnostic and it was a revelation to me that one could be a secular Jew. I knew nothing of Jewish culture, but I learned much about it from him: pastrami on rye, blintzes, egg cremes, bagels and lox, matrilineal descent, and much more.

Ray and I essentially lost touch after our freshman year. I withdrew from college in the spring of 1961 and did not return to classes until after my marriage in the fall of 1963 I regret that I was totally unaware of the senior year musical he composed. He died soon thereafter while at graduate school. Ray's sophomore year roommate told me more than fifty years later that Ray was in the theatre program at the University of California at Berkeley, and died of a gunshot wound. According to Ray's father, he had been cleaning a gun used as a stage prop.

Trinity was a liberal arts college, for which I'm now grateful, even though I wasn't too happy then. The first two years before declaring a major were devoted mostly to English, your chosen foreign language (French for me), European history, math, science, religion, and philosophy.

MY FIRST BIG academic shock was to learn that applied music was not part of the curriculum for a music major, which included music history and appreciation, harmony, counterpoint, and composition. Organ lessons, the main reason I was there, were an extra-curricular activity, and the cost of lessons was not covered by tuition.[2] One received neither grades nor credits toward graduation. I had to pay out of pocket.

Trinity College Chapel, an astoundingly beautiful 20th-century Gothic Revival edifice, stood at the centre of the campus and my life. I would describe it as Early English Gothic because it has a beamed wooden ceiling rather than stone vaulting. Unlike many college buildings, it was named after the college and not its benefactor, William G. Mather.[3] The principal architect was Philip H. Frohman, who from 1921 until his death in 1972[4], was the principal architect of the Cathedral Church of St. Peter and St. Paul in Washington, DC. (a.k.a. the Washington National Cathedral).

[2] It would have been the same had I gone to Yale. Only Michigan, of the three colleges to which I applied, offered a music degree.

[3] I was dumbfounded to learn that William G. Mather, class of 1877, was a direct descendant of the Massachusetts Puritan minister, Cotton Mather, one of the early architects of American racial and religious bigotry. He preached and wrote about the superiority of white Protestants over blacks, Muslims, and Roman Catholics. His understanding of correct Protestant belief also excluded Anglicans. That his many-times great-grandson donated an Anglican Chapel should have him turning in his grave. To learn more about Cotton Mather, see Ibram X. Kendi: *Stamped from the*

I was given a chapel key and had round-the-clock access to the building. I preferred to practice late into the evening after my homework was done. I could stay awake to practice the organ, but I was unable to stay awake for late-night academic work. There were four pipe organs in the building: a small unit organ on a landing about halfway up the carillon tower, the already-mentioned one in the crypt chapel, a Rieger positif, and the main organ. The latter was historically significant. Installed in 1932 soon after the opening of the new chapel, it was the first Skinner organ independently designed by G. Donald Harrison. The sound was powerful but a bit on the coarse side when compared with Harrison's later instruments. The reed stops were decidedly English rather than the more French ones of his later organs.[5] As a chapel assistant, I had freer access to the main organ than other organ students, who were each only allowed to use it for one hour before their respective lessons.

Professor Watters originally hoped that Harrison would rebuild the organ and relocate it to the west end in line with Harrison's later thinking, but there was no money in the college budget for such an undertaking. The project had to wait for a benefactor or benefactors to step forward. By the time I arrived in 1959, Don Harrison had been dead for three years. Professor Watters then hoped that the rebuild

Beginning – The Definitive History of Racist Ideas in America (Bold Type Books, New York City, 2016). See also William G. Mather - Wikipedia

[4] Even before a single architectural line was drafted, it was the stated intent of Remson B. Ogilby, president and college chaplain, "to construct a building without equal for beauty of design, one that would stand for all ages." Frohman was a logical and inspired choice. See Peter Grant, *The Chapel of Trinity College* (Trinity College, Hartford, 2007). See also Philip H. Frohman - Wikipedia

[5] Most people in my day thought of the 1932 organ as an Aeolian-Skinner, but the two companies did not merge until 1933. See also, G. Donald Harrison - Wikipedia

would be undertaken by Joseph Whiteford, Harrison's successor at Aeolian-Skinner. Watters' hope soon became my dream, finally realized in 1971 when the late Mary Lyman Brainerd bequeathed a new organ in memory of her husband, Newton C. Brainerd. He was a former mayor of Hartford and had served as a college trustee for 41 years. Mrs. Brainerd stipulated that the organ be built by Austin Organs of Hartford rather than an out-of-town builder.

We still got the instrument of our hopes and dreams because by-then-retired Professor Watters was the consultant. Everything was new, with the notable exception of the original bottom twelve open-wood pipes of the 32' Untersatz from the Harrison organ. These had always been under the rose window at the liturgical west end of the chapel. Such pipes were already prohibitively expensive by 1972 and would rarely be part of a new instrument today. The new organ was placed on a low gallery six feet above the nave floor and in front of the open wood pipes. It speaks directly up the nave toward the high altar. In 1986, a magnificent carved wooden case was added, and an image of Professor Watters features just above and to the right of the console. The organ is not only beautiful to hear but also beautiful to see, and has served the chapel longer than the original.[6]

[6] I have been invited back six times to play recitals on the new organ: in 1973, the same year I played Notre Dame de Paris; 1988, 25th class reunion; January 2003, Clarence Watter's centennial celebration recital (shared with other alumni students of Professor Watters during the month after his actual birthday); June 2003, 40th class reunion; 2013, 50th class reunion; 2023, 60th class reunion. I have also played for the class memorial services at our 50th and 60th reunions. It is worth noting that I was invited to play a carillon recital at my 45th class reunion in 2008, which I did in memory of Thalia. It is 112 steps each way to get to the carillon. After four trips up and down, plus the physical exertion of playing, I thought I was going to die. That was my final visit to the carillon, I shall never go up there again.

I STUDIED ORGAN and some piano privately with Professor Watters from September 1959 until the spring of 1962. From 1959 until March 1963, I also sang in the chapel choir. I am normally a baritone but I also learned to sing countertenor when the repertoire called for it. On special occasions, the chapel choir combined with the boys of St. James' Church, West Hartford, where Professor Watters was also organist-choirmaster. This combined choir was styled *The Cantores Sancti*. We sang at the Ceremony of Lessons and Carols every December in the college chapel.

The Cantores Sancti were invited to sing at the main Eucharist for the Second Sunday of Easter 1960 at the Cathedral of St. John the Divine in New York City. We also sang by invitation at special Evensongs in parish churches around the Diocese of Connecticut. The rectors were often Trinity College alumni. These parish Evensongs featured music by Thomas Tallis. A particular joy was singing some of our Tallis repertoire on the charter bus that returned the choir to Hartford. My favourite was, *Blessed are those who keep his testimonies*. I later included this anthem on the 1973 Te Deum Singers' compact disc, *In quires and places where they sing*.

Because the chaplain was a poor singer, Professor Watters invited me and a couple of others to become precentors. We chanted those parts of Evensong usually sung by the officiant. This was invaluable training for me later in my career when it became my role to train seminarians as well as parish clergy. I also learned to play the carillon. Chapel Choir members were paid about $100 per semester. I was Assistant Carillonneur in my second year and was paid for that also.

I was, thanks to Professor Watters, quickly able to replace my on-campus library job with better paying church positions. I was organist-choirmaster at the West Avon Congregation Church during my first academic year, and then moved to the Congregational Church in South Granby in the fall of 1960, remaining there until the end of 1962.

First-year academic classes included advanced algebra, basic calculus, English, European history from the Middle Ages through the 19th century, a survey of French literature, and harmony. Members of the class of 1963 who had successfully completed their first semester of academic work matriculated in a chapel ceremony in January 1960. Professor Watters played the march (*Marcia*) from Charles Marie Widor's Third Organ Symphony for the academic procession, as he would again when Thalia and I married in 1963.

My second-year classes included basic biology, basic German, religion (Judeo-Christian thought with E. LaB. Cherbonnier in the first semester and Old Testament with Theodore Mauch in the second), 18th-century French literature, and 16th-century counterpoint.

During my first two years as a student, and the following two living in an apartment near the edge of campus, I presented three organ recitals in the college chapel. Looking again at those printed programmes now, I am surprized at the technical difficulty of the repertoire.

I ENTERED THE 1962 National Organ Playing Competition of the First Presbyterian Church of Fort Wayne, Indiana. Contestants had to be under thirty-five years of age. The prize was a fully paid guest appearance in the church's annual recital series. The preliminary round consisted of selecting, recording, and submitting three major works: J.S. Bach, romantic, and contemporary. The submitted recording had to be continuous, witnessed, and unedited. There were, if I remember correctly, twenty-six contestants in the preliminary round. These taped performances, averaging 25-30 minutes each, were played for a panel of three local judges unaware of the performers' identities. Eight finalists were selected to come to Fort Wayne to anonymously repeat their three selections in person before a panel of three different judges, mostly university organ teachers. Each contestant was responsible for his or her own transportation to and from Fort Wayne but the church arranged and paid for nearby hotel lodging and food. I made the finals but did not win. The winner was Professor Eugen Gmeiner, Chapel Organist at Acadia University in Wolfville, Nova Scotia.[7] I tried again the following year but did not make the finals.

A. GRAHAM DOWN, a visiting summer school instructor, sought me out in July of 1962 because he had questions about the chapel organ and organs in general. He taught English, and perhaps history, at the Lawrenceville School in New Jersey, and was organist-choirmaster at Trinity Lutheran Church in Trenton. He was also chair of the

[7] Eugen was the only other contestant with whom I formed a friendship. We shared mealtimes and turned pages for each other during practice sessions and the final competition. If I had to lose, I am glad that it was to him. He was a landed immigrant in Canada from Austria. As such, he could not enter the USA without a visa. The Canadian Minister of Immigration therefore pre-emptively approved his citizenship application so that he could travel to Fort Wayne for the finals.

Eugen later addressed a letter to me simply as "Richard Birney Smith, organist – Hartford, Connecticut, USA" and the post office delivered it. I doubt that such a thing would occur today. We stayed occasionally in touch by mail over the years. He died much too young at 49 or 50 in 1977.

committee in charge of commissioning a new organ for the school. We became frequent luncheon companions and had long, interesting conversations. We made two field trips that summer. The first was a four-or-five-night trip to Montreal and Québec City to see specific recent organs.

In Montreal, we visited and played three organs by Rudolph von Beckerath of Hamburg, Germany: Queen Mary Road United Church in Westmount (1959), l'Eglise de l'Immaculée-Conception (1961), and l'Oratoire Saint-Joseph (1959) on top of Mont-Royal. We were hosted at each by the resident organist: Kenneth Gilbert, Gaston Arel, and Raymond Daveluy. They all wanted historically-informed mechanical-action (a.k.a tracker action) organs, but despite their searches in the mid-1950s, found that such instruments were not being built in North America. Kenneth Gilbert was particularly gracious. When he learned I was interested in the harpsichord, he invited me to play his personal Wittmayer instrument in the parish hall and gave me a phonograph recording of him playing it. I had no inkling at the time that he would later become a mentor who would change my musical perception and perhaps even my career trajectory.

Graham Down and I continued from Montreal to Québec City to hear and play the organ at l'Eglise des Saints-Martyrs-Canadiens. It was built by Casavant Frères of St-Hyacinthe, and while still electro-pneumatic, represented a turning point for this century-old Québec firm. Under the strong influence of Kenneth Gilbert and his Montreal colleagues, Casavant opened a tracker shop in 1961 dedicated to building historically-informed mechanical action instruments. We were warmly welcomed at Saints-Martyrs-Canadiens by parish organist

Claude Lavoie, who demonstrated the organ. He also opened my ears and mind to a style of improvisation that was less formal and more spontaneous than the practices of the disciples of Marcel Dupré.

We proceeded from Québec City to visit the basilica at Ste-Anne de Beaupré. I wanted to see it because I had played a piece during my high school years by Alexander Russell called *The Bells of Saint-Anne de Beaupré*. Going there was an anticlimax at the end of the trip because it turned out to be a holy tourist trap, but I'm glad we went.

The second trip with Graham Down was to visit the organ of his church, Trinity Evangelical Lutheran, in Trenton, New Jersey. This medium-sized two-manual organ was a gem. Like the instrument at Trinity College, it had one company's name on the console but was the inspired work of another organ builder within the firm. That person was C. Wilson Barry. Graham then took me to Princeton to meet Will Barry. Over the years, Will became a mentor, my favourite living organ builder, and a close personal friend.[8]

I played a carillon recital for the Southern New England Regional Convention of the American Guild of Organists at Trinity College on 25 June 1963. It preceded a choral performance of Ernest Bloch's *Sacred Service* in the chapel.

I RE-ENTERED TRINITY College in the fall of 1963 after a two-year absence from classes. I was now married.[9] Poor grades in biology had cost me my scholarship and earned me academic probation at the

[8] Our friendship developed for over sixty years to include his wife Louise, Thalia, all of his children, and several of his grandchildren, great-grandchildren, and later Rosie. I played the organ for his funeral in 2013, for Louise's funeral in 2023, and am an honorary member of the Barry family.

[9] See Chapter 15, "Thalia and I."

end of my third semester. Failure in biology earned me academic suspension at the end of my fourth. Passing a science course was a prerequisite for entering third year classes.

I took basic philosophy; repeated basic German; music history and appreciation with Clarence "Pete" Barber, Associate Professor of Music; and church music with McNeil Robinson, organist and choirmaster of the Church of St. Mary the Virgin, New York City. He replaced Professor Watters during the latter's sabbatical leave.

In early November of 1963, Thalia and I drove down to play a recital on the Wilson Barry organ at Graham Down's church in Trenton for the Central New Jersey Chapter of the American Guild of Organists. We were billeted at the Lawrenceville School. The recital went very well. I would have liked Will Barry to hear what I could do with his marvellous instrument, but he and his family had moved to Massachusetts that summer so he could take a position at the Andover Organ Company. Pete Barber was unhappy that I was skipping classes to play an out-of-town recital, but the trip was a clear indication that my priority was music performance rather than academics. I withdrew from college before the end of the semester.

I consciously carried guilt about not graduating for at least a decade. That was lifted by Pete Barber after my 1973 recital at the college. Over coffee in a local diner, I confessed my intent to return someday to finish my degree. He replied, "Whatever for?" and explained that I had already acquired enough knowledge and experience in my career that earning a degree would add little. That was a huge weight lifted from my shoulders. Despite this, guilt unconsciously survives and continues. In my recurring dreams about returning to campus as a student and graduating, I am about two decades older than the graduating seniors.

One of the curious details of my student life was that I formed no lasting friendships with my 1963 classmates. I spent my time locked inside the chapel practicing the organ. I attended only one football game in my first week as a college student and never witnessed another intercollegiate sporting event. It was not until I was invited back to perform an organ recital for our 25th class reunion in 1988 that I finally connected with classmates. Since then, I have been an active member and cemented numerous friendships. The Class of '63 is a unique group of men, the most successful in the history of Trinity. We regularly set records in the tens of millions of dollars for reunion gifts to the college. When in the past I have expressed discomfort at my lack of financial success, my classmates quickly reassured me that they were as proud of my artistic accomplishments as they were of other classmates' business achievements.

We are especially proud that we established the Class of '63 Scholarship at our 25th reunion.[10] One of our carefully-selected students, based on need and ability, enters the freshman class each year and graduates debt-free four years later. This continued until our 50th reunion in 2013 when we decided to support two students annually. More recently, we pledged $3 million toward much-needed repairs and renovations to our 90-year-old chapel.

After I participated in the 2003 Clarence Watters centennial recital, Professor Marjorie Butcher[11], a great fan of organ music, asked me a question: I don't remember it exactly, but it was phrased in such a way

[10] Trinity College began accepting female undergraduates in 1971. I am personally proud that the Class of '63 scholars are an ethnically, racially, and gender diverse group of people.

[11] Marjorie Butcher, Professor of Mathematics, began teaching at Trinity in the fall of

that I could not avoid mentioning the fact that I had never graduated. She quickly nominated me to the Board of Trustees for a Bachelor of Arts degree, honoris causa. My B.A. was presented at our 40th class reunion in 2003. Several of my classmates expressed surprise I had not graduated; they had not noticed that I was sitting in the audience rather than with them.

1959, the same year my class entered. She was the first female faculty member of the college. I never studied with her, and I doubt that we met before that day in 2003.

-15-

Thalia and I
(1963)

Thalia Bessie Anne Woodward Lumsden was the first great love of my life. One can only say that in retrospect; it is impossible to know such things at the beginning of a relationship.

I met her on 27 March 1963 on a blind date. She had turned twenty-one earlier that month. I was twenty-two and living in Hartford, Connecticut.

Completing a science course was a prerequisite to entering the third year of study at Trinity College. I failed biology at the end of 1960-1961, my second year in college and was therefore placed on academic suspension. I successfully completed a biology course the following academic year at the University of Hartford and transferred the credit back to Trinity. This ended the suspension, but I did not have enough money saved to pay tuition to re-enter college in the fall of 1962. I continued working as a door-to-door book salesman, church musician, and keyboard teacher while trying to accumulate the necessary funds.

I shared a third-floor apartment near the edge of campus with another Trinity student. In many ways, I continued much of my student life without attending classes. For example, I continued to sing in the chapel choir, function as a precentor at Sunday Evensong, and share occasional meals with friends on campus. Organ lessons were put on hold because I had little practice time outside what was necessary to maintain my church job.

In late February or early March, my roommate's girlfriend, Jan, told me she and a friend, Douglas, had found an interesting date for me: a young Scottish woman named Thalia. The funny thing was that Jan had never met Thalia and Douglas had never met me. They somehow figured out that we would make an interesting couple.

Thalia was born and raised in Cupar-Fife, Scotland, and had been living in the United States for only nineteen months.[1] At the time, she was working as a mother's helper for a Glastonbury family with eight children and, in addition, dancing a specially-created role in an amateur theatre production of the Broadway musical *Brigadoon* in nearby Bloomfield. Douglas was Thalia's bagpiper.

Earlier in March, I made a careless left turn into oncoming traffic while on a sales call in Thompsonville. My Volkswagen Beetle was demolished, and I ended up in hospital for observation. Jan came to visit while I was there. I asked if she and Douglas had made any progress toward setting me up with Thalia. She replied that they had not figured out how to introduce us. I, therefore, impatiently asked for Thalia's phone number.

It took a few days for Douglas to get Thalia's permission to give out the family phone number and for Jan to pass it on to me. I called almost immediately on Monday evening, March 25th. Thalia and I had a

---

[1] This was Thalia's second trip to the United States. She had visited in 1959 as a Girl Guide, an exchange between her hometown group and the Girl Scouts of Manchester, Connecticut. Her impression was that the carefully planned and scripted visit, including a brief audience with President Eisenhower at the White House, gave a false best-foot-forward impression of the USA. Thalia wanted to come back to live and see the real America. She therefore raised the money to return to live with a family in Manchester. She quickly obtained a job as a long-distance telephone operator. Direct-dial long-distance was just being introduced. Most long-distance calls still required operator assistance.

pleasant conversation for ten or fifteen minutes. She asked me whether I preferred to be called Richard or Dick. No one had ever asked me that before. It took only a second or two for me to decide that I preferred Richard. Only people who knew me prior to that day have since been allowed to call me Dick. I also warned her, as was necessary in those days, that I was Negro. She did not see that as a problem.

I invited her out on Wednesday. I decided on a luncheon invitation rather than an evening one to minimize the awkwardness of an interracial date. Meeting in broad daylight was simpler.

I arrived promptly at noon to meet Thalia at the family home where she worked. When a slender blonde, who did not match my pre-conceived notion of what a Scottish girl looked like, opened the door, I said, "Good afternoon, Mrs. Peek. I am Richard, here to meet Thalia." She replied, "Hello Richard, I'm Thalia." I had expected that I would have to pass inspection and engage in small talk with her employer before being allowed to proceed, but none of that happened. Thalia and I left directly.

We were both well-dressed for the occasion, as was normal then. She wore a smart, light-grey wool skirt and jacket, nylon stockings and high-heeled shoes. I wore a navy blue suit and tie.

I knew nothing about Glastonbury, so I took Thalia to lunch at Aunt Jemima's, a familiar restaurant in Wethersfield, not far from the college. Looking back from the 21st century, it seems inconceivable that an African American would patronize a place with such a racially stereotypical name and logo, but this was before such issues rose to public awareness.

We had a lovely and lively conversation for close to two hours over ham, eggs, and pancakes. Interracial couples were rare in 1963, and many restaurant patrons stared at us. Thalia noticed this, and innocently thought they were doing so because we were such an attractive couple. I did not want to end the afternoon by taking her home. I therefore obtained her permission to show her around the Trinity College campus. While there, I gave her a tour of the chapel and played the organ for her. All the while, the engaging conversation continued.[2] She eventually had to return home because Mr. and Mrs. Peek were going out for a Wednesday evening Lenten discussion group at their church. Thalia invited me in to meet the family, all ten of them.

They had already finished dinner and, before long, the parents left for church. I don't remember the next part of the evening in detail. I probably talked with the pre-teen children, and maybe watched a bit of television with them while Thalia cleaned up the kitchen. She then invited me to have some scrambled eggs with her. They were soft-cooked and I, unaccustomed to this, almost gagged and was unable to finish eating all of them. I am still embarrassed more than five decades later. I made the feeble excuse that I wasn't hungry. She should have immediately asked me to leave but didn't.

Thalia then absented herself to put the children to bed and I hung around, probably watching television. It would have been polite of me to say goodbye to let her get on with her work, but my manners failed me yet again. Shortly after, Thalia rejoined me in the living room as Mr. and Mrs. Peek came home. We made polite conversation for a while

[2] Thalia was so engaging that I completely forgot that I had that morning scheduled an impromptu evening celebration with an attractive magazine salesperson. My purchase of a subscription to Gourmet Magazine had pushed her over a sales goal which would earn her a prize or a bonus. This was the first and only time in my life that I stood up a date.

before Mrs. Peek, who was four months' pregnant, excused herself to retire for the night. Charlie Peek, an engineer for the Pratt & Whitney division of United Aircraft, asked me a question about what makes a pipe organ tick. Not sensing that he was trying to get rid of me, I gave him a detailed answer. As he later told the story, I talked and drew diagrams for more than two hours until he gave up and went upstairs to bed.

Thalia and I resumed our conversation which gradually warmed up romantically. Somewhere about 2 o'clock in the morning, I proposed marriage. Being a trained salesman, I gave her a choice between two things, both of which were acceptable to me: September or October. At that point, she teared up and said (in her beautiful soft Fife accent), "I can't. I've a son." Like many British women of her generation and earlier, she considered herself soiled linen and permanently ineligible for marriage.

She then explained that after arriving in the USA, she discovered herself pregnant by a boyfriend back in Scotland. She had written him, explaining her predicament, but he never replied. She incorrectly interpreted this to mean he was ignoring her and turning his back on the situation.[3] I assured her that my feelings were unchanged and that my proposal still stood. She said neither yes nor no but indicated that she would think about it. The time was now approaching 3 o'clock in the morning, and I finally had enough sense to leave.

[3] Thalia was likely impregnated the night before she left Scotland. She was in a relationship with a married man twelve-or-so years her senior. When it became obvious she was pregnant, her Manchester host and sponsor disowned and expelled her. A kind neighbour, Mrs. Ouellet took her in. Not long after, Thalia was fired from her job at Bell Telephone. It is a miracle she was not deported. She also managed to keep the pregnancy permanently secret from most of her family. Only her sister, Sonia,

Thalia got a few hours' sleep. Maxine Peek, after getting her husband off to work and the kids off to school, brought her a cup of coffee and asked how the date had gone. Thalia replied, "We're going to get married after the baby arrives." Seeing the horrified look on Mrs. Peek's face, she quickly added, "Your baby, Mrs. Peek; after *your* baby arrives."

Despite what she had said to Mrs. Peek, Thalia did not accept my proposal for a full four weeks. I saw her almost daily after that until I flew to Kansas City on April 13th for Easter. My mother, in the aftermath of the automobile accident, had arranged for me to come home for ten days or so. While there, I told her about Thalia but was too scared of my father's reaction to tell him. My lack of trust deeply hurt him. I consulted with Mother's favourite jeweller about an engagement ring, and suspect he gave me a cardboard sheet with holes in it to measure Thalia's ring size.

I next saw Thalia on Wednesday, April 24th. Her first words were, "When can we get married, Richard?"

We chose September 7th at Trinity College Chapel. The date was safely after Maxine Peek's due date. Thalia generously submitted to my desire to be married at Trinity with my teacher at the organ, even though she would have preferred to marry in the Congregational Church in South Glastonbury, which she attended with the Peek family. The minister there, Rev. Ted Hoskins, was an exceptional pastor, and

knew. Thalia spent the last weeks of her pregnancy in an unwed mothers' home in Bridgeport. Her son, whom she called Lachlan, was born on 30 May 1962. She was allowed only a brief time with him before he was whisked away. Children's Aid did not want an unwed mother to bond with the child and perhaps change her mind about giving the baby up for adoption. The letter she had previously written to Lachlan's father in Scotland was never forwarded.

had greatly helped her settle into the Peek family home after the trauma of giving up her child. Thalia had been raised in the Episcopal Church of Scotland but had drifted to the Free Church in Cupar because they had youth activities that were lacking in the rather staid Anglican parish.

The next four months are a blur. Thalia and I continued to meet almost daily after work. I would usually arrive at the Peek's home around 10 o'clock. I was useless as a book salesman; my concentration was off, and my heart wasn't in it. I started a new church job at Holy Trinity Church in Southbridge, Massachusetts sometime around the beginning of May. I was paid the princely sum of $200 per month with no benefits. It was a one-hour drive from home, but gasoline was only 29¢ per gallon. Looking back, I don't know how I survived with so little money, but I was accustomed to pinching pennies. My mother had been a good teacher.

Four memories stand out from that spring and summer. Thalia wanted a pearl engagement ring rather than the normal North American diamond solitaire. During my Kansas City trip in April, I had worked out a ring design: a slim band of white gold with a central pearl flanked on each side by three tiny diamonds. I presented it to her on May 4th in front of the whole Peek family, just before we left for the Trinity College prom. The Lester Lannin band was playing. The twist was still popular, but I liked the slow romantic dances more. It was a fun evening, and some of my classmates met Thalia for the first time.

The second stand-out memory was the struggle to find a place to live together after the wedding. Connecticut had yet to enact an equal housing law. This meant that any landlord could reject any potential tenant for any reason or no reason at all. We scoured the newspaper ads for suitable apartments to rent: apartment buildings, duplexes, and subdivided homes. We were always turned down with feeble excuses even before we were allowed to look at the place: the apartment is already rented, we only rent to teachers, we don't allow students. Even though we knew that the superintendents or owners were lying, we had no legal recourse. Moreover, who wants to live in a place where one is clearly unwelcome?

Finally, Ted Hoskins, the minister at the Congregational Church in South Glastonbury offered us a recently vacated apartment above the church offices. It was a temporary arrangement because the building was slated for demolition and the entire church building was to be moved and expanded on the corner lot occupied by the offices. He faced fierce opposition from some members of his congregation, including some whom Thalia considered to be friends, but prevailed in the end. The negative argument I remember most vividly was that the church would be setting a bad example for the neighbourhood children if an interracial couple were allowed to live there. Ted enlisted some of the men of the congregation to come and clean the place. It was a major job involving sanding, painting, and removing a significant amount of junk left behind by the previous tenants. As far as Ted was concerned, South Church was merely being Christian. The rent, including all utilities, was $90 monthly, which seemed like the earth to us.

I gave my Hartford landlord appropriate notice and moved to South Glastonbury on September 1st. Neither of us owned a stick of furniture, other than my phonograph, but various people generously gave us a card table, some folding chairs, and a sofa. We didn't own a bed, but a thick slab of foam rubber on the floor was all we needed. We were aware that Thalia's female friends were planning a wedding shower and that there were boxes and boxes of wedding presents arriving daily at the Peeks' home.

The third stand-out memory was the marriage preparation course we attended. It was a two or two-and-a-half-hour interfaith session once a week for four weeks in a Unitarian-Universalist Church in Hartford. The facilitators were Jewish, Christians of several denominations, and non-religious people. Even though birth control was still illegal in Connecticut, we were well-instructed by a gynecologist on how to avoid unwanted pregnancy, and conversely the most efficient ways to get pregnant when desired. Thalia's doctor was cooperative and gave her a prescription for the (then still new) birth control pill. She started taking them in late July as we had been instructed in the course.

Fourth, the blood test. When we went to get the blood test necessary to apply for a Connecticut marriage licence, the lab technician looked at us and asked, "Do you two know what you are doing?" We assured him that we did. After drawing the blood, he, looking embarrassed, said, "Well, at least the blood's the same colour."

My parents and siblings arrived the day before the wedding and stayed at the old Bond Hotel in downtown Hartford. The wedding rehearsal took place in the college chapel on Friday evening. There were three clergy: J. Moulton Thomas, the college chaplain; Ted Hoskins, from South Church; and Dad. Thalia and Dad met each other for the first time that evening. I would have preferred a Nuptial Eucharist on Saturday rather than just a wedding ceremony, but Thalia had never been confirmed in Scotland. Confirmation was, in those days, considered a prerequisite to receiving communion. We therefore privately celebrated the Eucharist in the Crypt Chapel after the rehearsal. Five were in attendance: Thalia and I; Dad presiding; Robert Harned, the best man; and Joan Onderdonk, the maid of honour. Only the priest, bride, and groom received communion, as was normal in those days. To end the evening, Thalia and I went to Giovanni's, our preferred romantic coffee house. We ordered our favourite pastries: cannoli for Thalia and rum baba for me.

The wedding day, September 7th, arrived bright, beautiful, and right on schedule. I went across the street to the drugstore for breakfast. The pineapple juice burned a little as I swallowed, but I didn't take much notice. I put on a suit and tie, walked two doors down the street to South Church, and played the organ for a morning wedding. Money was tight, and we needed every penny that we could get.

Thalia sewed dresses for the bridesmaids and the maid of honour as well as her wedding gown and going-away dress. I changed for our wedding around half past noon: full morning cutaway with striped trousers, wing collared shirt, waistcoat, and cravat. It was considered gauche in those days to wear evening formal wear before 5 p.m. My rented cutaway was a little too big, but I had to live with it. The best man picked me up sometime after 1 o'clock and drove me to the college chapel. We arrived by 1:30 and waited in the sacristy until the service began at 2.

Thalia and I each had one fear on our wedding day. I feared, as she had often intimated, that she would adhere to the Scottish tradition of arriving late. She feared the wedding ring, as I had joked, would feature a black pearl to contrast the engagement ring. We each had the good sense not to actualise either.

We had mailed three hundred wedding invitations, perhaps a third of them to friends of my parents whom we did not even know. Somewhere between 150 and 200 people attended, many were personally invited because we ran out of printed invitations. Bill Bowie, a good friend and Master Carillonneur of Trinity College, played the carillon for 20-30 minutes before the ceremony.[4] Daniel Peek, the eldest of the Peek children, along with Louis Otis (Skip) House III and Buckley (Buck) Johnson, both mutual friends from the Post-High Discussion Seminar (PHDs) at South Church were ushers. Clarence Watters, my teacher and College Organist, played *Marcia* from Charles-Marie Widor's Third Organ Symphony as the processional, which included six more Peek children. Marilyn, barely a year, and newborn Robert were too young to participate. Emily and John, the next youngest, led off as flower girl and ring bearer. They were followed by four Peek bridesmaids: Eileen, Lillian, Stephanie, and Catherine. Joannie Onderdonk, the maid of honour preceded the bride. Thalia's Scottish family was unable to attend, so Charlie Peek stood in for George Lumsden, the father of the bride, and escorted Thalia up the aisle.

Chaplain Thomas officiated. Ted Hoskins presided over the

[4] William T. Bowie was one of my few personal friends on campus. He became Noëlle's godfather in 1966. He returned to Trinity as an associate professor of chemistry in 1971: the first full-time black faculty member.

[5] More progressive denominations, such as the United Church of Christ, had recognized that "man and wife" were unequal terms, still the language of property, and had changed the phrase to "husband and wife." Anglicans would take another decade or so to do the same.

exchange of vows and pronounced us man and wife.[5] The congregation then sang *All people that on earth do dwell* with Clarence Watters providing a wildly modern free accompaniment to the final verse, *Praise God from whom all blessings flow.* Dad led the final prayers and pronounced the blessing. He brought a brand-new aspergillum, which resembled a black fountain pen, to sprinkle holy water on us during the nuptial blessing. Clarence Watters played the *Final* from Louis Vierne's First Organ Symphony as the recessional. It was normal for the bride and groom to exit very quickly, but Thalia and I took our time so that we could enjoy the music.

We lingered in the glorious sunshine on the lawn outside the chapel to greet our guests and allow movies and photos. Our volunteer official photographer used a brand-new camera for the first time and came up with nothing. We therefore have a scant photographic record of the occasion. My godfather's 8mm movie camera produced an overexposed record of the moments outside the chapel. This we later transferred to a videotape which I still possess.

The wedding was the first opportunity for Thalia to meet some of my friends and extended family. They included my mother, brother and sister; both sets of grandparents; my mother's sister and my father's sister, who had driven over from Detroit in three cars; and my godfather who had driven up from Queens. It also allowed me to meet some of Thalia's friends for the first time. The most important person was Mrs. Ouellet, the Manchester neighbour who had taken Thalia in during the awful early days of her pregnancy.

We then all proceeded to the Peek's home in Glastonbury for the reception, a gift from Maxine and Charlie Peek. The house was beautifully decorated. There was a formal receiving line in front of the living room fireplace. I remember thanking Mrs. Ouellet for "taking care of my girl" but not much else. I had sung the wedding hymn with great gusto and really irritated what had seemed a minor sore throat. The refreshments included hundreds of petit fours, a choice of alcoholic or non-alcoholic punches, and an authentic Scottish wedding cake. In Canada, we are accustomed to fruitcake at weddings, but it was brand new, at least to me, in the United States in 1963.

It was a joyous day for all, indoors and outside on the lawn. We lingered until 5:30 or 6 o'clock. Thalia changed into her going-away outfit, the bridal bouquet was thrown, and the best man drove us home, less than ten minutes away.

Arriving there, we discovered that the seats from our recently-acquired Volkswagen Beetle had been removed and placed in the apartment. Some friends from the Post High Discussion Seminar had decided to help us furnish our rather bare apartment. It was a cute prank but I, suffering from an excruciatingly sore throat, had lost all sense of humour. I called someone, said some regrettably unkind things, and they came over to reinstall the seats in the car.

After I changed into regular clothing, Thalia took me to her doctor, a wedding guest, who diagnosed a viral infection: strep throat. There is little you can do except take painkillers, gargle, and wait for your immune system to kill a virus. Thalia drove us to Sturbridge, Massachusetts, to spend our wedding night in a motel near my church. We simply could not afford for me to take a Sunday off.

Arriving at church on Sunday morning, we were surprised to discover a pew full of extended family members who had driven up from Hartford. We all went out for brunch after church. We received numerous cash gifts from parishioners and family to help with honeymoon expenses. This was before the days of credit cards, except for department store accounts. Almost everything was therefore paid in cash. Looking back, it was probably a blessing we could not overspend and go into debt for our honeymoon.

Thalia and I drove to New York City, about four hours from Southbridge, and checked in at the not-quite-finished Lincoln Square Motor Inn which was quite inexpensive. Lincoln Center, the future home of the Metropolitan Opera, New York Philharmonic, the New York City Ballet, and the Julliard School of Music, was still under construction across the street. We went out for supper at a nearby Chinese restaurant, a new gastronomical experience for me.

My sore throat was much better on Monday morning. I turned to Thalia and said, "Good morning, wife." She replied, in her inimitable soft Fife accent, "Good morning, maaaan." A tender moment that I treasure to this day. Our honeymoon was brief, three or four nights in New York City. We spent a lot of time alone together as newlyweds are wont to do. One detail was particularly notable: no one stared at us. New Yorkers, at least then, were considered cold and matter-of-fact. Interracial couples did not attract particular attention.

At the time, our marriage was illegal in 24 out of 50 states. Despite the constitutional provision that states are obligated to recognize each others' legal documents, we could have been arrested in many places for inhabiting the same hotel room or living together. Fortunately, Thalia and I wanted to get married in Connecticut. Dad could not have solemnized our marriage at our home parish in Kansas City. It was not until 1967 in the landmark decision Loving v. Virginia that the US Supreme Court declared anti-miscegenation laws unconstitutional. Richard and Mildrid Loving were legally married in the District of Columbia in 1958 but were arrested and sentenced to a year in jail for living together in Virginia. It took nine years for their various appeals to grind their way to the US Supreme Court.

Thalia and I loved New York City. I remember that we went to Basin Street East one evening for an enjoyable dinner show featuring edgy black comedian Dick Gregory, and the Stan Getz Quartet. We also visited the Playboy Club for inexpensive drinks and a meal. My parents and siblings were also in New York for a few days. I particularly remember my mother visiting us one evening. She and Thalia bonded well. I was however horrified when Mother commented that she and Thalia were very much alike.

We returned home on Wednesday or Thursday. Weekly choir rehearsals at Holy Trinity Church resumed that Thursday evening. On Monday of the following week, Thalia started a new job as a sales clerk at Sage-Allen, a downtown Hartford department store, and I re-entered Trinity College as a third-year student. I had arranged most of my classes in the mornings. I would often drop Thalia at work, attend class and then drive to Southbridge to teach piano or organ students at Holy Trinity Church. Thalia did some dressmaking on the side and picked up a few extra hours of work sewing in a Glastonbury shop that made curtains and draperies. It was a hectic life for both of us, but we seemed to survive — until catastrophe struck.

On Friday, November 22nd, I dropped Thalia at the shop for an afternoon of sewing and headed to Southbridge to teach some lessons.

Shortly after I drove away, the programme on the car radio was interrupted by a news bulletin that gunshots had been heard during a presidential motorcade in Dallas, Texas. The President's car had sped away from the scene. Within the next few minutes, the national network took over from local programming and confirmed that President Kennedy had indeed been shot. I was about halfway to Southbridge when his death was announced. I called the rector from a payphone along the highway. We arranged to meet at the church in thirty minutes. Father John P. Miller, my student Neil Hicks, and I then shared a requiem Eucharist in memory of President Kennedy.

From that Friday afternoon until President Kennedy's state funeral in Washington and his burial at Arlington National Cemetery on Monday, November 25th the world pretty much stopped for Thalia and me, and for millions of others. We were glued to the television in the Peeks' living room for most of the weekend.

Over the next four to six weeks I sank into what I can only describe as a serious depression. The concept of clinical depression had not yet reached popular awareness, and it never occurred to us that I needed medical or psychological attention. I managed to do my church work and teach lessons, but my academic work suffered. I attended some classes but fell behind in assignments. I was exhausted by supper time and could not stay awake over homework. I withdrew from college before the end of the semester.

I do not remember Christmas at all. I do vaguely remember that we had a New Year's Eve party with many of our friends from the Post-High Discussion Seminar. The only memory that survives is that one of the guys drank half a bottle of the lavender water I had been given for Christmas 1958 in France.

And so ended 1963.

-16-

Early Marriage Years
(1964-1965)

The first several months of 1964 seem to be lost in a fog. I was still recovering from undiagnosed and untreated depression following the assassination of U.S. President John F. Kennedy the previous November. Thalia and I continued living in our rented apartment in Connecticut above the offices of the Congregational Church in South Glastonbury.

She continued working as a clerk at Sage-Allen, a department store in downtown Hartford. I continued the five-days-a-week one-hour commute to Holy Trinity Church in Southbridge, Massachusetts. There I played Sunday morning Eucharists, conducted Thursday evening choir rehearsals, and taught numerous private students on the other days. Thalia accompanied me every Sunday morning and on Thursday evenings as often as her work schedule allowed. My work at Holy Trinity was, by and large, happy. The rector and the choir were supportive as I slowly began learning how to be a person among persons. My musical skills were excellent, but my interpersonal skills left much to be desired.

The choir at Holy Trinity had some good voices but had not been exposed to much of what I deemed to be the great music of the Church. With the rector's support, I quickly changed direction, a challenge which was enthusiastically accepted. We soon sang Tallis, Gibbons, Byrd, Palestrina, and others. On the previous Fourth Sunday in Advent, Bill Bowie (who played the carillon prelude for our wedding), came up to sing the solo part in *This is the Record of John* by the late-

Renaissance English composer, Orlando Gibbons (1583-1625). We had also added David Willcocks' recently published compilation, *Carols for Choirs*, in time for Christmas. One delightful bit of good fortune occurred when a thirteen-year-old soprano, Sandy Haig, auditioned for the choir. She possessed a natural, pure, bell-like voice that no one had yet had an opportunity to spoil. She was an excellent chorister who was also capable of solo work. I particularly remember her singing *If God be for us, who can be against us?* from Handel's Messiah. It quickly became and remains my favourite Messiah aria.

We formed several long-term friendships which lasted for years after we left Southbridge. The rector John Preston Miller and his wife Barbara were a great support to a young interracial couple who were virtually integrating the town. Will and Mary Hicks — she sang soprano in the choir — frequently welcomed us into their home, and their eldest son, Neil, studied piano and organ with me. Sof Kollios, short for Sofoclis, the son of Greek immigrants, sang bass in the choir. He ran a short-order restaurant which served breakfasts and lunches in downtown Southbridge. While McDonald's and its competitors were becoming established in major cities, fast food had not yet arrived in Southbridge. Thalia and I loved to go to *Sof's Central Spa* for Sunday brunch after church before driving back to Hartford. One of the peculiarities of our life as a young couple was that our close friends were fifteen to twenty years older than we were.

On Good Friday, 27 March 1964, the Holy Trinity Choir, the Rector, and I presented a major service of music and the spoken word. The musical centrepiece was *The Seven Last Words from the Cross* by Heinrich Schütz. It is scored for choir, soloists, and strings. Ernest Nordman, a keen amateur violist and member of the congregation, recruited a couple of violinists and another violist from Providence, Rhode Island, where he worked. I recruited one of Thalia's friends from Glastonbury to play violoncello.

Soon after this event, Ernest, the first violinist, the other viola player (who was also a violinist), and I decided to stay together to form a permanent organization. The ensemble was quickly named *The Gregorian Consort*. Our first concert was at Holy Trinity Church on May 22nd. The programme included a harpsichord piece by Handel, bass arias by Bach and Purcell, and ensemble pieces by Bach, Corelli, and Telemann. By then we had added a recorder player and a bass singer. Early rehearsals were held in the recorder player's living room in Providence. Jackie Walker[1] had a full family of custom-made Von Heune recorders and a large collection of Renaissance and Baroque sheet music. We played a wide variety of pieces for two to five instruments with harpsichord continuo. Ernest had earlier built the harpsichord from a Zuckerman kit.

In the late spring or early summer, Thalia and I upgraded our transportation from a used Volkswagen Beetle to a brand-new 1964 MG 1100. It was a two-door sedan with front-wheel drive which, while common now, was an innovation in 1964. Thalia and I also decided to

---

[1] Jackie Walker was an incredible character as well as a fine musician. She considered herself a moral atheist but, especially when we were playing religious music, expressed fear, dare I say terror, of God. Somehow she thought God would get upset at her for playing Christian music. I was therefore never convinced of her atheism. Bill Schoedel, violinist and violist, had lived in Canada for a significant period of time and was able to give Thalia and me a great deal of useful information about Canada later when we were preparing to move to Saskatoon.

leave the Hartford area and move to Southbridge. We found a pleasant and affordable second-floor apartment on Hamilton Street, a few blocks from the church, to occupy at the beginning of September.

I played a major organ recital at St. Thomas Church, 5th Avenue, in New York City on 5 August 1964, for the 50th Anniversary Convention of the American Field Service (AFS). I was thrilled to have an opportunity to play the large 1956 Aeolian-Skinner organ that some considered to be G. Donald Harrison's masterpiece.[2] In addition to playing significant works by Bach, Louis Vierne, and Marcel Dupré, I gave the first performance of my own *Four versets on O filii et filiae*. Newspaper clippings from before the recital indicated that I originally planned to play only three. The first three movements were complete on paper and were played on the chancel organ. The fourth and final movement was partially improvised. It juxtaposed *Victimae paschali* played on the full resources of the chancel organ with *O filii et filiae* which was proclaimed from the powerful *trompette en chamade* stop which spoke from high on the west wall above the main entrance to the church. I am still proud of this composition more than five decades later. It is dedicated to the memory of Stephen P. Galatti, President of AFS[3], who died unexpectedly on July 13th.

The St. Thomas recital was almost certainly Thalia's debut as my

---

[2] The organ at St. Thomas has a huge endowment. I have been told that it is larger than can ever be spent. The 1956 Aeolian-Skinner that I played has twice been extensively redesigned. In 1996, a separate mechanical-action Taylor & Brody instrument was built in the west gallery. The main organ was replaced in 2018 with a brand-new instrument by Dobson Pipe Organ Builders. It never occurred to me to ask AFS for complimentary registrations to the convention. I was not paid for the recital. Some form of reciprocity would have been appreciated.

[3] Stephen Galatti - Wikipedia

page-turner, a role she admirably and dependably fulfilled at all public concerts for at least the next twenty-five years.

BACK IN KANSAS CITY, my parents were rapidly heading toward separation and divorce. I was not there, but I suspect it was not a happy place for my siblings. My dad strongly disapproved of my sister's boyfriend, Howard Carney Jr. My later-in-life observation and experience indicate that strong parental disapproval drives couples closer together rather than apart. If I am correct, his disapproval worked in spades: Marris was pregnant before the end of 1963.

Mother had promised herself that she would stay with Dad until my brother graduated high school. Later in my life, my psychiatrist told me that this strategy, though common, was damaging to all concerned. Mother persuaded me, Thalia, and my brother Birney that it would be better if he came to live with us in New England. So after less than one year of marriage, we agreed to have a teenage son.

Thalia and I set out for Kansas City in mid-August. We stopped in Evanston, Illinois, for a day or two, staying with family friends. I remember our moment of arrival in Kansas City. Thalia bounded out of the car, barefoot, to enjoy walking in the grass. I quickly screamed for her to get out of the grass. She stopped and calmly asked why. "Chiggers!" I exclaimed. She had never heard of these pesky almost invisible arachnids whose bites cause nasty itching. She thought that I had exclaimed the N-word. Fortunately, none had bitten her. After a good laugh, we knocked on the door and entered.

I remember little of our visit. We naturally attended St. Augustine's on Sunday, August 30th. After church, I do recall a high-school girlfriend from 1958 mischievously telling Thalia that I had married the wrong person. Later that afternoon or, perhaps more likely, Monday afternoon, we received a telephone call announcing that Marris had safely delivered a baby girl, Angela Louise Carney. Birney's memory is considerably more sedate, but I remember he and I dancing around like fools and exclaiming to each other: "You're an uncle!"

We packed Birney and his belongings into the back seat of our car and headed home to Glastonbury midweek. It was tight. We drove straight through, stopping only for food, fuel, and bathrooms, with perhaps the occasional snooze in a rest area parking lot. We had no money for hotels.

On Saturday, September 5th, we rented a truck at reduced weekend rates for our move to Southbridge and loaded the truck that afternoon. Birney and I drove to Southbridge early Sunday morning. Massachusetts still had many blue laws in effect. Trucks were, thereby, prohibited from driving on Massachusetts highways on Sundays between sunrise and sunset. We had to leave very early to arrive at our new home shortly after dawn. I played the Sunday morning Eucharist as usual. The truck was unloaded during the day: neither Birney nor I can remember details. Thalia did not come to Southbridge with us. Perhaps she followed later in the car or stayed behind to clean the Glastonbury apartment. If the latter, she would have billeted with the Peeks. We returned the truck on Labour Day morning, and the three of us piled into the MG 1100 to go to our new home.

BIRNEY ENTERED SOUTHBRIDGE high school the next day for his senior year. Thalia opened a dance school several days weekly at the Sturbridge Recreation Centre. I continued playing Sunday services, conducting choir rehearsals, and teaching private lessons. Mother periodically sent some money to help defray the cost of feeding and housing Birney. Despite all this, there was never enough to make ends meet. I therefore made myself available as a substitute teacher at Southbridge High. I sometimes taught English, French, band, or history. I merely babysat at other times for math and science classes.

The generally favourable student reviews of my teaching were carried home by Birney. I remember two amusing stories. The first occurred while taking attendance on my first day. Numerous French-Canadian families migrated to Southbridge in the late 19th and early 20th centuries to seek employment opportunities, particularly in the textile mills. Proud that I spoke fluent French, I pronounced the students' names with my best accent. I was unaware until they started laughing that their names had, over the years, become quite anglicized. I particularly remember Jeanne Bourgeois, perhaps because she was near the beginning of the alphabet. I called out her name, and the class erupted into guffaws. As the laughter subsided, someone asked, "Do you mean Jeannie Bur-joyce?"

On another occasion, I referred to something as a polyglottal redundancy. The moment seemed unexceptional until my brother brought the story home. According to him, no one dared ask what I meant. The students loved "polyglottal redundancy", and the story quickly spread. At any rate, I enjoyed classroom teaching and was popular with the students and the administration. I was often called.

Thalia's dance classes were very successful. She had mostly girls but also a few boys from kindergarten age up to and including teens. We purchased a portable stereo phonograph for our home and for dance classes to replace the monaural Magnavox which I had carted from Kansas City in 1959. To end the season in June 1965, Thalia choreographed and mounted a complete performance of Stravinsky's *Petrouchka*. She was able to create a role for every one of her students, and knowing her, she probably sewed many of the costumes too. I conducted the stereo: Pierre Montoux and the Boston Symphony Orchestra.

FRIDAY EVENINGS SOON became a special event with rehearsals of The Gregorian Consort. Birney and I would pick Thalia up around 5 o'clock as she finished teaching. We then drove to Providence, stopping there at a drive-in fish-and-chips restaurant. (I still adhered to Anglo-Catholic discipline and did not eat meat on Fridays.) Each week before we arrived, Ernest tuned the harpsichord. He had arranged space in a local church where it could be stored and we could rehearse.

Our next concert was an organ dedication on October 25th at the Church of the Reconciliation in nearby Webster, Massachusetts. The programme included the *Carillon de Longpont* (a solo organ piece by Louis Vierne), ensemble pieces by d'Aquin, Albinoni, Hovhaness, and Telemann, and concluded with Handel's Concerto #2 in B-flat major for organ and orchestra. Later in the year, we added a husband and wife team who played oboe and flute. The Gregorian Consort was great fun and planted a seed which finally sprouted in Dundas, Ontario in 1968 and eventually evolved into the Te Deum Orchestra & Singers.

I played a major recital on 1 March 1965 at Grace Church,

Providence. It was called *The Birth and Passion of Jesus Christ as Expressed in the Music of the Church Year*. The programme featured numerous short pieces by Bach, Dupré, LeBègue, Pachelbel, and Messiaen before concluding with six movements from *The Stations of the Cross* by Marcel Dupré. I received my first major newspaper review from Ruth Tripp in *The Providence Journal* the following day. She said many kind things. Regarding my programming: "His program followed the Church Year in its sequence and it resembled a museum tour in the manner in which music works of distinction were displayed with consummate taste." She concluded: "The recital displayed well-grounded musicianship and excellent power of communication."

On Sunday, 28 March 1965, I played a complete performance of Dupré's *Stations of the Cross* before Evensong at St Mark's Church in Philadelphia, Pennsylvania. Thalia and I, of course, had to arrive on Saturday to prepare organ registrations. We attended Sunday morning Eucharist for the Fourth Sunday in Lent. That morning I learned, from St. Mark's music director Wesley Day, to introduce hymns with only the unharmonized melody line. While I have modified the procedure somewhat, I have continued to use it ever since.

The Fourth Sunday in Lent is also known as Refreshment Sunday or Mothering Sunday, when ancient Lenten disciplines were and are briefly and slightly relaxed. After the morning service, simnel bread was served at the parish coffee hour. It was new to both of us. I consider theirs to be the most authentic I have ever tasted. It is a somewhat dry poppy seed bread made without shortening. I, for one, am glad that ancient Lenten dietary disciplines are considerably relaxed in the modern world.

IN MAY 1965, I was invited to become Organist and Master of the Choristers at the Cathedral of St. John the Evangelist in Saskatoon, Saskatchewan, Canada. Thalia and I decided to accept the offer the following month.[4]

I made my first long-playing phonograph recording, *Richard Birney-Smith at St. John's Parish, Waterbury, Connecticut*, in late July or early August. The organ, by my Kansas City organ-builder friend and mentor Charles McManus, was one that I had long admired. I naively wanted unique repertoire to attract public interest. This was a complete misunderstanding of the classical music marketplace: people do not generally purchase music that is unknown to them. The centrepiece of the recording was Bach's Canonic Variations on *Von Himmel hoch*. This piece is gorgeous, and I am still proud of my performance, but it did nothing to increase sales. Other pieces on the disc include two noëls by Nicolas LeBègue, my recently completed *Four versets on O filii et filiae*, and the final movement of Louis Vierne's First Organ Symphony. These other pieces are an accurate record of my artistic development in 1965, but I have evolved a long way since these performances. Lacking previous recording experience, I laid down the entire recording between midnight and 4 a.m.[5] I learned that evening that a professional-quality recorded performance requires two or more sessions.

The Friday after Labour Day, September 10th, The Gregorian Consort presented a farewell concert at Holy Trinity Church. I

[4] The details of this appointment are outlined in Chapter 17: "We move to Saskatchewan."

[5] Most pipe organs are in churches. Modern-day traffic noise, especially trucks and public transit, is almost always a problem. Organ recordings are therefore usually made in the wee hours of the morning.

conducted the ensemble pieces from the organ or harpsichord. I now look at the size and complexity of that programme and wonder if I had lost my senses. In addition to three organ solos, the programme included Handel's Organ Concerto #6 in B-flat; Vivaldi's Flute Concerto *Il Gardellino*; and the first movement of Bach's Brandenburg Concert #5 which concludes with a huge harpsichord cadenza. The climax of the evening was Bach's Brandenburg Concerto #2. We hired Roger Murtha from the Hartford Symphony to play piccolo trumpet. The performance of this final piece was one of the greatest thrills of my young career. I do not remember any details of my final Sunday service.

We drove off toward Montreal on Monday morning.

We move to Saskatchewan
(1965-66)

A position-available ad appeared in the January 1965 issue of *The Diapason*, then the official journal of the American Guild of Organists (AGO), seeking applications for the position of organist-choirmaster at Knox United Church in Saskatoon, Saskatchewan. My first reaction was flippant: Superman wouldn't like that. The comment harked back to an old comic-book story of him rejecting full-face designs for an honorific postage stamp because he feared the possibility of the double 'o' in an Altoona, Pennsylvania, postmark circling his eyes perfectly and giving away his day-to-day secret identity as Clark Kent. I recognized the same possibility with a Saskatoon postmark. I was not yet ready to take seriously the possibility of applying for a position there.

When the ad appeared again in February, I discussed it with a United Church minister friend who lived near me in Massachusetts. We consulted his encyclopedia and learned that Saskatoon sat on the same latitude as London, England, was located in a semi-desert that survived as rich farmland because of the snowmelt, and often had winter temperatures as low as -25°F (-32°C). We also learned that Saskatchewan had some of the finest gravel highways in the world. This last fact reduced us to snickers.

When the ad appeared for the third time in the March issue, I said to myself, "Maybe God is trying to tell me something," and I applied for the position. Knox Church replied with a job description. We were not a good fit. I withdrew my application and thought the matter ended.

Meanwhile, The Very Rev. Elwood Harold Patterson, Dean of the Cathedral of St. John the Evangelist, two doors up the street on Spadina Crescent, decided it was time for a change in musical leadership. He therefore arranged to read the pile of applications at Knox and selected me as the person he was looking for. In late May, I received his letter. At first I thought it was from the Cathedral of St. John the Evangelist in Spokane, Washington, where I had been advertising myself for a possible recital engagement. Only after I opened the envelope and began reading, did I realize it was from Saskatoon. Dean Patterson offered me the position and invited me to telephone him collect.

Two aspects of this process would now be considered unethical. First, the position at the cathedral was not yet vacant. Second, the fact I was married was an explicit employment qualification.

On Monday June 13th, after my brother's high school graduation and patronal festival celebrations at Holy Trinity Church, I drove Birney and myself to Logan Airport in Boston. He departed for Chicago to rejoin our mother. At cathedral expense, I flew to Saskatoon via Winnipeg. While waiting there between planes, I met an Inuit gentleman dressed in a business suit, who was also between flights. It was, for me, a chilly evening but he was uncomfortably warm, a perhaps trivial memory but instructive for me. The Air Canada Vickers Viscount turboprop from Winnipeg landed into a brilliant orange Saskatoon sunset at 10:25 p.m. I had never seen anything like it. The beauty of the moment encouraged me to want to move there.

I was picked up at the airport by The Rev. Canon Roland Wood, Associate Rector of the cathedral parish. The next morning, after a good night's sleep and breakfast courtesy of Canon and Mrs. Wood, I was taken to the cathedral. I met Dean Patterson, affectionately known far and wide as Father Pat, who showed me around the church and the parish hall. I learned about the new Canadian maple leaf flag officially adopted earlier in the year, the approaching 1967 Canadian centennial celebrations, and that Dean Patterson was in remission — believed by many to be miraculous — from Hodgkin's Disease.

The wardens joined us later that day. I was surprised to learn that I was there not to be interviewed but rather to decide whether or not to accept their offer. There were no other candidates for the position. I obviously would have played the organ, and remember being impressed by the cathedral's beautiful reverberant acoustics, but unimpressed with the post-war Hill, Norman & Beard instrument. I stated clearly that it needed serious attention, probably a complete rebuild. This they agreed to investigate. The wardens explained that the organ had been problematic since its installation in the early 1950s. The extremely dry winter air in Saskatoon was desiccating the beautiful tongue-in-groove woodwork of the windchests. The builder had not thought to build the organ with local wood that could withstand the dry conditions of the Canadian prairie. On an occasion before my arrival, one or more swell shades had fallen off and crashed to the floor. The cathedral authorities installed a high-powered humidification system in the organ chamber, but it was never enough to solve the problem. When I enquired why the cathedral had imported an organ from England rather than purchasing a Casavant organ from Québec, I was told that the wardens of the time wanted an Anglican organ rather than a Roman Catholic one. Such a denominational distinction was imagined rather than real.

I returned home to Massachusetts to discuss the offer with Thalia.

Dad had often said that if a priest is asked to move from one parish to another, he should ask why. If he is asked to allow his name to stand for bishop, the question becomes "Why not?" It seemed to me that I, being offered a cathedral at the age of twenty-four, was in a similar situation. We asked, "Why not?"

THE CANADIAN IMMIGRATION procedure of the time was simple compared to what it is today. We had only to demonstrate that I had a job offer, take a simple physical examination which included X-ray proof that neither of us had active tuberculosis, and pay a small fee which was reimbursed by the cathedral. My doctor discovered only a spontaneously-healed tubercular scar from earlier in life. Immigration approval, never in doubt, arrived early in August. We scheduled our start at the cathedral for 15 September to allow for a farewell concert and final Sunday at Holy Trinity after Labour Day.

Shortly before leaving Massachusetts, we received a letter from Canon Wood that Dean Patterson's Hodgkins Disease had become active again. As we were busy preparing to move and knew little about Hodgkins, we did not appreciate the gravity of the situation.

Our furniture and belongings preceded us by van from the Mayflower moving company. Thalia and I drove from Southbridge to Montreal on Monday, 13 September. That evening we boarded a transcontinental Canadian National train for the forty-eight-hour journey to Saskatoon, while our car followed on a different train the next day. The trip was lovely. The food in the dining car was good, and the private sleeper was comfortable. One peculiar event occurred in Ontario: I picked up our drinks to join some people at another table only to be told that in Ontario you could not move your own drink, you had to ask the waiter to move it for you. That antiquated law and many others were fortunately modernized over the next few years after the liberalizing influences unleashed by the Expo 67 world fair in Montreal. We arrived in Saskatoon on time Wednesday evening in a blinding snowstorm. Thalia ruefully asked, "Where have you brought me?"

The cathedral had rented a lovely brand new apartment for us on Preston Avenue, near the edge of the city. We stayed with Canon and Mrs. Wood for the next few days awaiting the arrival of our furniture. Our car arrived on schedule, but our furniture did not. It was lost. Mayflower Van Lines had no idea where it was.

Choir rehearsals began almost immediately. I played all three musical services the next Sunday. I don't remember any musical details, but I do recall an old gentleman who spoke to me at the coffee hour following the 11 o'clock service. During our friendly conversation, he asked if Thalia and I had any children. When I replied that we didn't, he said, "You will. The winter nights here are long and cold."

THE CATHEDRAL PARISH had four services each Sunday: said Eucharist at 8, a contemporary family Eucharist at 9:40 (followed by church school), the main cathedral service at 11 (which alternated between sung Eucharist on the first, third, and fifth Sundays, and Mattins on the second and fourth Sundays) and Evensong at 4 o'clock.

The choirboys rehearsed for one hour, four times per week. This was on Tuesdays after school, and Thursday evenings at 7 for an hour with the choirmen to assemble and polish what had been learned in the other rehearsals. The choirmen then remained for additional rehearsal.

The boys were back for rehearsal Friday after school, followed by a dinner organized by their parents, and then Saturday mornings followed by floor hockey. We had an additional warmup every Sunday morning before the 11 o'clock service, and again in the afternoon on the few Sundays the choir was scheduled for Evensong.

The contemporary service wasn't, in my opinion, very contemporary. They were using the Elizabethan English of the 1962 Canadian revision of the *Book of Common Prayer*. The music was supposedly contemporary, but it was the pseudo-1930s-style music of Geoffrey Beaumont and others imported from England. The Dean wanted a full cathedral-style service at 11, with service settings sung by the choir, but the existing choir was far from capable of that. Evensong was a congregational, rather than choral, service. My work to raise St. John's to a cathedral-level musical programme was cut out for me.

Several members of the cathedral banded together to lend Thalia and me enough furniture to allow us to move into our apartment. We had packed some fall clothing to accompany us on our journey, but those items soon became inadequate in the wintry temperatures. Our belongings were finally located in a warehouse in North Dakota in mid-November, not by the company but by an individual driver. He was headed our way and had room in his truck for our small load. Thank God for small mercies.

My first big musical challenge was the annual University Service on the evening of my second Sunday in Saskatoon. This was a major event to open the academic year of the University of Saskatchewan nearby. Many faculty and students attended. I remember that the organ was uncooperative and I was stressed. I had little input into the service other than to do what I was told, as most of the music had been planned before my arrival. When Stanley Steer, Bishop of Saskatoon, finished the final prayer of Evensong, I uttered a sigh of relief and launched into the final hymn. A few seconds later, I heard his strong voice beside the console forcefully saying something like, "Young man! The Bishop of Saskatoon has yet to pronounce the Benediction." I wrapped up the phrase and stopped. I was told that the music had gone very well and that almost no one would have been aware of my mistake, but this is the only part of the service I remember.

We soon became aware that Dean Patterson was losing his battle with Hodgkin's Disease. I had a couple of private visits with him at his home where he shared his vision of what the cathedral's music could become, and he and I attended a few weekday Eucharists together in the chapel. I never played a service at which he presided. He returned to the hospital towards the end of October, and we were soon informed that he would live no more than a few days. The cathedral mounted an around-the-clock prayer vigil to pray for a peaceful passing. I participated but could not bring myself to pray for his death. I instead prayed for his complete recovery.

Dean Patterson died in late October. He was only forty-five. His funeral was set for Monday, November 1st, All Saints' Day. His wife, Mary Ellen, was not yet forty. His children, Janet and Michael, were eight and ten years old respectively. I vividly remember little Janet wandering aimlessly around the parish hall, a few steps from the dean's house, the afternoon of his death. Thalia, and perhaps other Scottish people, had a semi-automatic question when someone seemed disoriented: "Have you lost something?" Janet replied very quietly, "Yes.

My Daddy." It is one of those life moments I shall never forget.

The weekend before the funeral is now a blur. The main thing I remember is the Friday choirboys' rehearsal and dinner. The dean's son, Michael, surprised us by attending. As it was just a few days before Halloween, I was terrified that one of the choirboys would make a ghoulish comment. I think one of them tried when we were outdoors walking through the entrance procession, but he was quickly shushed. I also suspect Michael was away in his own little world and did not notice.

THE CATHEDRAL WAS packed for the funeral service and everything went smoothly. The single musical detail I remember was playing a majestic organ recessional, #3 in Bach's Orgelbüchlein: *Herr Christ, der einge Gottessohn*. Bach set it as an Advent chorale prelude, but I now think of it as a statement of faith, appropriate to the Feast of the Baptism of Christ. My favourite English translation is *"O thou of God the Father, foretold by ancient seers, by God the Father given, in human form appears. No sphere his light confining, no star so brightly shining as Christ, our Morning Star."* I never play this piece without thinking of Father Pat.

Mrs. Patterson, Michael, and Janet left a few weeks later to return to Welland, Ontario, their hometown, before moving west to Trail, B.C., and then to Saskatoon. Both children were given generous scholarships to Anglican private schools by a member or members of Father Pat's previous parish, St. David's Church. Michael attended Ridley College in St. Catharines. Janet attended Bishop Strachan School in Toronto and, for her final year, the previously all-male Ridley College. Michael was eventually ordained priest after attending Huron College in London. He spent his entire career in the Diocese of Niagara as the rector of several parishes, as well as Archdeacon of Niagara and Archdeacon of Trafalgar. He retired in 2022. (Boy, does that make me feel old.) Janet became a physician in Hamilton. She specialized first as an obstetrician-gynaecologist and then as a psychiatrist. Mrs. Patterson eventually remarried happily. After being widowed again, she moved to a retirement home in Oakville, near Michael. She died in 2022, well past the age of 90.

We quickly discovered that Halloween was locally considered the beginning of winter. We had a block heater installed in our car, and when plugged in, it warmed the engine oil so one could start in the sub-zero Fahrenheit (below -18°C) temperatures. Our MG 1100 was not designed for the prairie winter; the model was not even sold locally. The locally available Morris 1100 lacked the beautiful wood-panelled dashboard and glove compartment that our car had. We soon discovered why when the interior wood in our car cracked badly in the cold.

Thalia was invited to work at the university bookstore, which was conveniently located on the way from our apartment to the cathedral. This allowed me to drive her to work in the morning and pick her up at the end of the day. For most of the Saskatoon winter one went to work in the dark and returned home in the dark. To see the sun, it was necessary to go outside sometime during the day. The upside is that Saskatoon had more than three hundred days of sunshine annually.

Thalia did not work long at the bookstore before being offered a better job, assistant programme director at the YWCA. She was very happy and effective there, working with youth, young mothers, and Indigenous people. Thalia and Dixie Kee, the programme director, became lifelong friends, and continued to stay in touch long after each left Saskatoon for Ontario.

Back at the cathedral, I started a mixed choir to sing at the 9:40 service. I soon started updating the music to styles more akin to the folk music of the day. The backbone of the new repertoire was Herbert Draisell's mass setting called *Gloria*. Bert Draisell, who had been one year ahead of me at Trinity College, composed it while studying for the priesthood at General Theological Seminary in New York City.

Through parish and coffee-house connections, I was able to recruit a volunteer ensemble of several guitars and a five-string banjo as accompaniment. Notable among them were Graeme Card, Nancy Ward, Mairi McLean, and Michael Millar.[1] I first encountered *Nancy & Mairi*, a guitar-vocal duo, at a cathedral coffee house. I was so impressed that I rushed downstairs to my office and composed the tune *Diognetus*[2] for Francis Bland Tucker's Hymn, *The Great Creator of The World*, which is based on the 2nd or 3rd-century *Epistle to Diognetus*.

I soon discovered that the 9:40 service overlapped the men and boys' warmup for the 11 o'clock service. I therefore arranged to leave after the Nicene Creed and before the sermon. Alison Crabb, my organ student and member of the mixed choir, directed the remainder of the service.

---

[1] Graeme, Michael, and others who played from time to time in the cathedral folk mass went on to form Humphrey and the Dumptrucks, Nancy Ward went on to sing with Ian Thomas, David Wilcox, and Sylvia Tyson before launching her own solo career. Mairi McLean became a music producer for CBC Edmonton.

[2] I expanded *Diognetus* in 2019, adding a bridge as we would say in jazz, to accommodate the words in three verses rather than six. I have loved this tune ever since I first wrote it.

IN DECEMBER, I received a forwarded notice from the Hartford, Connecticut, draft board to report for a physical exam there. I had not realized that I was required by law to keep the draft board apprised of any change of address. They were none too happy that I had left the United States without notifying them. After several letters back and forth, I was ordered to appear for a physical exam in Minot, North Dakota. I had previously enjoyed a draft deferral as a student and exemption as a married man (introduced by President Kennedy, but rescinded by President Johnson as the Vietnam conflict intensified). Now I was in real danger of becoming cannon fodder.

The physical was scheduled over three days in January. I wasn't sufficiently perceptive to question why it took that long. The reason was that the Minot draft board had no medical facilities, so the exam had to take place in Fargo. Had I known that, I could have made a one-day drive there and saved myself two bleak winter days bouncing across the prairie on a school bus. One small joy of the trip was seeing the movie version of *My Fair Lady* one evening in Fargo.

While the drive from Saskatoon to Minot was relatively uneventful, the drive home through a blizzard was hellish. Visibility was near zero. In such conditions, the Royal Canadian Mounted Police patrols were removed from the roads. At one point, I followed the taillights in front of me and ended up in a stranger's driveway. Thankfully, I made it home into the safety of Thalia's waiting arms.

Needless to say, I passed the physical with flying colours. I also discovered that Minot had a very high Indigenous population who were exempt from the draft. I was therefore a scarce commodity: a draftable male. It was time for Thalia and me to discuss our options, of which only two were available: take my chances, hoping that I would not be drafted, or change my Selective Service classification, which at the time categorized individuals based on their eligibility and suitability for military service.

During a moment of discouragement after failing biology and being placed on academic suspension at Trinity College in 1961, I investigated my military options with a recruiting officer in Hartford. I asked if I might enlist as a chaplain's assistant or French interpreter. I was told that one could not choose chaplain's assistant before enlistment. I was also told that the military would only allow me to work as an interpreter in a language that they taught me, rather than a language in which I was already fluent. Thus neither desired option was available. The recruiter further told me, off the record of course, that I had nothing to offer the military and that I should do my best to avoid military service. I took his advice seriously: our only acceptable option was to change my draft classification.

Our original family planning goal was to conceive our first child in the fall after two years of marriage. Thalia did not want to be pregnant during the heat of summer. When the fall of 1965 arrived, we decided to postpone for two more years because we had just moved to Saskatoon and could not afford a family. This situation was however an emergency: it was time to get pregnant as quickly as possible. We had received very good pre-marital instruction. We learned that many couples fail to get pregnant because they have sex too often. The human male is infertile for about thirty-six hours after intercourse. One exponentially increases the probability of pregnancy by having intercourse every other day. Thank you, Dr. Grody, for giving us such sound advice.

We consulted Thalia's obstetrician who gave her a green light after a thorough physical. She then discontinued her birth-control pills. After normal menstruation resumed in February, we put the plan into action. It was not very romantic. By this time, Thalia was working at the YWCA. Sometimes we arrived home from work exhausted, but it was our scheduled day. Other times, we might be feeling mutually affectionate, but it was not our scheduled day. Thalia had a positive pregnancy test sometime around the first day of spring. The baby was due in mid-November. We were elated.

I notified the Selective Service Board in Hartford that we were expecting. They, of course, would not take my word for it. Dr. Brown, our obstetrician, had to respond on a form they supplied, file a progress report every ninety days, and then submit a notarized birth certificate.

THE NEW DEAN, the Very Reverend Douglas Ford, began his duties at the cathedral on Palm Sunday, 3 April 1966. I composed a new anthem for the evening service which endeavoured to relate Passover and Palm Sunday. It was based on Psalm 24, *Lift up your heads, O ye gates*. It juxtaposed Hebrew cantillation, sung by a Yemeni rabbi/cantor from a local synagogue, with Gregorian chant and *fauxbourdon*. I have never tried to revive it. The score probably still exists somewhere in my files, but I cannot easily put my hand on it. I do not remember any other detail about Holy Week and Easter except that on Easter morning, the ice broke on the South Saskatchewan River which ran in front of the cathedral. It was one of nature's spectacular moments, but also an incredibly cold day for those of us who equated Easter with springtime.

Life went on normally week by week. The summer had two highlights: a two-week choir school seminar at St. Olaf College in Northfield, Minnesota and a one-week diocesan choir camp for choirboys somewhere near Lloydminster, a small city which straddles the Saskatchewan-Alberta border. The choir school seminar was a Lutheran event, but none of their local choirmasters was available to attend. I was therefore recruited to attend at Lutheran expense. Thalia and I drove to somewhere near Winnipeg and stayed the night. We proceeded the next morning to the United Lutheran Church in Grand Forks, North Dakota, to play the 1964 Casavant mechanical-action organ.[3] I loved the instrument. I learned much later that the organ and voicing were the work of Karl Wilhelm, who was the tonal director of Casavant before starting his own company. He and I would interact on numerous future occasions.

Thalia and I arrived in Northfield for the choir school seminar on Saturday afternoon or evening to check in at St. Olaf's. On Sunday morning, we drove half an hour or so to attend Westwood Lutheran Church in suburban Minneapolis to hear and meet Ronald A. Nelson. Ron was to be one of the instructors at the seminar which began the next day. The anthem that morning was *God be merciful*, a simple contemporary hymn-setting by Daniel Moe of Psalm 67, which I adore to this day.

[3] Pipe Organ Database | Casavant Frères Ltée. (Opus 2790, 1964) United Lutheran Church.

The other two instructors at the choir-school seminar were Lindon J. Lundstrom[4], founder of the Choir School Guild, and Pastor Mandus Egge. I soon became the seminar's resident organist, playing the daily chapel services on the impressive large Schlicker gallery organ[5] in Boe Memorial Chapel at St. Olaf College.

The seminar's focus was the organization and running of a parish choir school to instruct children in the Christian faith, and to train them to sing. Ron Nelson, a full-time church musician, began that training at baptism by presenting each family with a long-playing phonograph recording of the first verse of perhaps forty hymns. These, if played frequently, allowed children to learn each by rote and participate in Sunday worship long before they were able to read from a hymn book. I learned, to my surprise, that a young child has no problem singing the first verse over and over while the congregation sings a multiple-verse hymn. Westwood Lutheran Church had multiple children's choirs for various age groups. A choir-school participant would progress through the system until adulthood, able to sing in tune and read music.

I also learned, I believe from the Suzuki violin method, to play the same music daily during the first year of a child's life. That was probably the idea behind Ron Nelson's hymn recording. My yet-to-be-born daughters listened to Handel's *Coronation Anthems* (Noëlle) and the Bach *Magnificat* (Monique) daily for the first year of their lives.

Pastor Egge gave us a thorough grounding in Lutheran hymnody (the art and practice of composing and singing hymns), a gift that has enriched the worship experience of my congregations throughout my

[4] Linden Lundstrom - Wikipedia

[5] The Schlicker Organ that I played has since been incorporated into a larger instrument by Holtkamp.

career. I also gained a better knowledge of the three North American branches of Lutheranism and their respective publishers.

There were no conference sessions on the weekend; most of the conferees returned to their homes and/or home churches. So while we were in Minnesota, we enjoyed a weekend drive to admire a few of the many lakes. While preparing to make our day trip, Thalia asked one of the conferees if they might have a map. The lady, misunderstanding Thalia's Broad-Scots accent, looked puzzled and promptly returned with a floor mop. All three of us enjoyed a good laugh.

On the Sunday morning between the two weeks of the conference, Thalia and I attended St. John's Lutheran Church in Northfield, Minnesota, to worship and hear the 1965 mechanical-action Andover Organ there.[6]

While I was in conference sessions, Thalia created her one-and-only oil painting, *Integration*. It was almost pointillist in style, each small brush stroke representing a person or group of people. The people on one side were all black; white on the other. There were a few black dots on the white side and a few white dots on the black side. The painting was divided into four quadrants by two walls of flame in the shape of a cross. Thalia, very aware of American segregation and South African apartheid, believed that true integration could only be achieved by people crossing through the flames of violence and war. At the time, no one thought South Africa could make its eventual peaceful transition under the leadership of Nelson Mandela and Desmond Tutu. As I write these words in 2022, many improvements have occurred, but we are a long way from anything resembling true equality.

[6] Pipe Organ Database | Andover Organ Co. (Opus 51, 1965) St. John's Lutheran Church

The Diocese of Saskatoon summer camp was turned over to choirboys for one week each summer. The attendees were mostly my own choristers augmented by a few from other parishes. We had two choir rehearsals each day, enriched with sports activities. Camp staff provided meals and other necessities. Thalia, now several months pregnant, was a big help to me and very popular with the boys. The summer weather in Saskatchewan, fortunately for her, was mild, and she avoided the discomforts that she had feared. The main thing I remember from the choir camp was a skit, created by the boys, that made fun of me. They were incredibly good at mimicking my mannerisms, including what Thalia called my "guppy mouth".

At the end of camp we returned to Saskatoon on Saturday to rehearse for a special Sunday morning Mattins, which featured the music we had learned during the week. The boys did us all proud.

-18-

Life in Saskatoon
(1966-1967)

Life in Saskatoon presented both Thalia and me with significant culture shock. The move from halfway between New York City and Boston to halfway between Regina and Prince Albert felt like deprivation. No quick trip to the big city for concerts or other activities. To me, the Saskatoon Symphony Orchestra seemed less skilled than the Evanston Township High School Orchestra of my early teens. Many brands in the supermarket were new to me too, though Thalia recognized some British ones. The Sunday edition of the *New York Times* did not arrive until Tuesday afternoon. The three cultural bright spots were the Greystone Singers (a university *a cappella* chorus directed by Robert Solem), the Mendel Art Gallery, and CBC Radio. The upside of this is that isolated from both American television and press, I was unable to live an American life. I slowly but surely became Canadian. The two years in Saskatoon were consequently an important period in my life.

Sometime between spring and fall, Thalia and I moved from Preston Avenue to an apartment in a small building on Fifth Avenue. We were now both within walking distance of our respective jobs.

My relationship with Dean Ford was not great. We struggled to work together. He probably had more patience than I did. I wanted to get on with what Father Pat had hired me to do, but the dean, naturally, had a different vision of church music. I had a high level of musical skill but lacked people skills. In later correspondence with someone, he acknowledged my musical skills but said that I had a "prickly personality." He got that right. It did not take long before I began to search for a new post.

Meanwhile, Thalia and I applied our new knowledge from the choir school seminar and started a small Saturday morning choir school in the parish hall. The students were very young, ages four through seven. We had several adult volunteers who helped. The session involved rhythm training (such as clapping and marching to recorded music), learning hymns mostly by rote, a brief worship service in the cathedral, and crafts. The part I remember best is the service where the dean and I worked well together. It lasted less than twenty minutes. One particularly effective part was the Bible lesson. I would first tell the story in simple language that a child could understand. The dean then read the story from the Bible. I thought it worked very well.

On 16 September 1966, Michael Ramsey, Lord Archbishop of Canterbury, visited the cathedral on a transcontinental tour. It was the feast day of St. Ninian, Apostle to the Southern Picts and Bishop of Whithorn, in what is now Scotland. We sang Evensong. Dean Ford officiated and Archbishop Ramsey preached.

I composed an anthem for the occasion, *Prayer for Bishops*. The text was the collect for the Consecration of Bishops.[1] The musical style was inspired by Josquin des Prez. As this was a diocesan event, I was directed to invite choir members from other parishes. I had been taught in college that a collect is usually in three sections. It opens with an invocation and acknowledgement of God, followed by a petition asking for what we want, and a conclusion acknowledging the mediation of

---

[1] *The Book of Common Prayer*, 1962, Canada, p. 657.

Jesus Christ.[2] Not happy with being forced to include singers of unknown skill, I composed the invocation and conclusion in a style I thought a massed choir could deliver, but reserved the petition for more skilled alto, tenor, and bass members of the cathedral choir. It worked.

Prayer for Bishops was sung again at Douglas Ford's request when he was later consecrated Bishop of Saskatoon. The Te Deum Singers sang it at least twice more in concert. I am still proud of this piece more than five decades after its composition and hope to have at least one more opportunity to perform it before I retire.

Thalia always shone when around British aristocracy. Glowing and seven-and-a-half months pregnant with Noëlle, she made a special dress and hat for the reception after the service. Archbishop Ramsey complimented Thalia on her hat. He did not comment on the music. ☺

Our child was supposed to arrive in mid-to-late November. Ultrasound imaging to determine a child's sex was not widely used in North America until the 1970s. Even if it were, we probably would not have wanted to know our child's sex in advance. We both wanted a European name that worked in both French and English. English speakers would badly mispronounce many of the names we liked. That eliminated Karen (with a broad "a"), Françoise, Geneviève, and a host of others. We eventually decided that our first son would be named Alistair Lumsden-Smith, as we both admired Alistair Cooke. Our first daughter would be named Noëlle Lumsden-Smith, partially in honour of a French cousin I found enchanting during my student days in France.

---

[2] Other authorities may describe the structure differently. More recent liturgical revisions will usually follow the ancient practice of including a doxological phrase acknowledging the Father and the Holy Spirit as well as Jesus Christ in the conclusion.

I was elected Chair of the Saskatoon Centre of the Royal Canadian College of Organists (RCCO). The two accomplishments I remember in this role were a large and well-attended hymn festival at Knox Church, which I programmed and led from the organ, and inviting Sir Francis Jackson, Organist and Master of the Choristers at York Minster, to play a major recital at Knox Church at the fall of 1967.

I also undertook two additional part-time jobs in the fall of 1966: the first was music instructor at the College of Emmanuel & St. Chad, an Anglican seminary, where my role was to teach future clergy to sing the Eucharist, Mattins, and Evensong; the second was as music director of the University of Saskatchewan Nurses' Choir.

Towards the end of their academic year, the nurses at the university presented an all-Canadian concert in honour of the Canadian Centennial.

THALIA'S NOVEMBER DUE date came and went with no sign of labour. This was the first, though unrecognized, trait of our elder daughter who has, throughout life, marched to her own drummer and never let others tell her what and when. When we reached the two-week mark, Dr. Brown directed that labour should be induced on Friday, December 2nd. Thalia agreed. I took her to University Hospital, just across the bridge from the cathedral. I spent most of the afternoon with her, left to rehearse the choirboys, and returned to wait, and wait, and wait.

When Thalia was finally sufficiently dilated, I was not allowed to follow her into delivery. Pre-natal classes for couples and the practice of allowing fathers in the delivery room were just becoming normal in the

Eastern United States but not yet in Western Canada. Dr. Brown thought that fathers would only get in the way, even possibly faint and require distracting medical attention. I was therefore ushered into a waiting room with four to six other expectant fathers. We sat in front of a black-and-white television watching an inane comedy show or movie. Saskatoon had only one channel and colour TV had only been introduced in Canada three months earlier.

Noëlle Lumsden-Smith arrived as the clock approached midnight. She was born a night owl and has so remained throughout her life. We soon learned that the hyphenated surname was not permissible under Saskatchewan law. All legitimate children had to carry the surname of the father. The same was true in Ontario when Monique was born twenty-six months later. Many people incorrectly assumed that Noëlle was so named because she was born in December, but her name had been chosen months before when we expected her to arrive in November.

After an hour or so, I was permitted to briefly visit Thalia and Noëlle in recovery. I thanked the nurses, at least one of whom sang in the nurses' choir, for taking "such good care of my girl." I remember that now with embarrassment. Such language, referring to a grown woman as a girl, was acceptable then but is no longer.

It was well after midnight when I left the hospital. The visitors' parking lot did not provide plugins for visitors' cars so my lovely MG1100 would not start. The only thing I could think of was to impose on my friend, organ student and chorister, Dennis Essar, who lived in a nearby dormitory. Good news: he was not asleep. The bad news: he was not in his room. Home was within walking distance, but I was not dressed for that cold. Buses were still running, so I took one.

Arriving home, I telephoned Dennis who had by then returned from doing laundry. He drove over to our apartment, picked me up, took me back to the hospital and used his battery cables to start my car. We then drove back to the apartment where I cooked a celebration breakfast in the wee hours.

Under the leadership of Premier Tommy Douglas in 1962, Saskatchewan had instituted universal medical care that covered both physicians and hospitals. Noëlle's birth therefore cost us nothing. We did pay a few dollars for a private hospital room for Thalia because she had to continue working by telephone. Dixie Kee, her boss, was away in Vancouver dealing with family illness or death. We should have asked the YWCA to reimburse us those few dollars, but we were so thankful for Noëlle and Saskatchewan healthcare that it didn't occur to us.

Thalia and Noëlle came home within a few days, and we resumed our busy lives. We juggled our schedules so that one of us could be home to care for Noëlle and enlisted the help of neighbours when we both had to work. All three of us attended a Greystone Singers Concert when Noëlle was only one week old. We sat in the back of the balcony. Thalia was dressed so she could easily nurse the baby if she got restless. Noëlle was very quiet.

She was an exceptionally beautiful baby. Don't all parents think that? I remember one friend asking, "How did the two of you manage to produce such a beautiful child?" The slightly insulting question is unanswerable.

Noëlle was baptized on Sunday 10 December 1966 at the cathedral during the 11 o'clock Mattins. Her godparents were Mary Hicks, John and Barbara Miller, and Bill Bowie.

I remember one unusual evening in January. Thalia and I were both home and we decided on the spur of the moment to see a movie. We jumped in the car and headed downtown, suddenly realizing within a few blocks that we had a baby at home. Oops! We quickly returned, enlisted the help of a neighbour, and were still able to go out.

Life went on. Dennis Essar and his friend Ken Gordon soon moved into an upstairs apartment in our building. They were great friends and a huge help in caring for Noëlle when Thalia and I both had to work. Noëlle's first sounds were "ha-da". Dennis tried to coax her into uttering Hadassah as her first word. He didn't succeed but had a lot of fun trying.

THALIA, NOËLLE, AND I flew to Detroit on 28 February 1967 where I was to present a benefit organ recital for St. Matthew's Church. More than one hundred donors were listed on the back of the programme, listing St. Mathew's Choir as the sponsor, but I'm sure most of the fundraising was done by Grandpa Smith. The donors included many family members and friends from the Detroit, Chicago, and Kansas City areas as well as St. Matthew's parishioners and the Vestry (parish council) of St. Cyprian's, another historically black parish in Detroit.

Aunt Ina, Dad's sister, picked us up at the Windsor, Ontario, airport a few days before the recital. Her son Wayman tells me that the US Immigration officer was confused that I could be American, Thalia British, and Noëlle Canadian. The recital took place in St. John's Church, Woodward Avenue, a significant detail that was somehow omitted from the printed programme. The musical selections were identical what I had played in Providence, Rhode Island, during Lent of 1965.

My brother Birney drove us to Chicago the next day to spend time with him, Mother, and her husband John. Mother threw a party with numerous family members and friends. John's daughter Harriet and his granddaughter were among them. Mother found it highly amusing that Harriet was a little older than she was. It was a lovely visit for which I am very grateful. John, a great fan of Oscar Peterson, was a quiet and kind man who was good for my mother. This was the only time we met him; he died unexpectedly in the fall of 1968.

GEORGE MAYBEE, ORGANIST and Master of the choristers at St. George's Cathedral in Kingston, was the unofficial dean of Canadian cathedral organists. I enlisted his aid in my search for a new position. The first one I applied to was at St. Matthias Church in Montreal. Moving to the Province of Québec was very appealing to this francophile. However, I did not even make the shortlist.

A position at St. James' Church, Milwaukee, Wisconsin, was advertised in one of the professional magazines. I applied. It looked very promising. They flew me down in the spring for an interview, but my hopes were dashed when the rector turned out to be a Southerner. He accused me of filing a misleading application because I had failed to mention that I was Negro.[3] The upside of the trip was that I was able to visit two honorary uncles who were in Wisconsin at the time: Jack Bunday, who was enrolled in a doctoral programme in French at the University of Wisconsin in Madison, and Joe Turnbull, rector of a

[3] See Reflection #1: "Racism."

parish in Milwaukee.

George Maybee then suggested I apply to two parishes in Ontario who were seeking church musicians. They were St. Peter's, Brockville and St. James' in Dundas. I applied to both. George wanted me to take the Brockville position. There was an established choir of men and boys, a complementary private school teaching appointment, and therefore more money. But St. James' had a rector with an exciting liturgical vision, and I liked it better. The church had to stretch to match my Saskatoon salary but somehow did. However, they only paid half of our moving expenses.

This appointment took place at a time when rectors everywhere were beginning to relinquish their authority to choose church staff, and it was the last time I applied to a rector rather than a search committee. St. James' turned out to be the one-and-only church to which I have ever successfully applied. On all other successful occasions in my life, I have been called by the church to fill a position or to help out temporarily and later asked to stay.

AN OLDER PARISHIONER from St. Andrew's, Evanston, invited herself up for a visit sometime before July 1st, Dominion Day, as it was then known. Nancy West was a housekeeper and cook for the Kennedys, an affluent white family. I remember our family attending dinner at their home with them and Father William St. John Brown, the rector at St. Luke's Church in Evanston, which the Kennedys attended. Nancy, however, attended our black parish whenever she could. She was a very intelligent woman who had never had an opportunity for much formal education. I wonder what she could have accomplished had she been born several decades later than the turn of the 20th century.

Nancy, Thalia, Noëlle, and I attended *Pion-Era*, an annual outdoor exhibition of turn-of-the-century steam tractors and other farm equipment. We also watched the RCMP Musical Ride. This being the Canadian Centennial Year, everything was presented with extra polish, enthusiasm, and pride. Nancy was a generous guest who paid our admission to everything and gave us extra money for groceries. She then decided that she wanted to see the Rocky Mountains. Our MG1100 was too small for the four of us, so she paid for the rental of a suitable car for our drive to Banff. Using Thalia's connections, we secured a lovely cabin at the Banff YMCA/YWCA. Noëlle, somewhat advanced for her age, decided it was time to teach herself to turn over on the bed. She succeeded admirably but fell onto the wooden floor and scared the daylights out of the rest of us. She bounced well and was soon back to her normal cheerful self with a minimum of tears. We enjoyed the Banff hot springs and made a day trip to see Peyto Lake, and ride on a multi-passenger tracked vehicle on the Columbia Ice Fields. It was a delightful trip for all four of us.

I had earlier filed a letter of resignation from the cathedral. We departed Saskatoon, probably on Monday, July 31st. As our car had previously departed by train, Dennis Essar and Ken Gordon drove us to the Canadian National train station, and bade us farewell.

-19-

We Move to Ontario
(1967-1968)

The Rev. Canon Joachim Carl Fricker had been rector of St. James' Church, Dundas, since 1965. He persuaded his wardens that it was time to seek a professional organist-choirmaster to begin in September of 1967. He received and rejected thirty-nine applications for the position. The fortieth application was from Stephen Crisp, who was then serving as sub-organist at Canterbury Cathedral. Canon Fricker, affectionately known as Father Jo, offered the position to Stephen. My application, number forty-one, then arrived.

Father Jo had been Father Pat's successor as rector of St. David's, Welland. Upon receipt of my application, he immediately called Mrs. Patterson as a reference. She had returned from Saskatoon to Welland with her children after Father Pat's death. Whatever she said about me was kind enough to convince him that I was the musician he was looking for. He then called me in Saskatoon to explain that he wanted me to come to St. James but had offered the position to a previous applicant. Meanwhile, Stephen Crisp seemed unable to make up his mind. I was, of course, not privy to the discussions that followed between the two of them. At any rate, Canon Fricker gave Stephen a firm deadline for a decision. The deadline came and went and I was subsequently hired. The entire process took place via telephone and letter. The mail was a lot faster in those days. Canadian postage was 4¢ local and 5¢ for out-of-town.

Thalia, Noëlle, and I arrived at Toronto Union Station a day later than scheduled, probably on Thursday morning, August 3rd. There had been an accident on the rail line ahead of us and our train had to be rerouted. Our car, which had travelled ahead on a freight train, was simply delayed and was therefore not waiting for us in Toronto as planned. I telephoned Canon Fricker at St. James'. He advised us to rent a car and proceed to Dundas. We stayed with the Fricker family in the rectory next to the church for the next few days. August was our month of vacation. My new appointment would officially begin on September 1st.

Father Jo gave me a tour of the church building. As St. James' had never had a professional musician on staff, he showed me the spaces in the tower basement that he thought could become the choir room and my office. I played the 1962 Keates organ. It was nothing to write home about but was in much better condition than the Saskatoon organ. I played some hymns and organ music for Father Jo, and remember playing what later became the second of my three versets on *Veni Emmanuel*. The brief dance movement had been saved from a longer improvisation and written down in Saskatoon. I asked Father Jo if he recognized the theme; he said, "O come, o come, Emmanuel." I was impressed by his discernment.

We soon departed Dundas to enjoy the rest of August. I drove Thalia and Noëlle to Glastonbury, Connecticut, to spend most of the month with the Peek family. I returned to Kingston to attend a week of training for choirboys and choirmasters at Camp Hyanto, the summer camp for the Diocese of Ontario. It began with Evensong on Sunday evening at St. George's Cathedral followed by an organ recital by David Willcocks, Director of Music at King's College, Cambridge.

The camp began on Monday morning. The faculty were David Willcocks, Leo Sowerby from St. James' Cathedral in Chicago, George Maybee from St. George's Cathedral in Kingston, and Peter Partridge from Ridley College in St. Catharines. Peter did the sectional rehearsals for the boys, while the other three divided up the choirmaster training, men's sectional rehearsals, and full rehearsals. There were no women in attendance, which seemed normal at the time but strange and unacceptable now. David Willcocks was one of my heroes. I showed him my anthem *Prayer for Bishops*, which I had composed for the visit of the Archbishop of Canterbury to Saskatoon the previous November. He was kind but unimpressed.

The week concluded with a festive Evensong at St. George's Cathedral. I was a proud member of the alto section. I remember singing a major anthem by Leo Sowerby, and Sir Charles Hubert Hastings Parry's majestic coronation anthem, *I Was Glad*. The Parry coronation anthem was first composed for Edward VII, then revised and expanded for George V. Peter Partridge did admirable organ accompaniments for the musically ambitious service.

After Evensong, I headed for Toronto to attend the once-each-decade International Congress of Organists (ICO). The first took place in England in 1957. This, the second, was in Toronto, Ottawa, and Montreal. It was a joint convention of the (British) Royal College of Organists (RCO), the American Guild of Organists (AGO) and the Royal Canadian College of Organists (RCCO). The gathering was an outstanding series of musical events and warm conviviality. For two weeks, several hundred attendees enjoyed listening to a wide variety of organs, organ recitals, choral concerts, choral services, and the finals of an organ improvisation competition. I also began to meet Hamilton RCCO colleagues who introduced me around.

A life-changing moment during my time in Montreal was meeting privately with Kenneth Gilbert who had been so kind and welcoming during my visit to play Montreal's Beckerath organs in 1962. I told him I was trying to save money to purchase a harpsichord. He explained that the one I wanted and the one he had shown me in 1962 reflected yesterday's thinking. The three Beckerath organs in Montreal represented the revival of historically informed mechanical-action organ building, while the McGill University harpsichords, each built in Massachusetts, exemplified the revival of historically informed harpsichord building. We made an appointment to meet at McGill where he showed me into a room with three harpsichords: a Frank Hubbard, a William Dowd, and a William Post Ross. He left me alone to stay as long as I wished to play them. It was a revelatory experience.

The words *historically informed* in the above paragraph mean that the builders of such organs and harpsichords were trying to recapture the sounds of 17th and 18th Century instruments. This often requires painstaking research into long-forgotten construction techniques and performance practice to discover how those sounds were achieved. I also purchased a copy of Frank Hubbard's 1965 book: *Three Centuries of Harpsichord* .[1]

This being Canada's Centennial Year, many ICO attendees lingered

[1] Frank Hubbard: *Three Centuries of Harpsichord Making* (second printing) © 1965 & 1967, Harvard University Press, Cambridge, Massachusetts, USA.

in Montreal to enjoy Expo 67. I could only spend one day there, but vividly remember the movie *A Place to Stand* at the Ontario Pavilion, and the geodesic dome of the USA Pavilion. I visited the Swiss Pavilion with a scintillating group of international musicians, and enjoyed an outstanding dinner featuring cuisine from the Romansch-speaking area of Switzerland. This was the first time that I truly understood the name of the world-famous orchestra founded and conducted by Ernest Ansermet: *L'Orchestre de la Suisse Romande*.

I returned to Toronto to pick up our car and then drove to Connecticut for some downtime with Thalia, Noëlle, and the Peek family. We also spent time with friends in Massachusetts, including three of Noëlle's four godparents. We returned to Dundas sometime before the first of September to begin work. We stayed in the rectory with Jo and Shirley Fricker and their five children while we looked for a place to live.

Meanwhile, unbeknownst to me, Neil Hicks, my former student from Southbridge, decided to give me a harpsichord. He had been given a harpsichord and a grand piano when his father Will sold his business, Mosaics Fabrications, to the Bendix Corporation for more than a million dollars, endowing his wife and each of his children with substantial sums.

Neil, knowing that I wanted but could not afford a harpsichord, decided to give me one as a gift. He consulted with Thalia hoping to find out my exact desire. The new knowledge I had gained through my recent meeting with Kenneth Gilbert in Montreal now made the surprise he intended impossible; they had to bring me into the decision-making process. In late 1967, I chose to commission an instrument by

William Post Ross of Boston. I negotiated with Bill Ross, Neil sold some stock, and a contract was signed. The custom-made harpsichord was scheduled for delivery in early 1969.

FATHER JO DECIDED that I should play my first service on the second Sunday in September rather than on the Labour Day weekend. He and I, along with his two eldest sons Michael and Stephen, attended St. Thomas' Huron Street in Toronto for high mass on the first Sunday of the month. Although I was raised Anglo-Catholic, I found the service extremely pompous. Stephen had never experienced incense. At one point in the service, he leaned toward his dad and asked, "What's that?" His dad told him what it was, but Stephen heard "insects" which confused him more than ever.

The Frickers thought there were several people we should meet, and invited them to the rectory one evening after Labour Day. I remember Tom and Emily Cain, and Tom and Dorothy Kellett, but I am sure others were included. Tom Cain eventually sang bass in the choir of men and boys as well as in the Te Deum Singers. He was a substitute organist when I needed to be away, my mentor in English language usage, and my authority on Latin translations. He remained a steadfast friend for the rest of his life. Tom and Dorothy Kellett were very welcoming and periodically invited us to their home for dinner, including our first Thanksgiving in Dundas.

I recall only one detail of my first Sunday. Tom Kellett came to me after the service and said that the Bach *Prelude and Fugue in G Major*, which I had played before the service, reduced him to tears. He told me he had waited his whole life to hear music like that at St. James'.

Father Jo and I agreed on a music programme that included three choirs. A men and boys choir was to be created from scratch to sing the 11:15 service. Like Saskatoon, this service alternated between Eucharist on the first, third, and fifth Sundays, and Mattins on the second and fourth Sundays. Tom Cain recruited a tenor, Paul Clifford, from the McMaster Geology Department. I sang alto. We initially had about twenty boys audition. Over time, the number of boys stabilized at around twelve. The boys rehearsed Tuesday after school, and again on Saturday morning with floor hockey afterward. They also rehearsed Thursday evening for an hour with the men, who, as in Saskatoon, remained for an additional hour-and-a-half sectional rehearsal.

The girls' choir and the mixed choir sang at the 9:30 family Eucharist. This latter combination worked well because in the early days, the mixed choir I inherited had no sopranos. The girls' choir filled that gap. Church School was attached to the 9:30 service, with the children leaving during the hymn before the sermon.

Before our arrival, Father Jo put our names on a waiting list at the Helen Park Apartments, a four-storey subsidized low-income accommodation that included many McMaster graduate students. A vacancy soon appeared, and we moved in around the first of October. As our two-bedroom with balcony apartment was on the top floor at the end of a corridor, we had no one above us or on the bedroom side. The living/dining room shared only one wall with a quiet neighbour. There was a Dutch-Canadian couple straight across the hall with young children who eventually became occasional playmates with Noëlle. Alice, their mother, was particularly memorable because she was the most meticulous housekeeper we had ever encountered. We often said that it would be safe to eat dinner straight from her floor.

Meanwhile, my work at St. James' progressed. Father Jo and I worked well together. He was the boss and I, a trusted advisor, was free to speak my mind. We were a great team. He could work with my "prickly personality," and I had no difficulty accepting his decisions when he did not take my advice.

We soon began dreaming about moving the 9:30 Family Eucharist in a more contemporary direction. When the English Church moved from Latin to English in 1549, one of the principal tenets of Anglicanism was that it was repugnant that public services happen "in a tongue not understandeth of the people."[2] We will quietly ignore the fact that many people in 1549 spoke local dialects and could barely understand English, if at all. *The Book of Common Prayer* was first published in 1549, revised in 1552, and again in 1604. There were later editorial revisions in each national iteration of the Anglican Communion, but we became more or less stuck with Elizabethan English, which remained in the 1962 Canadian revision, even though this new version was hailed as a major step forward.

As much as we admired the language of Shakespeare for its sublime beauty, it certainly was not — and perhaps never was — the language of the people. The Roman Catholic Church had already moved from Latin to the local vernacular as a result of the Second Vatican Council[3]; it was time for Anglicans to offer an alternative to Elizabethan English.

---

[2] See article 24 of the *39 Articles: 39 Articles of Religion - The Anglican Church of Canada*
[3] The first vernacular masses took place in Ireland on 7 March 1965. English was used in some places, Irish in others. American Roman Catholics began using the mass in English less than a month later. I am not sure when the use of English and French began in Canada.

Beginning in the fall of 1968, we tried many revised Eucharistic liturgies at St. James'. We used the *Green Book* and the *Zebra Book* from the USA, the *New Zealand Liturgy*, the *Scottish Liturgy*, the *Qu'Appelle Liturgy* from Regina, and we wrote our own. Musically, we adopted Bert Draesell's *Gloria* mass which had been so successful in Saskatoon. Our first guitarist was Paul Weiss, and we later expanded to include others. Ian Thomas, Nora Hutchinson, and Oliver MacLeod joined us on occasion. Ian asked me to join the group on harpsichord, but I declined his offer and suggested he talk to Nancy Ward in Saskatoon. He did, and she joined them in the fall of 1969 as harpsichordist, guitarist, and singer. The group soon changed its name from *Ian, Oliver & Nora* to *Tranquility Base* and signed a contract with RCA Records.[4]

I did not realize at the time that St. James' Church was on the cutting edge of Canadian liturgical renewal in the years 1968-1973. I have a vivid memory of a circa 1971 conversation with the Rt. Rev. Ted Scott[5], then Bishop of Kootenay and soon thereafter Primate of the Anglican Church of Canada. We were heading out the back door of St. James' after a special evening service at which he preached. He was on the way to his car and I was on my way home. He asked me why Jo Fricker's liturgical ministry at St. James' was so effective. I answered him at some length. He thought for a few seconds after I finished and said, "Dignity without stuffiness; informality without sloppiness." Bingo! I have tried to follow and teach Ted Scott's succinct summary ever since.

Father Jo went on to become Dean of Niagara in 1973, then

[4] Both Nancy Ward and Ian Thomas have gone on to significant musical careers. There is copious information about each of them on Google and other search engines.

[5] Ted Scott - Wikipedia; "The charisma and complexity of Ted Scott" - *Anglican Journal*

Suffragan Bishop of Toronto (informally styled Bishop of the Credit Valley), and chair of the Doctrine and Worship Committee of General Synod.[6] This latter appointment eventually led to the publication of *The Book of Alternative Services* (BAS)[7] in 1985. I occasionally quip that Jo Fricker, Tom Cain, and I wrote the BAS at St. James' between 1968 and 1973. I am exaggerating my role, but neither of them ever contradicted me. A crucial contributor to the work of the Doctrine and Worship Committee and the BAS was The Rev. Dr. David Holton from the theological faculty of Trinity College, Toronto.

Paul Clifford and his wife Barbara were active members of the Bach-Elgar Choir in Hamilton. I was soon invited to play harpsichord continuo for the Bach-Elgar Choir's December *Messiah* performance at First United Church, Hamilton. An instrument built by John Baker of Ancaster was supplied for my use. This concert was an opportunity to begin building a network of musical connections within the community. Robert Morrow, son of a prominent Hamilton musical family, organist of First United, and future mayor of Hamilton, played organ continuo.

Now that my harpsichord was on its way, I began realizing my dream of a baroque ensemble to continue the work I had begun in Southbridge with the Gregorian Consort. My first objective was three free concerts in the 1968-1969 season. After obtaining permission to

[6] The Rt. Rev. Joachim Fricker was suffragan bishop - "The Diocese of Toronto" (anglican.ca)

[7] The 1985 publication was proposed as the *Book of Common Prayer for the Anglican Church of Canada* but a conservative faction had enough votes to block its official authorization under that name. *The Book of Alternative Services* has since then become the de facto Canadian prayer book without ever being authorized as such. The 1962 prayer book remains official but is used in very few parishes. The Episcopal Church USA revised their *Book of Common Prayer* in 1979. The Canadian committee was able to use that as a resource to improve our own *Book of Alternative Services*.

present the concerts at St. James', I started recruiting patrons and sponsors through personal acquaintances. While the Gregorian Consort had been a volunteer group, my three concerts at St. James' were to be performed by professional musicians.[8] I first approached Marta Hidy, concertmaster of the Hamilton Philharmonic Orchestra. She either was not interested or did not have time. She did however, kindly recommended musicians for me to approach. I also spoke at a Rotary Club breakfast and probably to other groups. In addition to all of the above, I taught several private piano students and organ students while trying to be a husband and a father.

THALIA AND I had married in September of 1963, and her parents had been unable to attend the wedding. They and I had yet to meet, and they now had a one-and-a-half-year-old granddaughter. Thalia and I decided that we must get ourselves to Scotland. Noëlle was still young enough that she could travel on our laps for free. We managed to finagle a return Toronto-London charter flight in August of 1968, and off we went for three weeks.

Our first stop was with Thalia's sister, Sonia. Her husband, John White, met us at Gatwick Airport and drove us to their home in Pinner, Middlesex, not far from London. We stayed pretty close to their home for a few days. There was not much opportunity for tourism because we had a small baby. Sonia teased me a lot. She called me "Dicky Birdy,"

---

[8] I became a member of the American Federation of Musicians of the United States and Canada (AFM) in Saskatoon. Robert Solem asked me to play organ continuo for a performance of two sections of Bach's Christmas Oratorio in December of 1966. In North America, union and non-union musicians are rarely allowed to perform together.

which made me very uncomfortable. I just had to get used to it for the next few decades. John was an alcoholic and a racist, to which, of course, he was blind. He was a supporter of Enoch Powell, a right-wing anti-immigration politician from Ulster.[9] John stated that there were no race problems in Britain except where there were too many outsiders: a classical example of blaming the victim.

Thalia and I met or visited her younger brother, Robin, who was engaged to be married that September. He was living with Sonia and John but moved out for a few days to make room for us. We also managed to attend Sunday Evensong at Westminster Abbey. We thought the music left much to be desired. It was not the same standard we were accustomed to hearing on King's College, Cambridge, recordings.

We proceeded to Cupar-Fife by train to spend nearly two weeks with Thalia's parents, George and Marie Lumsden. We stayed at their home at 9 Kirkwynd. They were warm and welcoming. George owned a barbershop and hair salon. He did the gents' hair and hired someone to do the ladies' hair. Both Thalia and her older brother, Gordon, had previously worked in the shop. We visited Gordon, his wife Jean, and their young children at their home nearby.

Thalia's dad thought that all black men were natural boxers, and he wanted to box with me. Thalia's mum shared one of her favourite television programmes, *The Black and White Minstrel Show*. It featured formally dressed men in blackface dancing with bewigged and formally dressed white ladies. She was surprised and bewildered that I did not like the show.

We visited two of Thalia's closest childhood friends, Virginia Nelson

---

[9] Enoch Powell - Wikipedia

(née Reekie) in St. Andrew's and Morag McRoby in Cupar. We were very well fed everywhere. Beverages and pastries around 4 o'clock were called afternoon tea. The evening meal was generally called tea, short for high tea. I was surprised to find that Scottish dinners usually included potatoes prepared in two different ways: boiled and roasted, for example. If you were offered a second helping of anything, you were expected to decline. If they didn't insist or offer it again, that was the end. If they offered a second time, you were free to accept or decline. My North American, "Yes, please," or, "Yes, thank you," after the first offer were considered rude. I had a lot to learn.

Thalia loved St. Andrews and shared it with me during Lammas Fair. I spent some time in the ruins of St. Andrews Cathedral looking for Birney family tombstones, but have yet to find a connection there with James Gillespie Birney. We made an automobile day trip to Loch Lomond with Thalia's mother. Thalia must have done all or most of the driving. I don't think I was yet ready to drive on the left side of the road. Thalia, Noëlle, and I made a three-day trip to Inverness, picking up a lovely recently-married young couple of Danish hitchhikers. We adored Inverness. I would love to go back sometime.

I am amazed at how much we packed into our first year in Dundas.

-20-

New Directions
(1968-1970)

We returned from Scotland and England in late August, ready to start our second year in Dundas.

Soon after our return, Father Jo suggested to Thalia that St. James' needed a free, weekday group for young mothers. This would encourage them to get out of the house and spend time with their peers. Their discussion led Thalia to start such a group in October. It met for an hour and a half on Tuesday mornings in the church gymnasium. Childcare was provided. The members spent approximately thirty-five minutes in physical exercise, twenty minutes for coffee and casual conversation, followed by a thirty-five-minute programme of spiritual or intellectual nourishment. Father Jo and Thalia dubbed the group *Body and Soul.*

Body and Soul continued under Thalia's direction until the latter part of the 1970s when she began full-time employment. The group carried on without her, although she was always available by telephone when her counsel was desired. The mandate changed over time to include older members as well as young mothers. Thalia was the guest of honour at their twenty-fifth-anniversary celebration in 1993, and meetings continue to this day, interrupted only by the Covid-19 lockdown.

One of my favourite Body and Soul stories is when June Solntseff called to inquire about joining. Thalia explained what the group was about and wanted to emphasize that membership was free of charge.

"There are no dues," said she. There was a moment of stunned silence on the other end of the line before June said, "But I'm Jewish." In Thalia's Fife accent "dues" and "Jews" were pronounced identically. A few minutes of conversation cleared up the misunderstanding. June joined the group and remained a friend for the rest of Thalia's life.

I was looking forward to my series of three concerts to celebrate the arrival of my new harpsichord in early 1969. The opening event was set for 4 November. Marta Hidy recommended three or four musicians. Three accepted. They were violinists Karoly Sziladi and Natalie Mysko, and violist Don DiNovo. If she recommended a cellist, that person did not accept. I asked James Burchill to play organ continuo. As the string players sat at the top of the chancel steps, with the organ console out of their line of sight, it was not feasible for me to play and conduct. I played two organ solos and the string programme featured baroque music.

I had wanted to sign with a professional organ-recital manager when we lived in Southbridge, but none was willing to accept me. Thalia and I therefore created our own management and called it Te Deum Concerts. When we initiated the three self-sponsored concerts in Dundas, the heading on the printed programmes said, "Te Deum Concerts presents Music for Organ & Strings." The instrumentalists had no formal name, and were simply listed on the programme as *The Musicians*. Lorne Betts, music critic for *The Hamilton Spectator*, assumed *Te Deum Concerts* to be the name of the event. The name stuck.

I had initially hoped that the men and boys choir of St. James' would be able to sing major choral works, such as Bach cantatas, with instrumental accompaniment. It soon became clear that they were years away from acquiring that level of skill. Early in 1971, I created the Te Deum Singers to fulfil that function. In 1982, I added paid section leaders. Still later, when I was counselled to drop the Te Deum name in favour of something that better described our product, the board of directors accepted my suggestion of the Te Deum Orchestra & Singers.

EARLY IN OUR relationship, Thalia and I had decided that our two children would be spaced about two years apart. We had also agreed that the second child would be adopted. Quite likely before our summer trip, we called the Hamilton Children's Aid Society to start the adoption process so that the new baby would arrive before the end of 1968. Thalia wanted the child to be as young as possible and would have liked to be in the delivery room waiting for the child to be born. This was of course not possible. The earliest age a child could be adopted in Ontario was about six weeks.

We also wanted to adopt, in the language of the time, an Indian or Eskimo child. We thought that this would be socially responsible. We rightly or wrongly believed that Indigenous children often ended up in orphanages because they were difficult to place. We were unwittingly positioning ourselves to participate in *The Sixties Scoop*.[1] Somewhere in the application process, we were told there was growing resistance to adopting children outside their ethnicity. The example given was that a

[1] The Sixties Scoop refers to the large-scale removal or 'scooping' of Indigenous children from their homes, communities and families of birth through the 1960s, and their subsequent adoption into predominantly non-Indigenous, middle-class families across the United States and Canada. This experience left many adoptees with a lost sense of cultural identity. The physical and emotional separation from their birth families continues to affect adult adoptees and Indigenous communities to this day. Sixties Scoop | *The Canadian Encyclopedia*.

child born to a Jewish mother should be placed with Jewish adoptive parents. We then stated that we would willing to consider any difficult-to-place child. Thalia and I had soul-searching discussions about how we might react to a handicapped child. We decided to cross that difficult bridge if and when it were in front of us.

There was a lot of paperwork and several interviews before prospective parents were judged eligible to adopt. We were approved sometime in the fall. Then we waited and waited and waited for a call from Children's Aid. When that didn't happen, we called them early in the new year only to discover that our paperwork had been filed as incomplete. Contrary to what we had been told earlier, we lacked a blood test necessary for final approval. We were therefore not even being considered when adoptees became available. The blood test was soon done, and the waiting began again.

I MADE AN organ recital tour of England and Scotland in late January and early February while Thalia and Noëlle stayed with the Peeks in Connecticut. English organ builder Peter Walker was my primary contact and facilitator. Peter and I had originally connected at the International Congress of Organists in 1967, and he was invaluable in arranging recital engagements for me. When in London, I stayed with an old male friend of Thalia. I had a British Rail pass that meant I could hop on and off trains whenever I wished. I often changed trains in Leeds. My recitals, in order of occurrence, were at Bradford Cathedral and the Doncaster Parish Church (now known as Doncaster Minster) in Yorkshire; McEwan Hall, University of Edinburgh; Trinity Church, Brompton, in London; a small church or college chapel in Lancaster; the

Parish Church in St. Andrew's, Fife; and Queen's College, Oxford. I was picked up at the train station in each town, billeted or put up in a hotel, fed, paid either £20 or twenty guineas (£20 and 20 shillings), and delivered back to the train station for the next leg of the journey.

In those days, transatlantic passengers had to stay at least twenty-one days to get the least expensive airfare. I consequently had some open spaces between engagements. In Canterbury, I visited an American Field Service friend, Anne Sellers who had been an exchange student in Kansas City in 1958-1959. While there, I was able to spend some time in Canterbury Cathedral and attended a special processional service of lessons and carols. Anne was a member of the philosophy department at Keynes College, University of Kent. She arranged for one of her colleagues to invite me to dinner at the university's high table, which was literally that: a faculty-only table on a raised platform at one end of the dining hall. We not only had a superior position, we also had a better menu. Looking back, I remember everyone in the hall was male. A lot of the conversation was directed towards me, which caused me to eat more slowly than usual. When the others finished eating, they patiently waited for me to finish. I noticed the situation and asked them to proceed to the next course. My faculty host replied imperiously, "Wouldn't think of it."

Another vivid memory from Canterbury: LSD was very fashionable at the time, but Anne explained why she was not interested in trying drugs. "I have all the perception that I can stand," said she. I have frequently borrowed her sentence over the past six decades.

During a Friday train change in York, I was able to meet Dr. Francis Jackson and play the York Minister organ for more than an hour. I know that it was a Friday because there was no Evensong. The Friday evening service is plain (spoken without music). The cathedral was undergoing major restoration work at the time. The magnificent organ, atop the rood screen, was surrounded by a huge plastic bag to protect it as much as possible from airborne dust. The sound of the full organ inside the bag was deafening, but I was still able to appreciate the beauty of the instrument, and hear the music reverberating around the building.

I was also able to visit Derek and Enid Maishman in Nottingham. We had become friends at the cathedral in Saskatoon while he, an engineer, was working for a nearby potash mine. On February 2nd, Derek and I attended a superb Candlemas Lessons and Carols service at King's College, Cambridge. On the way there, we passed Ely Cathedral but were unable to gain entrance.

During an open space between recitals, I flew to Paris for a few days to visit my French brother, Jérôme. This was my first return to France since 1959. He had a modest apartment on rue Aubriot in the Marais. Jérôme kindly arranged for me to play the 1964 Kern mechanical-action classic organ in the nearby Church of Notre-Dame-des-Blancs-Manteaux. This beautiful instrument from Strasbourg was my first experience of a Kern organ.

I played a wide variety of organs during the tour. They ranged from a one manual positive in Lancaster to three or four manual symphonic instruments in St. Andrews and Edinburgh to a classic Frobenius from Denmark at Queen's College, Oxford, where the tour ended. I had to mix and match repertoire to construct programmes to suit each instrument. While in Oxford, I heard the excellent men and boys choir at New College. I was invited to another high-table dinner where, this time, I knew not to fall behind the others. I was given a guest apartment with a student valet who polished my shoes overnight and delivered my breakfast the next morning. The inequality between my honoured guest status and students was striking and embarrassing. I was delivered directly from my Oxford noon-hour recital to Heathrow for the flight to New York. There I met Thalia and Noëlle at LaGuardia Airport for our return to Toronto.

The tour was a wonderful experience. There were two significant disappointments. First, Gillian Widdicombe of *The Musical Times* was supposed to review my London recital but somehow did not attend. She said something nice in the next issue, but hearsay is not a review. Second, I had an appointment at Wigmore Hall with a potential European concert manager. He said that organ fees were just too low for him to justify the effort necessary to arrange engagements. On the other hand, I learned I did not enjoy living out of a suitcase while travelling from place to place. I never again undertook a similar tour.

IN LATE FEBRUARY or early March 1969, Te Deum Concerts presented the second of our series: *Music for Oboe and Strings.* As my harpsichord had not yet arrived, I borrowed John Baker's. The guest oboist was Frank Morphy from the Toronto Symphony. The centerpiece of the programme was the Marcello Concerto for oboe, strings, and basso continuo. I think we had added a cellist to the group by then. We had two rehearsals with strings and harpsichord, with the soloist joining us on Monday morning for the final practice.

The concerto begins with a brief introduction before the oboe plays. When Frank played his first few notes, we all were jolted. The soloist and the accompaniment were in different keys. Both brothers Allesandro and Benedetto Marcello claimed to have written this concerto. The Alessandro Marcello version, which we had prepared, was in D minor; the Benedetto Marcello was in C minor. I had to scramble, with Marta Hidy's help, to find string parts for the version that Frank was playing. The concert went well even though the string players and I were virtually sight-reading our parts. I learned an important lesson that day: always make sure that the soloist and orchestra are using the same edition.

I am convinced Allesandro Marcello wrote the original concerto. We performed it on several occasions in succeeding decades.

IN EARLY APRIL we received a call from Children's Aid stating that they had a difficult-to-place baby girl for us to consider. We asked about her background and were told that her father was black and her mother was of Scottish ancestry. Thalia and I dissolved into laughter. We then explained to the bewildered social worker on the other end of the call that these were our own backgrounds. The birth parents were Hamilton teenagers. We were told that he was an outstanding basketball player. (This turned out to be incorrect. His forte was actually football.) Beyond that, we were told very little.

We wanted to see the child immediately, but she was not at the Children's Aid office. We had to wait a day until she could be brought there. We drove to the office on Friday, April 11th, spent an hour with the baby girl and decided to bring her home. She had been born in Toronto on February 7th. We named her Monique Lumsden Smith. She was baptized in St. James' Church by the Rev. Paul Jackson on the

Second Sunday of Easter, April 13th. Some parishioners reacted with great surprise, saying that they hadn't noticed Thalia was pregnant. Monique's godparents were Michael Doran, a musician and close friend from Dundas; Alison Crabb, organ student and chorister from Saskatoon; and Enid Maishman, the Saskatoon friend I had recently visited in Nottingham.

When we applied for a new birth certificate with the name that we had chosen, someone in the registry office made a mistake which revealed the name given by her birth mother. By a surprising coincidence, Monique's initials were MLS in both cases. Eighteen or so years later, Thalia and I combined our knowledge of her birth name with the sparse details supplied by Children's Aid to discover the identities of her birth parents.

THE FINAL TE DEUM concert of the season was in late April. The centerpiece of the programme was Bach's Brandenburg Concerto #5, which features an extended harpsichord cadenza near the end of the first movement. But alas, my new harpsichord had still not been completed. I learned yet another valuable lesson: never expect a commissioned harpsichord or organ to be delivered on schedule. The exceptions to this rule are rare.

John Baker's harpsichord was not large enough to project the necessary volume for the cadenza, so I scrambled to borrow a larger instrument from someone in Woodstock. It was not a historically-informed instrument, like the William Post Ross I was awaiting, but I had to make do. My instrument was to be, as far as I know, the first historically-informed harpsichord in the province of Ontario. The concert was successful, but without the new harpsichord, the raison d'être for the three-concert series, we needed to have a second season.

I HAVE LITTLE recollection of the summer of 1969. There is a photo of Monique, Noëlle, my Grandparents Smith, and me taken in 1969 in Brighton, Michigan. Thalia was presumably behind the camera. The four of us must also have visited Detroit relatives on the same trip. I wonder if we continued on to Chicago to visit my recently-widowed mother. We may also have taken the available opportunities to get to know Southern Ontario. The Royal Botanical Gardens and Webster's Falls were only a few minutes from home. Some Saskatoon friends had moved to Toronto and Stratford. We likely visited them. Niagara Falls was also good for a day trip. My dad visited us at the Helen Park Apartments as did my sister, who had changed her name to Micki Demarris, and her husband, Jimmy Paulk. Jimmy was the bass in a vocal group performing in the Ballroom of the Royal York Hotel in Toronto. Jimmy and Micki treated us to dinner and a show, an evening that we could never have afforded.

MY HARPSICHORD WAS finally delivered in the fall, just in time to open the second season of Te Deum. We had it delivered to the rectory and shared it with several friends one evening soon thereafter. We probably moved it to the church next door on Sunday after services. Bach's Harpsichord Concerto #5 in F Minor was the centerpiece of the Monday evening programme, which likely included one or two harpsichord solo pieces as well. The long wait was finally over. I now had to settle in and master the art of tuning the instrument. In the early months, it took me about three hours to do the job of tuning 183 strings. I eventually could do it in 30-45 minutes.

After the concert, we moved the instrument again, this time to the living room of our apartment which was on the fourth floor. The single elevator at Helen Park was narrow. We had to put the point of the harpsichord up towards the ceiling with the keyboard end resting on the floor. It did not take long for us to realize that it was time to stop imposing on our friends and to start using professionals. One mover would ride in the elevator with the harpsichord. The other two would run up or down the stairs to meet the elevator at its destination. It was awkward for all concerned and punishing for the instrument. When word got out that I had the only instrument of its kind in the area, the Hamilton Philharmonic Orchestra, the Bach-Elgar Choir, and other groups began hiring me for continuo jobs.

IN JANUARY OF 1970, while walking to church for Body and Soul, Thalia noticed a for-sale sign in front of a house on Victoria Street, just behind St. James'. She telephoned me from church and gave me the phone number of the real estate agent. Thalia and I had never even discussed buying property, but she was way ahead of me. She knew that, with two young children and a harpsichord, we had outgrown our apartment. They were asking $18,900 for the pre-World War I home. We offered $16,900 and were surprised our first offer was accepted. That amount still seemed like the earth to us. My mother helped with the small down payment. David Lee, a local lawyer and avid ragtime pianist, did the legal work and took the first mortgage. The owner, Jean McGillivray, hesitated a bit before taking back a small second mortgage.

She was persuaded by her friend, neighbour and St. James' parishioner, Nellie Chappel, that we were good people who would make our payments on time.

The deal was rapidly concluded and we moved into 105 Victoria on March 1st. Now we were homeowners with two kids and two mortgages. Victoria Street, depending on how you count, is only four to six blocks long. It is divided in half by Sydenham Street. The houses east of Sydenham are larger and more expensive. The houses to the west were, at the time, more modest. Some newer construction has since modified what we used to call the working-class end of the street. According to hearsay, number 105 was once owned by a local carpenter who, aside from creating very nice woodwork in his own home, did much of his work at the more expensive end of the street.

In the 1960s, it was fashionable to strip the paint from old wood and refinish it to look natural. However, we were persuaded to respect the original style and leave it painted white. Thalia was a modernist and expressed herself by painting three sides of the kitchen and the living room each in a bright colour and wallpapering the fourth side with wild floral patterns. It remained that way until we toned things down in the later seventies and early eighties. Outside, the house was whitewashed stucco on frame.

The front room became my music studio. There had been sliding doors between the front and middle rooms of the main floor. They were long gone, leaving an open rectangular arch. We hired a carpenter to lower the arch to fit a standard folding door, which was less expensive than commissioning custom-made folding doors. They were not soundproof but offered a degree of privacy to music students from family members passing through to the stairway to and from the second floor.

The kitchen was at the back of the three downstairs rooms. Upstairs were four small bedrooms and a bathroom on three sides of a central landing, which originally had probably been the upstairs parlour. The kitchen and the two back bedrooms were a later addition to the original house. The fourth side was the staircase. A full unfinished attic was accessible by ladder behind a door next to the bathroom. There was a basement with a concrete floor under the original house, and an unfinished crawlspace for plumbing and heating ducts under the kitchen.

The garden was twice the length of the house on a hill that began rising about four metres from the back door. There was a central concrete stairway with a peach tree to the left. We were told there were a few flowers but decided to do nothing until after the snow melted to see what was growing. To our surprise, up came dozens of crocuses, daffodils, tulips, grape hyacinths, foxgloves and other spring perennials. We later learned we had inherited the neighbourhood's horticultural showpiece.

Life was good.

-21-

The Halcyon Years
(1970-1973)

Thalia and I met and were married in 1963. From then until March of 1970, we moved household seven times. Now that we were parents and homeowners, we entered a period of greater stability. Thalia was a full-time mother and homemaker as well as the facilitator for all things related to Body and Soul at St. James'.

My work at the church and with Te Deum Concerts was both exciting and challenging. While separate entities, the two musical programmes were interconnected: several individuals sang in one of the church choirs and in the Te Deum Singers.

Someone suggested that the harpsichord stay at St. James' rather than be transported back and forth between the church and our house. A pew was removed at the back of the chapel, and the harpsichord lived there. It was playable for lessons and personal practice. We also used it on the nave floor to the right of the chancel steps quite a bit during the folk mass setting at the 9:30 Eucharist, and it was moved to the chancel aisle for concerts where I would face the altar with my back to the audience. Instrumentalists were grouped around the harpsichord between me and the altar.

Dad moved from Philadelphia to Trinity Church, Wall Street, New York City sometime in 1969. Jo Fricker was already involved in liturgical renewal through an organization called Associated Parishes. Dad put Father Jo and me on the mailing list of Trinity Church. We thereby became even more aware of new and fresh thinking in the wider church.

When Trinity encouraged congregants to wear something red for Pentecost, we immediately incorporated that practice at St. James'.

Trinity made a big deal of celebrating their patronal festival, Trinity Sunday. They invited former parishioners back to celebrate the day with a grand liturgy and a parish picnic. We soon followed with St. James' Day at the end of July. Many of our parishioners, who might normally have been away on the last Sunday in July, began organizing their summer holidays around St. James' Day.

Trinity created a large outdoor banner: "TRINITY CHURCH IS ALIVE & CELEBRATING." We soon followed with, "ST. JAMES' IS ALIVE & CELEBRATING" in bright red letters on a white banner across the top of the parish hall. I particularly remember how Trinity influenced us during those times when many other thinkers and writers were talking about the death of God and the imminent demise of the institutional Church.

Father Jo and I had our own ideas too. I remember preparing for an Easter Vigil in 1970. It was, in my opinion, a rather dreary little evening service on Holy Saturday at which the Paschal Candle was lighted. Few attended. I asked Father Jo why we did this. He explained that this was "the most important service of the year" with a rich tradition dating back to the Early Church. I reacted strongly that we were not treating it as such. He agreed and we started planning to celebrate the following year's Easter Vigil as the most important service of the year.

IT DIDN'T TAKE long for Larry King, music director at Trinity Church, to invite me to play a recital there. Their weekly recitals followed the Thursday noon Eucharist. I chose Canada Day 1971 to play an all-Canadian programme. The church had two Aeolian-Skinner organs playable from either of two four-manual consoles. One was located to the right of the altar (it may have been movable), and the other was in the west gallery. The chancel organ included about forty stops. The gallery organ was about sixty stops. I chose to play from the gallery. I started the programme with *O Canada* on the full chancel organ and then proceeded to alternate between the two organs until the final piece that used both simultaneously. Composers represented on the programme included Raymond Daveluy, Barrie Cabena, Healey Willan, and others. I concluded the recital with my own *Four Versets on O filii et filiae*, using the combined resources of the two organs.

Trinity Church, or possibly Dad, arranged to billet Thalia, the two girls, and me in dormitory rooms at General Theological Seminary. The girls were too young to attend the recital, but a babysitter was provided so Thalia could attend. Afterward, the four of us visited the Bronx Zoo on our way to visit my old Trinity College friend and Noëlle's godfather, Bill Bowie, and his parents in New Haven, Connecticut. From there, we spent a few days with the Peeks in Glastonbury, Connecticut, and then visited Noëlle's godmother, Mary Hicks, and her family in Sturbridge, Massachusetts. It was a wonderful, but very challenging, trip. We had very little money and had to count every nickel and dime. This is the stuff of sweet memories.

We bought a family-sized tent and began summer camping. The seed had been planted the previous winter by Jane and Paul Dixon, friends from St. James', who owned a tent trailer. They told us about a place called Skycroft near Chaffey's Locks on the Rideau Canal. Skycroft was 2,000 acres of pristine woodland. The main camping sites were on

Lake Opinicon with plentiful swimming, rowboats, canoes, fishing, woodworking, and a barn for indoor gatherings. The holiday started as a two-week venture that first summer and gradually grew over the coming decade. Camping was affordable. Thalia was an experienced Girl Guide and a great cook over an open fire. I had been a Boy Scout in my youth, although never in Thalia's league, but over time I learned to find, saw and chop wood to supply the fire.

Late in the summer of 1971, I was called on short notice to become organist-choirmaster at Temple Anshe Sholom, a Reform Jewish synagogue in Westdale, the Hamilton neighbourhood near McMaster University. For some reason, they were without an organist and choirmaster just before the High Holy Days. These begin with Rosh Hashanah (the Jewish lunisolar New Year) and run for nearly a month through Yom Kippur (the Day of Atonement); Sukkot (the feast of tabernacles, a fall harvest festival and time of thanksgiving); Shemini Atzeret (the eighth day of Sukkot), and finally Simchat Torah (when the annual reading of the Torah is completed and begun again from the beginning). While I had some Jewish experience during my teen years substituting for my teacher, Edna Scotten Billings, at Temple B'nai Jehudah in Kansas City, this was a totally new experience. I now had to make decisions, in collaboration with the cantor, about the week-to-week music for Friday evening Sabbath services, as well as periodic Saturday morning Bar Mitzvahs and Friday evening Bat Mitzvahs for thirteen-year-old boys and twelve-year-old girls respectively. It was a steep learning curve, but I enjoyed the challenge as well as the additional income.

I remained at Temple Anshe Sholom for slightly more than two years, beginning with the 1971 High Holy Days. During my time there, I learned a lot which has deepened my understanding of Judaism and enriched my understanding of the roots of Christianity. Both Conservative and Reform Jewish liturgies were undergoing transformation at the time, shifting away from Ashkenazi (European) practices toward Middle Eastern ones. This included a noticeable shift in Hebrew pronunciation from Ashkenazic to Sephardic. This was not unlike the great vowel shift in British English except that it also included some consonants. For example, sholom became shalom, bas mitzvah became bat mitzvah, and Adon Olom became Adon Olam.

This shift in language also encouraged a gradual shift in musical culture from European to Middle Eastern.

This change was very challenging and exciting for me because I was not very fond of Ashkenazi music, which I described as bad Brahms. When I was learning church music, the churches were gradually moving away from a steady diet of Victorian hymnody to a more eclectic mix of both older (e.g. plainsong, Renaissance, and baroque music) and newer music (e.g. Ralph Vaughan Williams, Healey Willan, and others). This was both exciting and painful. Some wanted change (a breath of fresh air), while others resisted and wanted to cling to "the way we always did things." Roman Catholics, Anglicans, Lutherans, and Jews were each having similar challenges within their respective traditions.

When I returned home from my April/May 1973 trip to France, I discovered the president of the congregation had, for his son's Bar Mitzvah, replaced my excellent student with a more well-known local organist. While he was entirely within his rights, I considered his action unethical. I tendered my resignation effective at the end of the fall High

Holy Days. Looking back, I wish I had remained at Anshe Sholom longer than two years. Did I resign as a matter of principle, or was it a fit of ego? From a distance of nearly fifty years, I do not have a definitive answer to that question.

I have few specific memories of 1972. My work at St. James' continued and Te Deum Concerts grew stronger. The family returned to Skycroft for summer vacation under canvas. It is quite likely this was the year that Father Jo hosted a meeting of Associated Parishes at Camp Canterbury Hills in Ancaster, and asked me to accompany him to the founding conference of the Canadian Liturgical Congress in Ottawa. My work as organ consultant for St. Christopher's Church in Burlington and Church of the Redeemer in Stoney Creek likely began about this time.

1973 WAS A banner year. The first of many things that made it so were the celebrations of the 24-year tenure of Walter Bagnall, Bishop of Niagara. He had announced his retirement effective June 30th. Christ's Church Cathedral, Hamilton, would have been the natural location for such celebrations but the cathedral was, in my opinion, a dreary place liturgically and architecturally. In those days I described it as "dead from the ankles up". Meanwhile, St. James' was at the cutting edge of liturgical renewal in Canada, of which I was unaware at the time, but in retrospect can now see clearly.

Bishop Bagnall asked to have three major pre-retirement cele-brations at St. James', and Father Jo agreed to host all of them. The first was the bishop's final diaconal ordinations on Easter Day in the afternoon. The second was his final confirmation service. The third was a Pentecost Day concelebration of the Eucharist with the priests who were his first diaconal ordinands in 1952.

As I write, some fifty years later, I occasionally cross paths with retired priests, deaconed on Easter 1973, who recall that service as one of the high points of their life. It was for me too. It was at the end of a very exciting, satisfying, and exhausting Holy Week which included Palm Sunday, Passover service and seder, Maundy Thursday, Good Friday, Erev Shabbat, the Easter Vigil with choirs and brass[1], Easter morning, and the ordinations. I provided music for a dozen or so liturgies during the eight days from Palm Sunday through Easter Day. Two or three of them were at Temple Anshe Sholom, and the rest were at St. James'. A particularly tender memory is that of my choir member, John Davis, now a retired priest in Australia, chanting the Litany of the ordination service.

We were in the process of raising money to rebuild the organ at the church, and held four fundraising recitals in 1972-1973. I played the first and third recitals. The second was a twelve-hour marathon called *Pipe, Pedals, and Pistons* which involved twelve local organists each playing a thirty-minute programme on the hour. My cherished French-trained colleague Dennis Driscoll and I took turns playing a thirty-minute programme on the half hour.

[1] The Easter Vigils of 1971-1973 were each recorded by Ed Ballik, a physics professor at McMaster University. While he was an amateur musician, his recordings were of professional quality. In 1973, we conflated the best parts of the three services into a long-playing phonograph recording and issued it as *EXULTET* (Te Deum Records 001). While it was criticized in professional publications for congregational noises, it in my opinion captured the immediacy of live worship in a way that an empty church recording (to which it was unfavourably compared) could not. The disc is now out of print but I plan to upload it soon at SoundCloud. Stream Richard Birney-Smith music | Listen to songs, albums, playlists for free on SoundCloud.

I had learned from hard experience that the great organists of the world were unknown in Dundas and Hamilton. I therefore hired an organist from a famous building and marketed the building: Sir Francis Jackson, Organist & Master of the Choristers at York Minster in England. I chose Dr Jackson because he was a first-class musician who, I was confident, would make the most of the limited resources of the St. James' organ. He did not disappoint.

Dr. Jackson played the fourth and final recital of the series at St. James' on the Friday after Easter. I particularly remember his oral introduction to, and stellar performance of, Maurice Duruflé's *Prelude and Fugue on the Name of Alain*. Even though Duruflé composed this piece in 1942, only two years after Jehan Alain died in the Second World War, I was unaware of its existence until I heard Dr. Jackson play it.

The next morning, I boarded a plane for Boston. I played four recitals in the next eight days: Sunday afternoon at St. Anne's Church in Lowell, Massachusetts; Tuesday or Wednesday noon hour at St. Paul's Chapel of Trinity Parish; Thursday noon hour at Trinity Church, Wall Street; and Sunday afternoon at Notre-Dame Cathedral in Paris. I had also been asked to play at Salisbury Cathedral in England during this trip but the invitation got lost in the mail. By the time the problem was discovered, my inflexible airline reservations had been made.

MY RECITAL AT Notre-Dame de Paris was one of the biggest thrills of my life. I had wanted to play Notre-Dame ever since I first met Pierre Cochereau in the tribune there in 1958. The organ there had undergone several "improvements" since then, with which I disagreed, but Notre-Dame is still Notre-Dame. I arrived in Paris Friday morning,

May 4th. I had always wanted to see April in Paris thanks to the great recording of that song by Count Basie and Ella Fitzgerald. Mother Nature granted my wish by delaying spring. The horse chestnut trees, emblematic of April in Paris, were still in full bloom.

I STAYED WITH my French sister, Brigitte Bost, in her apartment on rue de la Glacière. She was still single, working as a bilingual administrative assistant for J.-B. Pontalis, a psychoanalyst whom she would eventually marry. Pierre Cochereau, titular organist of the great organ at Notre-Dame, was busy recording for Philips Records that weekend. Organ recordings usually take place in the wee hours to avoid, or at least minimize, traffic and other noises that occur in the vicinity. Notre-Dame was no exception. In addition to that limitation, the cathedral organ could not be played when the building was open to the public except for religious services, recitals, or concerts. My assigned practice time was therefore from 5 am until 7:30 am on Saturday and Sunday mornings.

Public transit was not yet running at 4:30 am, so I walked thirty minutes from Brigitte's apartment. I met François Carbou, curator of the cathedral organs, who let me in and accompanied me to the gallery overlooking the nave. The tribune at Notre-Dame is higher than any other to which I have ever climbed. Unlike other French churches I know, the stairs up to it were entered via an exterior door. From there one takes a well-worn stone spiral interior staircase up to the base of the south tower.

The console faces the altar rather than the organ case, and the view down the entire length of the nave is awe-inspiring. One of the cathedral canons orally introduced the weekly Sunday organ recital, which in those days preceded the 6 p.m. mass. I was tasked with writing programme notes to introduce each piece. I composed a first draft, and Brigitte corrected my French. I then printed the final version in my clearest block script. It was difficult for me to understand these introductions at such a great distance from the lectern, but there was a small television with a loudspeaker on top of the console.

I was allowed to play anything I wanted with one caveat: it could not be anything that had been performed within the previous twelve months. Fortunately for me, none of the pieces I had in mind was off-limits. I worked hard to make sure my selection was international and suited the instrument. I opened with the *Passacaille* from *Sonate en sol* by Montreal composer Raymond Daveluy. I continued with a four-movement voluntary by English Baroque composer John Stanley. The quietest piece on the programme was *Contemplative Canzone* by 20th-century Flemish composer Flor Peeters. I then played *Offerte du 5e Ton: Vive le Roy* by French Baroque composer André Raison, and tried as much as humanly possible to use the François Thierry pipes from the 1730-1733 rebuild of the Notre-Dame organ. I also enjoyed — and was even a little proud — that I could play this on the five-manual console without changing a single stop during the performance. All the contrasts that the composer demanded could be achieved by changing manuals.

I concluded the recital with *Toccata* (1958) by American composer Milton Gill. I met Milton in 1963 at an organist's convention. He was on the music faculty at Dartmouth College. His toccata had won the American Guild of Organists composition competition in 1962. It was a great piece, but almost no one played it because it was so difficult.

Milton somehow intuited that I was up to the task, and gave me a copy of the not-yet-published manuscript, a year before its publication. I finally mastered it in time for my 1973 recitals at Lowell, Massachusetts; Trinity Church, Wall Street; Notre-Dame de Paris; and Christ's Church Cathedral, Hamilton. I don't remember ever playing it again, and I don't know of anyone else who plays it. Tragically, Milton was killed in a plane crash in 1968 at the Hanover, New Hampshire, airport as he was returning to Dartmouth. His toccata is a great composition that deserves to be heard, but is, unfortunately, not an audience pleaser.

Notre-Dame was probably the largest audience of my career. A few hundred perhaps came to hear the organ recital, while a thousand or two were there as tourists or to attend the evening mass. At least six people came to hear me. My French father and mother, Charles and Eva Bost, drove down from Normandy; my French sister, Brigitte; my Saskatoon friend, Bill Egnatoff, took the train over from Lausanne, Switzerland, where he was teaching; Randy Seaby, a young Hamilton organist, came in from Strasbourg where he was studying; and an Australian friend-of-a-friend, Kirsty Healy, flew in from London. They were given privileged seats in the north triforium not far from the organ tribune, courtesy of Monsieur Carbou, curator of the cathedral organs. After the recital, Bill, Randy, Kirsty and I went to a local brasserie for supper. It was a memorable day.

Monsieur Carbou was sad that Thalia had not accompanied me to Paris. Without my knowledge he made a monaural cassette tape of my recital, and gave it to me afterwards to take home to her.[2] It remains one of my most precious possessions.

[2] Stream *Notre-Dame de Paris* (1973) by Richard Birney-Smith | Listen online for free on SoundCloud

The airline required that I remain in France for three weeks but my memories of that time are spotty. I took the train to Rouen at some point. While wandering outside the cathedral, I bumped into my former organ teacher, Marcel Lanquetuit. We had a cordial conversation. I told him about my Paris recital, and he asked me to write to him from time to time. I never did, and sadly regret it to this day.

I HAD A MEMORABLE visit to the harpsichord collection at the *Conservatoire National de Musique* in Paris. As 1973 was long before the instant communication of email and the internet, appointments to visit and play instruments such as those in the conservatoire collection had to be arranged by mail well in advance. One could not just walk in off the street. The curator of the collection was Madame La Comtesse de Chambord. The France aristocracy was officially abolished in 1790 during the French Revolution, but with specific permission from the Ministry of Justice[3], some individuals are allowed to continue their titles, though without legal status or privilege. There were numerous instruments in the room at the Conservatoire. I don't know how frequently they were routinely tuned, but the one I came to see had been prepared for my visit. It had been built by Andreas Ruckers in Antwerp in the 17th century, then subsequently enlarged and extended by Pascal Taskin of Paris and Versailles in the 18th century.[4] I remember having to crawl to get to it. I sat down in great anticipation expecting a revelation. This was, after all, the real thing, neither an instrument inspired by Ruckers and Taskin, nor a copy. The revelation was that

[3] The post-revolutionary history of the French nobility is more complicated than my one-sentence summary above. French nobility - Wikipedia

[4] Ruckers - Wikipedia There were actually two Andreas Ruckers, father and son.

there was no revelation at all. It sounded just like my 1968 William Post Ross harpsichord which had been inspired by instruments like this one. I was dumbstruck. Wow![5] Before leaving the building, I had an emotional moment in front of the memorial wall of the conservatoire commemorating students and faculty who died in war. I recognized several names, but the one that brought tears to my eyes was Jehan Alain (1911-1940).[6] He was an important composer who was destined for greatness. He and Olivier Messiaen were friends and mutual admirers. Perhaps he could have been equal to or even greater than Messiaen.

I attended a Sunday noon organ mass (in other words, one without choir) at *La Trinité*, the church where Messiaen had been titular organist since 1931. Messiaen was not the only titular who preferred to play an organ mass rather than high mass; it gave them a greater opportunity to choose repertoire and improvise. I have no idea whether I was hearing Messiaen or his assistant, Jean Bonfils. The latter had so absorbed Messiaen's style that one could not tell the difference by listening from the nave.

We were then still only a decade or so after Vatican II and the switch from the Latin mass to the local language. Congregational singing was still new and unfamiliar to most Roman Catholics. I was approached by one of the priests who heard me singing. He wanted to invite me to greater participation in the parish. He was very disappointed when he learned that I was just passing through. *"Vous êtes seulement de passage? Dommage,"* said he.

[5] This may indeed have been the instrument that I visited in Paris: ClavecinRuckersTaskin - Pascal Taskin - Wikipedia

[6] Jehan Alain - Wikipedia

One evening, Brigitte treated me to an all-Bach concert at the Hôtel des Invalides. The highlight of the programme was countertenor Paul Esswood singing one of my favourite cantatas, BWV 170, *Vergnügte Ruh, Beliebte Seelenlust*. During the interval, I was able to gaze at Napolean's tomb.

BACK HOME, FATHER JO was appointed rector of Christ's Church Cathedral and Dean of Niagara sometime that spring. He was to begin his duties around Labour Day. On the Day of Pentecost, Bishop Bagnall gathered his first four diaconal ordinands, by then mature priests, for a major celebration at St. James'. It was, I'm sure, a huge service with a lot of music but I retain only a visual image of the five of them celebrating the Eucharist together behind the altar.

At its 1972 meeting, the American Cathedral Organists and Choirmasters Association, with the encouragement of the Joint Commission on Church Music of the Episcopal Church USA, decided that it needed to widen its membership. I was invited to the first meeting of the new organization at the Cathedral of St. John the Divine in New York. In June, we met to discuss the "Loyalties and Ethics of the Church Musician" and to receive hymn settings commissioned by the association. A couple of them make useful solos or anthems, but looking back from 2023, these intriguing settings seem unsuitable for a congregation of amateurs to sing. I was however able to make new professional connections and renew some old ones. The conferees also recommended that the organization be renamed *The Association of Anglican Musicians*. This was ratified by the membership the following year.

There was one more big day to prepare: Father Jo's final Sunday at the end of July. Again, I have little recollection of the event itself. While it would have been a big celebration of his seven-year ministry at St. James', it was a sad day for me to have such a happy working relationship come to an end. I found a brief handwritten letter from Father Jo on the music rack of the organ when I arrived at church that morning. In it, he thanked me for my work and stated that hiring me was the most important decision he had made during his tenure. I am sad that over the following years, I somehow lost track of that letter.

Soon after Father Jo's departure, we packed up most of the smaller organ pipes (4-foot pitch and above) and shipped them to Wilson Barry, organ builder in Andover, Massachusetts. There he cleaned, rearranged, and revoiced them. A few small pipes were replaced with new ones to achieve the final disposition. His assistant, Bill Poleatewich, was also his son-in-law. He had married Will's daughter, Marta, the previous June.

The two men packed the pipes into Will's Ford van, affectionately known as the "the red item," and brought them back to Dundas late in the fall. The sticker on the back of the vehicle read: *Don't blame me, I'm from Massachusetts*. It was the middle of the Watergate crisis, eight or nine months before Richard Nixon resigned, despite sweeping the 1972 US Presidential election. Only Massachusetts had voted for George McGovern.

The revoiced and rearranged pipes were put back into the organ and then tonal finished. This is a process of meticulously adjusting each pipe to sound right in the particular and peculiar acoustics of the building. It can only be done in the space where the organ will live. It cannot be done elsewhere in advance.

We had a wonderful week or so. Will was not only my favourite organ builder and mentor on many levels, he was also a dear friend. My friendship with him continued until he died in 2012.[7]

I continue to be a close friend and honorary member of the Barry family to this day. I remember sharing an episode of the PBS television series *Upstairs Downstairs* with them. Will, an egalitarian American down to his toenails, was scandalized. He had no idea that such a two-tiered home had ever existed. I daresay that he would not be a fan of *Downton Abbey* either. On another occasion, Thalia served roast beef and Yorkshire pudding. Will had heard of Yorkshire pudding but never seen nor tasted one. He was surprised to discover that it wasn't a dessert.

Once the pipes were re-installed and the tonal finishing complete, the organ was tuned in quarter-comma meantone and the St. James' choirmen and I recorded *Meantone Organ*. The visit ended sadly as Will seriously sprained his back while retuning the organ to equal temperament after the completion of the recording. He returned home flat on his back in the rear of the red item while Bill drove.

I loved the resulting instrument that Will created for St. James'. It was only the first redesign step, but it changed the character of the organ. The blend was better and the whole thing was more flexible. The instrument, though not large, accompanied congregational singing and choral music with improved clarity and also became capable of playing a wider variety of organ repertoire. I was very happy.

[7] Clarence Barry Obituary (2012) - Andover, CT - Boston Globe (legacy.com)

-22-

Crisis at St. James'
(1974-1976)

ON MY WAY home from Paris in May 1973, I stopped at Karl Wilhelm's organ shop in Mont-Ste-Hilaire, Québec, as part of my work as an organ consultant. While visiting Wilhelm instruments in the greater Montreal area, I played a one-manual moveable organ he had built for Gerald Wheeler. I was impressed. Such an instrument would be very useful at St. James' and for Te Deum Concerts. Later that year, Karl Wilhelm offered me a similar instrument that was in progress in his shop. I borrowed money from a friend and made a down payment.

I was already a member of the Diocesan Liturgical Commission. Our task was to disseminate information to parishes to assist in liturgical renewal. We were also beginning to think forward to the diocesan centennial celebrations in 1975. The Canadian Liturgical Congress was planning a major meeting in Hamilton in the spring of 1975, and I was invited to do a musical event for them.

Back in Dundas, we were barely into 1974 before I realized that I was in deep trouble professionally. My working relationship with the new rector of St. James' was not healthy. The Rev. Philip Jefferson and I did not make a good team. It would be too easy, at a distance of nearly fifty years, to simply point the finger at him as the problem. That would be neither fair nor accurate.

I have since discovered that the new bishop, John C. Bothwell, had warned Father Phil to expect trouble. Why, I will never know. The deck was stacked against me from day one. The bishop's warning became a self-fulfilling prophecy.

The bishop and the parish also made a disastrous mistake. A search committee does not usually begin work until the outgoing rector has departed. The process had however begun and concluded soon after Father Jo's appointment to the cathedral was announced in the spring. Phil Jefferson began his ministry at St. James' the Sunday immediately following Jo Fricker's departure. There was no interval to allow the parish to grieve. A gap between rectors is now considered normal.

Father Phil and I had vastly different ways of communicating. I am a very direct communicator, while his style was indirect.[1] I try hard to say what I mean and mean what I say, which some find difficult to receive, even rude and/or offensive.[2] Phil was suspicious of academics and almost any form of expertise. This was awkward in a congregation with a high percentage of McMaster faculty. He valued perception over fact, and told me that a committee chair should know little or nothing about matters over which he or she is responsible, but rather should be able to listen and learn from ordinary people.

An opinion based on misinformation was therefore just as important as an opinion based on fact or experience. This made no sense to me. He wanted to lead by consensus. I understood my job to be advisory. I would, therefore, give my best advice to the rector and then allow him to make the final decision. My direct manner was, I discovered later from others, intimidating to him.

---

[1] Historian George Grant, McMaster professor and father of one of my choirboys, said that Phil was, "so indirect that he didn't know that he was indirect."

[2] As recently as 2017, a diocesan official I considered a trusted friend described me to a warden at Grace Church as "opinionated". Fortunately for me, the warden thought that more than sixty years of experience allowed me to have gathered some opinions.

I had yet to learn about these differences or personality type indicators. My Trinity College education trained me to value facts and logic over emotion. I now think that it trained me to overvalue facts and logic. It was not until I was working at Melrose United Church (1981-1992) that I took a Myers-Briggs personality test and discovered that my approach to life was out of step with my nature.

I also later discovered there was a major power differential between us. He was the boss and I was an advisor but, in reality, the actual dynamics were not as simple as I understood them to be. I had been at St. James' for six years before he arrived. I had earned a great deal of respect and trust during my time at church, which amounted to power I did not realize I possessed.

I tried my best to give Father Phil good advice on a week-to-week basis. Sometimes this meant trying to save him from himself. He loved to sing but was not a good singer. He had a hearing problem, wore hearing aids, and sang out of tune. On one occasion he wanted to begin the First Sunday in Advent by singing the solo song, *Prepare ye the way of the Lord* from *Godspell*, while leading the entrance processions at the Eucharists that day. I persuaded him not to do it but, very likely, bruised his ego by giving him advice he did not want to hear.

In the fall of 1974, my portable Wilhelm organ was completed. I sought and obtained permission from the rector and wardens to place the instrument in the baptistry, behind the congregation. I borrowed a van and drove with a friend to Mont-St-Hilaire to pick it up. It sounded wonderful in our space. We often used it during communion for hymns, organ music, and choral music. A few church members objected to the parish spending money on a second organ. Father Phil, valuing perception over facts, reported this to me as a problem. He did not think it important to inform these individuals that it was my personal instrument that had cost the congregation nothing.

In the spring of 1975, the Te Deum Singers, soloists, flute, oboe, audience, and organ, presented *Psalms and Hymns and Spiritual Songs* at Christ's Church Cathedral for the Canadian Liturgical Congress. It attempted to trace the history of liturgical music from early psalmody up to the present day. The climax of the concert was, for me, *An Infinite Alleluia*, an aleatory piece that I wrote to approximate the experience of singing in tongues.[3] The concert was a triumph. I received a standing ovation the next day as I entered the room for the morning conference session.

On the Day of Pentecost, I conducted the music for the Diocesan Centennial Eucharist at the McMaster gymnasium. The congregation and a massed choir of choristers from many parishes were supported by a large Rodgers electronic organ and a brass quartet. Choir, organ, and instrumentalists were on a balcony above more than a thousand congregants. The music included a new hymn composed by St. James' chorister Thomas H. Cain, and the first performance of *The Niagara Mass* by Derek Holman which the Diocesan Liturgical Commission had commissioned. The service was yet another triumph.

Within weeks of those two events, Father Phil imposed a set of guidelines for music at St. James' which prohibited plainsong, singing in any language other than English, *a cappella* singing during hymns, and free hymn accompaniments, along with several other restrictions. I no

---

[3] The piece was inspired by melodic fragments from William Albright's *An Alleluia Super Round* which I had encountered in the spring of 1972 at the Association of Anglican Musicians conference in New York City.

longer had control over any musical decisions other than tempo.

The wardens and I appealed to the bishop to mediate, or perhaps arrange counselling to help us improve our working relationship. This was a huge error on our part. His job is, among many other things, to support his clergy. The wardens and I were mistakenly asking him to be impartial. The choirmen, without my knowledge, wrote a carefully-worded letter to the bishop. He assumed that I was behind it.

I was optimistic when he invited me to meet him in the fall at the diocesan office. Instead, he surprised me with further directives. He disbanded the men's choir and gave the wardens detailed instructions on improving the interpersonal dynamics between the rector and me. If these did not work, I was to be dismissed immediately. If these were successful at improving the working relationship, I was to be dismissed anyway at the end of six months. He then laid his hands on my head and gave me his apostolic blessing. I left his office feeling betrayed.

It became clear a few months later that a new rector's warden, a close friend of the bishop, would be appointed at the January annual meeting. This would tip the balance of power in the parish corporation. I was in an impossible situation.

I TENDERED MY resignation in November, effective 31 August 1976. I chose that date in order to have time to find a new position. The rector would have liked it to be accepted earlier than the end of August, but neither the corporation nor the parish council would agree. My resignation was received but never accepted. From that moment until I departed St. James', I walked a tightrope as best I could, trying to live within the straightjacket of the guidelines while producing the best music I could.

I remember, in particular, the Easter Vigil of 1976. It was a major celebration with choirs, brass, and a large congregation. After the service, we adjourned downstairs to the parish hall for a joyous party. I had far too much to drink and, was feeling no pain by the time I left. A bunch of choir members continued to party at Grant and Doreen Dixon's home. I asked Ron Vickers to drive me there because I was too drunk to get behind the wheel. Mercifully, we made it safely. I had failed to notice that he was drunker than I was. On the ride over I made silly statements about the irrelevance of the Easter Bunny. I don't remember participating in the gathering but rather I took a nap in their young son's outdoor fort.

The next morning, I arrived at church bright-eyed and bushy-tailed with no hangover. Ron Vickers greeted me with my own nonsense from the previous evening: "The Easter Bunny is dead; Christ is Risen." I gave him a blank stare; I had no idea what he was talking about.

Sometime in May or June, some parishioners hosted a large farewell dinner in the parish hall. My friend and colleague, Dennis Driscoll, gave a delightfully humourous after-dinner speech. I was surprised with a purse of about $2,500. It was a memorable evening.

As I was entitled to a month of vacation, my final day at St. James' was the last Sunday in July, St. James' Day. The service was joyous. Phil Jefferson did not interfere with the music selection. The highlight of the service for me was the world premiere of *Windows in the Sky*, Richard Felciano's setting of *Ye Watchers and Ye Holy Ones* for congregation, organ, and electronic tape which I had commissioned the previous spring at the San Francisco meeting of the Association of Anglican

Musicians.

The events at St. James' had severely damaged both Phil Jefferson's reputation and mine. I was unable to secure another position in the Anglican Church and soon after these events, he lost out on a major academic appointment. I learned from a confidential source that retired Bishop Bagnall had quietly given me a recommendation for a position to which I had applied in another diocese, stating that an injustice had been done at St. James', but it was not enough even to get me an interview.

-23-

Life Goes On

My career troubles at St. James' were not all that happened between 1974 and 1976. Family and professional life continued. I had been celebrating Bach's birthday, on or near March 21st, for several years. Sometimes it was part of the Te Deum Concert Series for orchestra and/or choir, and sometimes it was part of the Te Deum Recital Series and featured only organ and/or harpsichord. Since the St. James' organ had been so beautifully rebuilt by Wilson Barry the previous fall, 1974's *Happy Birthday, Johann* featured the organ. I played the recital at least three times in 1974: at Christ Church Cathedral in St. Louis, Missouri; at St. Andrew's Church in Kansas City, Missouri; and at St. James'.

St. Louis was exciting because the cathedral had been redesigned. Now nicknamed "the flexible cathedral," the 19th-century furnishings had been removed and replaced with lean, modern fittings. The altar was moveable and the organ was completely rebuilt by Aeolian-Skinner and moved, along with the choir, to a west gallery. Instead of pews, there were chairs that could be turned around to face the back of the cathedral for concerts and recitals. The St. Louis redesign became the inspiration for numerous other church buildings, including Hamilton's own Christ's Church Cathedral in 1978.

Kansas City was exciting because it was my first return since 1963. While I was disappointed that none of my high school friends, acquaintances, or teachers attended the recital, my heart was warmed that

Edna Scotten Billings, the now-retired organ teacher who lit the fire under me during my teen years, was there. It was the last time that I saw her before her death.

It was a delight to play the recital at St. James', Dundas, and do justice to Bach's music in a way that had never been possible before. I repeated a major portion of the programme for broadcast on *Organists in Recital* on the CBC-FM network.

THALIA AND I attended the 1974 convention of the American Guild of Organists in Cleveland. We drove to Canton, Michigan, to leave Noëlle and Monique with cousin Ruth Ellen Davis, her husband Bruce, and their children. Ruth's Grandma Cookie (Olivia Bryan Cook), whom I loved and treated as an honorary grandmother, was also living there at the time. The girls had a delightful time with their young cousins. There has been regrettably little contact between them since. This is the downside of having our family spread all over the map.

We arrived at the convention a day early and were able to attend the Sunday morning Eucharist at Trinity Episcopal Cathedral. John Brombough had built and temporarily installed a brand-new mechanical-action organ tuned in meantone temperament. It was delicious. That organ is now permanently installed, with a milder temperament, in a church in Toledo.

The main convention programme focused on contemporary music. Much of it was, in my opinion, ear-splitting and ugly. One two-organ concert in Oberlin, by Jean Guillou and Cherry Rhodes, had most of its audience, including us, walk out before it was over. Perhaps it is important to note here that one person's noise is another person's music.

The late Jean Guillou was one of the great organists of the world. He was titular organist of St-Eustache in Paris from 1963 until 2016. Whether or not I liked his music that night is no more than a personal opinion. A small coterie of devoted fans who loved this concert remained afterwards to show their appreciation. I must, in all humility, recognize that some people would use similar adjectives to describe my music.

We were, on the other hand, excited to hear Gerd Zacher play Bach's *Art of the Fugue*, and William Albright play William Bolcum's *The Black Host*. I'm sure some found the Bolcum, performed at the Cleveland Museum of Art, to be ear-splitting and ugly, but we loved it. I bought the score and the recording but never learned the piece. The recording was very useful a few years later when I was testing stereo equipment for my studio, though patrons and managers of the stereo shops were not very appreciative.

Gerd Zacher played the Bach on the beautiful 1956 Rudolf von Beckerath organ at Trinity Evangelical Lutheran Church. Known for his contemporary performances, I suspect Zacher took many liberties with the written score, but he still exposed the inner beauties of Bach without getting in the way. The final fugue was performed in Kabuki theatre, physical gestures without a sound being made. I could practically hear the music in my head as he acted it out.

An unexpected bonus was a surprise engineered by Thalia. She recognized someone's nametag as belonging to a person I admired and said something like, "I think that you and my husband ought to meet each other." She introduced me to Marilou DeWall Kratzenstein. Neither of us knew that the other was attending the convention. I had learned much from Marilou's articles in professional journals and had exchanged correspondence with her regarding French Baroque organ music. She even corrected some misinformation I had learned during my time at college. We stayed in touch and collaborated for years, subsequently attending two weeks of Kenneth Gilbert harpsichord masterclasses at Wilfrid Laurier University together. On other occasions, she was a guest organ recitalist at St. James'; I shared a two-harpsichord recital with her at the University of Northern Iowa; and I lent her my harpsichord for a solo performance with orchestra in Flint, Michigan.

I had a once-in-a-lifetime liturgical experience that same summer. I attended a large gathering of professional church musicians in the months preceding the resignation of US President Richard Nixon. It might have been part of the Cleveland AGO Convention detailed above. We sang G.K. Chesterton's hymn O *God of Earth and Altar* to the Welsh tune *Llangloffan*. Even though the words were written for *The English Hymnal* of 1906, they seemed to have been written specifically for that moment. I was moved to the depths of my being. I have wanted to use this hymn and tune on other occasions, but things have never again seemed bleak enough to justify it. If I were still living and working in the United States, I probably would have used it during the presidency of Donald Trump. Here is Chesterton's text:

> *O God of earth and altar, bow down and hear our cry,*
> *our earthly rulers falter, our people drift and die;*
> *the walls of gold entomb us, the swords of scorn divide,*
> *take not thy thunder from us, but take away our pride.*

From all that terror teaches, from lies of tongue and pen,

from all the easy speeches that comfort cruel men,

from sale and profanation of honour and the sword,

from sleep and from damnation, deliver us, good Lord!

Tie in a living tether the prince and priest and thrall,

bind all our lives together, smite us and save us all;

in ire and exultation aflame with faith, and free,

lift up a living nation, a single sword to thee.

ON A BRIGHTER note: Thalia, the girls, and I continued our family summer camping under canvas at Skycroft. Monique entered kindergarten in September 1974. At about the same time, I was invited to become the regular continuo player for the *New Chamber Orchestra of Canada*. Mathieu Duguey, their harpsichordist, moved to the Maritimes and I took his place. Concerts were held in the auditorium of the Diocesan Centre, attached to The Cathedral Church of St. James in Toronto.

Thalia and the girls went to Scotland in December 1974 to spend Christmas with her family in Cupar-Fife. I made the regrettable decision to remain behind because I had never in my entire career been absent from my organ post on Christmas, Easter, or Pentecost. Thalia and the girls crossed paths in Toronto International Airport with Giles Bryant, organist & choirmaster at Toronto's Church of St. Mary Magdalene. He was on his way to England for Christmas while I stayed behind to fulfil my duty as I perceived it. The family had a wonderful time away, and were joined for a few days by our Australian friends, John Davis and

Peter Cahalan, who had finished their studies at McMaster and gone to England to undertake doctoral research. I wish I had been there.

Dad married Ada Viola Peters, a widow and chair of the English department at Tuskegee University, on Grandpa Smith's 90th birthday, 27 December, at St. Andrew's Episcopal Church in Tuskegee. Dad and Ada then flew to Toronto, rented a car, and came to Dundas. After visiting with me, they proceeded to Brighton, Michigan, to spend a few days with Grandpa and Grandma Marge. On their return from Scotland, my daughters immediately dubbed Dad's new wife "Granada." She loved it, and the nickname stuck for the rest of her life.

THALIA AND I flew to San Fransisco in the spring of 1975 for the annual conference of the Association of Anglican Musicians. The girls stayed with Donna Freeman and her children down the street in Dundas. The conference hotel in San Francisco was too expensive for us. We stayed instead as paying guests with a friend of a friend in a private home in Oakland. The conference sessions took place in three principal locations: Grace Cathedral, Church Divinity School of the Pacific (CDSP), and the University of California, Berkeley.

The Episcopal Church USA was still four years away from the publication of its revision of the *Book of Common Prayer*; the Eucharistic liturgy at CDSP was sensitive and traditional yet contemporary. This was small wonder as the Rev. Dr. Massey Shepherd was one of the leading minds there.[1] I had a chance for a semi-private conversation with him. I was in the throes of composing a Eucharistic setting for congregation and wanted to do two things with the text that I had never seen anyone

[1] Massey H. Shepherd - Wikipedia

else do. I wondered if either would be acceptable. First, I wanted to use the opening line of the *Gloria in excelsis* as a refrain that would be repeated after the priest (or cantor), and then again thrice more during the setting, *Glory to God in the highest and peace to his people on earth*. Second, I wanted to repeat the word *hosanna* three times at the end of the *Benedictus qui venit:* *"Blessed is he who comes in the name of the Lord. Hosanna, hosanna, hosanna in the highest"*. Dr. Shepherd assured me that both ideas were liturgically sound. Although I was then unaware, I would not be the first to do such things.

At the university's School of Music, we visited the electronic studio of composer Richard Felciano.[2] He had written several pieces for choir and electronic tape on commission from Trinity Church, Wall Street, and we had performed one or two of the simpler ones at St. James'. I was frustrated that these pieces never included a part for the congregation to sing, so I suggested we set a familiar hymn for congregation and electronic tape. Felciano liked my idea. We agreed on *Ye Watchers and Ye Holy Ones*, and a very low price. He normally charged $500 per minute of finished product, but he only charged me for the first minute. (By contrast, Stravinsky charged $1,000 per minute in the early seventies.) Needless to say, I was paid on a much lower scale when commissioned to compose later in the decade.

One evening that week, we were invited for dinner and a formal wine tasting at the home of a CDSP faculty member. He was a collector of Napa Valley and Sonoma Valley wines. It was the first time I had ever encountered the discipline of a formal wine tasting, and while it was a valuable learning experience, I wasn't particularly impressed with

[2] Felciano, Richard | Encyclopedia.com

that evening's selection. I wonder what I would think of them now?

The *Mass of St. Andrew* was successfully introduced at St. James', Dundas, on the first Sunday in Advent, 30 November 1975. Its structure was inspired by the setting John Merbecke wrote for the *Book of Common Prayer Noted* in 1550, a melody that could be sung without accompaniment. My melodies and rhythms were influenced by the exuberance of the Hassidic music I had encountered at Temple Anshe Sholom. In the early months after the mass's introduction, I improvised accompaniments. The following spring, I heard another organist improvise accompaniments to it, and I was not happy. I then wrote mine down based on my improvisations.

The piece has worn very well. After nearly fifty years, I really should get it published. I named it *Mass of St. Andrew* to honour the parish where I got my start as a church musician in 1951. St. Andrew's Day is also normally on November 30th, except when it occurs on a Sunday and is displaced by the First Sunday in Advent.

We rang out 1975 with a rather sad New Year's Eve party in Dundas with friends from St. James' and hoped for better times. Looking back over this chapter, things were not nearly as bad as they seemed at the time. Life, indeed, goes on.

THE CHURCH OF THE REDEEMER in Stoney Creek, for which I was organ consultant, ordered a small two-manual mechanical-action pipe organ from Karl Wilhelm in 1973 or 1974. It was scheduled to arrive in January 1976. Karl was exceptional in that he routinely underpromised and overdelivered. It was his intention to install the organ before Christmas of 1975. Canada Customs failed to notify him that the blower had arrived at a warehouse in Montreal. Work on the organ was suspended until the voicing could be completed with its permanent blower. Even though Karl knew it had been shipped from Germany, no one at Canada Customs could find evidence of its arrival. Instead, it sat in the warehouse for about six weeks until someone tracked it down.

The instrument was delivered to the church, assembled, and tonal finished near the end of January. I was then called to give final approval that it conformed to the contract. This I did. The assembled church officials, organ builders, and I laughed when I observed that it was still completed three days ahead of the contract. I played the dedicatory recital a month or two later. In 2019, I visited the church to show the instrument to my student assistant from Grace Church, Milton. It was as beautiful and reliable as when it was first installed.

The year 1976 brought many challenges. The first among them was to find a new venue for Te Deum performances. St. James' had been our unique venue since 1968 but we were no longer welcome there. The harpsichord, the portable organ, and the Te Deum Singers were now homeless.

A friend volunteered space for the harpsichord, a church welcomed the organ, and another church let the singers rehearse on Tuesday evenings without charge. While generous, these arrangements were cumbersome at best. The harpsichord and the organ were frequently moved in and out for our concerts, as well as when I was performing with the Hamilton Philharmonic Orchestra, the Bach-Elgar Choir, or the New Chamber Orchestra. Thalia and I soon realized we either needed to buy a larger house or build a music studio behind our home at 105 Victoria. After careful investigation, it became clear that a new music studio was the better option. We opened design discussions with architect Anthony Butler sometime in 1976.

A highlight of the New Chamber Orchestra's 1975-1976 season was a pair of March concerts conducted by Sir Neville Marriner, Founder and Music Director of the Academy of St Martin in the Fields. He immediately relaxed us before we made a sound at the first rehearsal. He lifted his baton for Bach's *Orchestral Suite #3 in D*, held still for a moment, then said quietly, "Trumpets, you are too loud." We all dissolved into laughter.

I was a soloist at Neville Marriner's second concert where I played Handel's most popular organ concerto, #13 in F, nicknamed *The Cuckoo and the Nightingale*. He paced it faster than I liked, but my preference could not prevail against Sir Neville. The performance was successful. That concert also included the world première of Milton Barnes' Violin Concerto, with his wife, Nancy Mathis, as soloist. She was named concertmaster of the New Chamber Orchestra in September of 1976, and soon thereafter also became concertmaster of the Te Deum Orchestra.

The Te Deum Concert Series divided its 1976-77 season between St. Paul's United Church in Dundas, and St. Christopher's Anglican Church in Burlington. The Te Deum Singers rehearsed at St. Paul's Anglican Church in Westdale.

Grandpa Smith died in July of 1976. Thalia and I flew to Detroit and back on Thursday, July 15th to attend and play the organ for Grandpa's funeral.[3] The New Chamber Orchestra had received a grant to play four weeks of evening concerts in various parks throughout Metro Toronto, and I was still able to play that evening's concert on our return.

[3] For details, see Chapter 5: "My Paternal Grandparents."

-24-

Picking up the Pieces
(1976-1979)

After my final Sunday at St. James', our family attended Sunday morning Choral Eucharists at Christ's Church Cathedral in Hamilton. Thalia and the girls felt uncomfortable there, as it was not their parish. They soon returned to St. James'.

I also sensed that my continuing presence at the cathedral made the incumbent church musician uncomfortable. Sad, but that is my experience. Other organists did not like having me, an unemployed organist, around. I was perceived as a threat, in the same way that single or divorced individuals are seldom invited to socialize with couples.

I also felt abandoned by my professional colleagues, and no longer welcome at meetings of the Hamilton Centre of the Royal Canadian College of Organists (RCCO). I soon let my membership lapse. No one called to remind me to renew. I did not rejoin until sometime after 2011.

Blair Havers, then Music Director at the Church of the Ascension, would periodically call me. "How's Mr. Smith today?" he always began. His calls were friendly and welcome. At least somebody cared. He and Dennis Driscoll — who had been turfed out of the Roman Catholic cathedral in Hamilton a year or two before I left St. James' — were my only church musician friends.

I switched to attending the 8 a.m. Eucharist at Christ's Church Cathedral. I made yogourt and listened to CBC Radio *Sunday Morning* while Thalia, Noëlle, and Monique attended the 10 a.m. Eucharist at St. James' across the street.

Writing this, I wonder how we survived financially. We were the almost stereotypical family with two kids and two mortgages. Thalia had always contributed to our income from the beginning of our marriage. When we lived in Glastonbury, Connecticut, she worked full-time at a department store in Hartford, and did some dressmaking on the side. It is also important to acknowledge that she saved us significant money by making almost all the clothing for herself and the girls. On occasion, she even tackled men's tailoring by making ties and an overcoat for me. In Southbridge, she ran a dance school. In Saskatoon, she worked in the university bookstore before being invited to a specially created position at the YWCA.

When we moved to Dundas in 1967, Noëlle was ten months old. Thalia had stayed home and focused most of her attention on being a good mother. Ever industrious, she bartered haircuts for babysitting, made candles and potpourri for sale, did dressmaking and tailoring for cash, and even occasional housecleaning. She worked from home until Monique entered grade one in the fall of 1975. At that point, Thalia gently re-entered the workforce outside of home. Her first part-time job in Dundas came that year when our friend Audrey Nicol opened *The Keeping Room*, a speciality kitchen shop.

Since moving to Dundas, I had always come home for lunch and dinner. Noëlle and Monique could walk back from school to have lunch with both of us, or just me if Thalia were working. Both girls remember having lunch with their mother at The Keeping Room on Thursdays, when on some occasions, a special treat would be a sandwich from

Links' Delicatessen next door: spiced ham on a Kaiser. Our family lunch gatherings continued until 1983 when both girls were in high school with a proper cafeteria.

THALIA WAS INVITED to a new position at the Mountain YWCA. Her job there was to create and organize lunch programmes in public elementary schools for children who did not or could not go home during the noonhour. The goal was to ensure the kids had a safe place to eat their brought-from-home food, and were adequately supervised for the better part of an hour and a half until classes resumed. Teachers were not available for this role, as their contract exempted them from lunchtime duties. Thalia's responsibilities included interviewing, hiring, and supervising part-time staff and emergency substitutes to be in the schools or outside on school property.

The need for these programmes was much greater than anticipated as more and more mothers entered the workforce. After perhaps two years, the Hamilton Board of Education realized they were paying the YWCA a substantial sum for little more than Thalia's office space, so the contract was allowed to expire, and Thalia transitioned to full-time employment at the board. This position continued to grow under Thalia's guidance to the point where she had an assistant and student interns.

I continued earning a bit by teaching private piano and organ lessons, as well as taking on substitute organ work where needed. Plans for the studio extension at 105 Victoria matured in the first half of 1977. Our architect, Anthony Butler, drew plans, they were tendered, and a contractor was selected.

Building began in September. Thalia's parents visited from Scotland for several weeks, in time to witness the groundbreaking. Thalia's father, we called him "Grump," loved to go for long walks in the countryside around Dundas. He frequently used the word "lush" to describe it. Granny was more of a homebody. She loved to cook for the family. Thalia benefited by rediscovering dishes from her childhood. She particularly learned that you can't give fish and chips the right flavour if you fry them in vegetable shortening; you must use lard. We visited Grump's brother in Toronto, as well as both the Canadian and American sides of Niagara Falls. We even went to a parish dance at St. Luke's in Hamilton. I was amazed that, despite being a large woman, Granny was feather-light on her feet.

Our next-door neighbour to the east protested to the Town of Dundas about the studio construction as soon as excavation began. We had anticipated his displeasure, and Tony, our architect, ensured that every detail of the construction complied with the building code so we could avoid any hearing necessary for an exception request. We put extra soundproofing on the side of the studio that faced our unhappy neighbour's property. One detail was particularly amusing. Long after our early 20th-century house was built, a bylaw was adopted that required space to be allowed on one side of the house for a driveway. Instead of building the studio directly behind the house, the studio was designed to be offset to the right to allow the required driveway space on the left. It could, of course, never be used as a driveway because the house blocked access. This situation created two benefits: the studio was now visible from the street on the right, and the driveway space to the left of the studio became a patio.

There were several other unique features. Because our back garden sloped upward, Tony designed a split-level building. Family members entered it from the kitchen via the existing back door. Visitors entered the new building from a porch and side door. Either way, you were in a vestibule immediately behind the kitchen door. With your back to it, and facing upward (north) into the studio, there was a wide closet to the left. Six steps led directly up into the studio, and to the left of this stairway was a three-piece bathroom with a shower. My office was to the right of the stairway.

The studio itself was twenty-feet-square with a twenty-three-foot cathedral ceiling, built for acoustical reasons. Since the bathroom, closet, entrance space, and office did not need such high ceilings, a floor was laid above them to create a loft that housed the furnace and left lots of room that soon housed the music library. A full-sized double-glazed sliding patio door was installed on the west side, and there were no windows on the east side to protect the cranky neighbour from any escaping sound.

The right (east) side of the peaked roof was three feet higher than the left. Three-foot-high windows ran the full length of the building. The far end of the studio, about four feet below grade, was stabilized by a retaining wall that went deep into the ground. A weeping tile behind carried water from the hill around the right side of the building down to the front yard and a dry well that was covered with gravel to create a driveway long enough for two cars.

Thalia, quite reasonably, thought that if I were getting a new studio, she deserved a new kitchen. Our early 20th-century house was likely originally built before indoor plumbing. When we bought the house, the kitchen sink was on the east wall, vertically between the basement water heater and the second-floor bathroom. The main upstairs closet had been sacrificed to create the bathroom. We designed kitchen renovations around the general store marble-topped ash counter for which Thalia had bartered while enumerating for an election a few years previously. The trade consisted of $5.00, a loaf of home-baked bread, and a jar of homemade jam. The marble top measured six feet by two feet and was about an inch thick. The height of the counter was two to three inches below standard which suited 5 foot ½ inch Thalia well. It ran at a 90-degree angle from the back (north) wall of the kitchen, just to the left of the door. A double sink, dishwasher, and counter were installed running west along the back wall, along with copious orange laminated cupboards. Thalia loved bright colours.

The renovation made the pantry on the west wall unnecessary, so it was demolished. Its window now brightened the whole kitchen, with added light coming in from a new windowed door. This was installed just to the left of the stove, now moved back to the west wall. We thereby had access to the yard and patio without going through the studio.

The kitchen and studio construction were supposed to take six to eight weeks. We learned, to our dismay, that residential construction was non-union, and union contracts elsewhere took precedence. Our building site remained idle for long periods as we waited for the various subcontractors to fulfill higher-priority jobs. It was not until mid-February that the piano, harpsichord, and portable pipe organ were moved into the studio, and I was ready to begin keyboard lessons as well as rehearsals with the Te Deum Singers. The front room of the house could now return to being a dining room.

1978 BEGAN WITH DISASTER. We were awakened in the wee hours one morning by a phone call from a neighbour. "St. James' is a ball of fire!" I looked out the bedroom window to see exactly that. Quickly throwing on some clothes, I rushed across the street to the church parking lot. It was a bitterly cold and windy January night. Soon after my arrival, the roof caught fire. It didn't take long for it to collapse. I walked around the outside of the flaming inferno in horror. The fire department was pouring tons of water onto and into the building, but the church was being gutted. Several friends and churchwardens gathered afterwards in our house. Still shivering, we huddled in the living room and exchanged what little information we had. It was very crowded because the kitchen furniture was crammed into the two front rooms during construction, but I was able to make hot chocolate to warm us up.

The next morning, a bunch of us inspected the interior of the burnt-out church. The sanctuary, chancel, and sacristy were completely gone. There was no evidence that the organ console, on the left side of the chancel near the sacristy door, had ever existed. The organ, in a chamber next to the right side of the chancel, was also destroyed. I looked for pipe metal on the floor, but could find none. All I found was a small piece of charcoal which I believed to be a remnant of a wooden organ pipe.

We learned that the fire had started at or near the altar, and had probably smouldered for hours there. The howling wind prevented the smoke from being detected and reported by nearby residents. The fire department suspected arson, but did not have enough evidence to name the culprit. The most common theory was that a young person was playing church and perhaps left some candles burning. No one believed that whoever was responsible intended to destroy the building.

We had no suspicion that our morning visit was dangerous. We were later told that the church floor was being held in place by ice that formed as a result of the fire department water. We were lucky no one fell through to the basement. Had I still been organist-choirmaster of St. James', my harpsichord would have been destroyed, and my portable organ likely damaged beyond repair. I soon discovered that the two instruments were seriously underinsured for their respective purchase prices rather than their replacement values.

THE TE DEUM Concert Series celebrated its 10th season with a major Bach Handel Festival from February 24th through March 17th. Four concerts for choir and/or orchestra were presented in Christ's Church Cathedral in Hamilton. A fifth concert for solo harpsichord took place in the Art Gallery of Hamilton. The events were well-presented, well-performed, and well-attended but we were, as usual, a little short of breaking even.

I was still without a church position two years after leaving St. James'. The debacle there had sullied both the rector and my reputations. We were labelled difficult to work with, maybe worse. I know he had been shortlisted for a major academic position but was blackballed by one of the trustees because of his human-relations performance at the church. I applied for numerous positions, but was seldom able to get an interview.

The Rector of St. Stephen's Episcopal Church in Providence, Rhode Island (near Brown University), was a close friend of mine from college days. He asked me to become his organist and choirmaster, and I was flown down. I met with the rector and wardens and decided it would be a good move.

In the meantime, I used some Dundas connections to get a bargain rental for a summer vacation week at a condo in Cocoa Beach, Florida. We drove south via Detroit to Knoxville, Tennessee, stopping to visit a horse farm in Lexington, Kentucky, where the famous racehorse, Man o' War, had been born and raised. We spent the night in a Days Inn in Knoxville, and continued to Cocoa Beach on the second day.

We had an enjoyable time there, relaxing. Ever aware of our tight budget, we prepared our meals in the condo, and were happy to use the swimming pool a lot in the sweltering heat. We encountered some teenage girls from Dundas there. As they were older than our daughters, no real connection was made, but it was an amusing coincidence. From our balcony, we also were able to witness a rocket launch from nearby Cape Canaveral. Even though miles away, the roar was incredible. You could feel the sound waves hitting your body. One gets little sense of that when watching a liftoff on television.

Our one excursion was to Disney World in Orlando, about an hour's drive away. It was monstrously expensive, and one was forbidden to bring one's own food. We nevertheless had a good time. The heat was also unbelievable, hotter than Cocoa Beach but less humid. We stayed until evening for the electrical parade and fireworks. 1978 was Mickey

Mouse's 50th birthday, and the parade was spectacular. Thalia and the girls enjoyed it, but I had more fun because Mickey was so much part of my American childhood.

We drove along the east coast for our trip back north, passing through Atlanta and vowing we would return someday. We saw wild alligators outside a lunch stop in South Carolina. We spent our next two nights and a day visiting Noëlle's godfather, Bill Bowie, who taught at Howard University in Washington. From there, we proceeded north to Providence, Rhode Island, to show Thalia and the girls where we would move in the fall. We stayed in the rectory. Thalia and the rector's wife did not bond at all, and I don't think Noëlle and Monique were particularly comfortable either.

From Providence we continued to Bangor, Maine, to visit Noëlle's other godfather, John Miller. He had been my rector in Southbridge, Massachusetts, from the spring of 1963 until Thalia and I moved to Saskatchewan in the fall of 1965. Somewhere along the way, we stopped for a traditional clambake. Rocks and seaweed were heated by a fire in the open pit, and once hot, the clams, lobsters, and potatoes were buried inside and the coals scraped to the side. We were amused when nine-year-old Monique called the lobsters "monsters". A good time was had by all, and Monique enjoyed eating the monster. She tells me that she wrapped an empty lobster shell in paper towels and toilet paper to keep as a souvenir. As we travelled, the stench got higher and higher, until she finally threw it away before the rest of the family "voted her off the island."

From Maine, we proceeded to Sherbrooke, Québec, to visit Sue Webber who had been an across-the-hall neighbour in our first apartment in Dundas. Her daughter, Heidi, had been best friends with Noëlle until we moved into our own home. It was great seeing Sue again, but the two girls had little remaining connection.

One morning, in a nearby park, I tried to strike up a conversation with a pre-teen boy. His reaction was "Je ne parle pas anglais". My French was so far from his Quebec *joual* that he did not even recognize I was speaking French.

From Sherbrooke, we proceeded home. I am exhausted just writing about the trip.

I HAD CLOSED the Te Deum Concert Series the previous spring in anticipation of our move to Providence. My good friend, Paul Goodrow, who was Treasurer of the Te Deum board ran a fundraising drive that successfully retired our significant but manageable deficit.

In August, the move fell through. I had taken out Canadian citizenship in 1971. At the time, part of the oath to her Majesty and all her rightful heirs and successors included a renunciation of all other citizenships. I erroneously assumed that the United States government would somehow be aware that I had taken this step and would automatically revoke my citizenship. Wrong! My friend was well-connected in the State Department and assured me he could speed up my approval to return to the US. He too was wrong. His connections were useless because applications for immigration to the United States go to the Department of Justice, not State.

I was still in fact an American citizen, and did not need to apply to return to the United States as an immigrant. I will spare you the intricacies of what followed. The bottom line is that I had outed myself as a Canadian citizen at a time when the USA was not friendly to dual citizens. I stupidly signed a form that caused me to lose my American citizenship. My application to immigrate to the USA got bogged down in the process, and I could not start the new position on September 1st. St. Stephen's then withdrew the offer.

In the fall, I created a new board of directors for Te Deum and we planned a three-concert season at Christ's Church Cathedral beginning in February 1979. We also decided that it was time to incorporate. We became the Te Deum Concert Society Inc. Over the next few years, between then and 1988, the board suggested that neither Te Deum Concerts nor the Te Deum Concert Society described our product. They felt that the words *Te Deum* meant nothing to most people, and that we should eliminate them. Richard Birney-Smith Concerts was one of the suggestions. I thought that suggestion to be egotistical. I also wanted the concerts to survive my retirement or death. I finally suggested *Te Deum Orchestra & Singers*. It satisfied my desire to keep the name and it described our product. The board adopted my suggestion. It became our operating name from that day forward.

In January of 1979, I was invited to become interim organist & choirmaster at the Church of the Holy Saviour in Waterloo, Ontario.[1] This parish, with its tiny building, is the oldest Anglican Church in Waterloo. It had, and still has, a distinguished choral tradition. A very British congregation filled the pews every Sunday. Holy Saviour had a decent pipe organ and the most skilled Anglican church choir of my entire career. Their repertoire was cathedral-like in its scope. They were also some of the friendliest choristers I ever met. We presented two

[1] https://holy-saviour.on.ca/history/

festal evensongs in the spring in addition to our normal Sunday morning duties, and sang an all-Tallis evensong at Christ's Church Cathedral in Hamilton. I was always addressed as Mr. Birney-Smith. I soon stopped correcting people and allowed the hyphen to become part of my name. Everyone now, except the Ontario Ministry of Transport, recognizes that I am Richard Birney-Smith.

After several months at Holy Saviour, I was invited to accept a permanent appointment. The nastiness of the winter commute along Highway 8 convinced me to decline their kind offer. I finished my brief tenure at the end of June, just in time to gather our equipment to set up camp at Skycroft.

THAT SUMMER, Thalia and I attended the Evergreen Conference in Evergreen, Colorado.[2] The conference was a rustic, small (under 50 people) but distinguished two-week summer school for Episcopal (Anglican) church musicians, begun in 1903 by Canon Winfred Douglas. I was on faculty, Thalia was on holiday with me, and the girls stayed in Ontario for Girl Guide Camp. I had been recommended by Dr. Thomas Matthews, my first organ teacher, who had been dean of the conference for many years, but was by then retired. He still attended the conference in an honorary role. The invitation from the current dean surprised me because Dr. Matthews and I had had virtually no contact since I moved from Evanston, Illinois, in 1955. He told me that he had been following my career in professional journals. He and his wife stayed in a comfortable cabin on the campus, and it was very satisfying to spend quality time visiting with them.

[2] The Living Church: Search Results (episcopalarchives.org)

The Dean of the conference that year was Dr. Alastair Cassels-Brown, Professor of Music at Episcopal Theological School in Cambridge, Massachusetts. The other faculty members were Alec Wyton, Music Director at St. James' Episcopal Church in New York City and the Rev. Dr. Jeffery Rowthorn, Associate Professor at Berkeley Divinity School and the Yale Institute of Sacred Music. Jeff, later Suffragan Bishop of Connecticut and Bishop in Charge of the Episcopal Dioceses in Europe, wrote the words to many hymns now in use in the United States, Canada, and elsewhere. It is interesting and curious that I was the only born North American on the faculty that year. Alec and Alistair were both born in England; Jeff in Wales. My focus at the conference was hymn playing and congregational singing. I also played an organ recital in St. John's Cathedral, Denver, during the second week.

In 1977, the Episcopal Church USA published its first revision of the *Book of Common Prayer* since 1928. The *Hymnal 1982* was now in the works, the first hymn book revision since 1940. Alec Wyton, a member of the General Convention's Standing Committee on Church Music, and one of the prime movers behind the new book, brought us a wish list from the editors. Among other things on that list were a baptism hymn for Lent and new words for the Genevan Psalter tune *Old 124th*. The tune had been included in the *Hymnal 1940* to Clifford Bax's words: "Turn back, O man, forswear thy foolish ways." Bax had written the words in World War I at Gustav Holst's request for a motet, based on the *Old 124th*, which Holst was composing. As of 2023, those words appear in fifty-seven different hymnals. The words are, however, hopelessly Pelagian.[3] The committee wanted to outfit the now popular tune with Christian words.

I took the wish list back to Thomas H. Cain, friend, chorister, and mentor. He wrote words for four of the hymns on the wish list. Tom killed two birds with one stone by writing a baptism hymn for Lent to fit the Old 124th tune: *Eternal Lord of love, behold your Church.*[4] The Church avoids baptisms during Lent, but Tom's hymn transcends the original request and is simply, in my opinion, a great Lenten hymn. It was published in the *Hymnal 1982*, set to the *Old 124th* tune. It has been set to a different tune in numerous other hymnals, including *Common Praise of the Anglican Church of Canada*, but I always stick to the original tune.

[3] The Pelagian heresy posits that humankind can perfect itself by its own free will. Mainstream Christian theology teaches that one can only be saved by the grace of God.

[4] Eternal Lord of love, behold your Church,
walking once more the pilgrim way of Lent,
led by your cloud by day, by night your fire,
moved by your love and toward your presence bent:
far off yet here the goal of all desire.

So daily dying to the way of self,
so daily living to your way of love,
we walk the road, Lord Jesus, that you trod,
knowing ourselves baptized into your death:
so we are dead and live with you in God.

If dead in you, so in you we arise,
you the firstborn of all the faithful dead;
and as through stony ground the green shoots break,
glorious in springtime dress of leaf and flower,
so in the Father's glory shall we wake.

© 1982 Thomas H. Cain (reproduced by permission of the author).

I was to write tunes for the other three of Tom's hymns but none was accepted for publication.

Thalia, not content to be just a spectator at the conference, taught dances to some of the hymns proposed for the new hymnal. One of them was an Israeli *hora* which gets faster with each repetition. The result, at 2,184 metres elevation (7,165 feet), was a room full of people on the floor gasping for breath.

My *Mass of St. Andrew* quickly became a favourite of both faculty and conferees. They especially liked that it was originally composed to be sung without accompaniment, like John Merbecke's setting composed at Archbishop Cramer's request for *The Book of Common Prayer Noted* (1550). Father Rowthorne, who could not carry a tune, appointed me lay deacon to sing the *Sursum Corda and Proper Preface* in his stead at the daily Eucharists. I had never before, and never since, heard of a lay deacon, but I enjoyed my role standing next to the presider behind the altar.

Both Alec Wyton and Alastair Cassels-Brown strongly suggested that I apply for the vacant Director of Music position at Trinity Church, Boston. This I did as soon as I got home. My friend and colleague, Ronald Arnatt, from Christ Church Cathedral in St. Louis, won the position. Sadly, he was fired almost immediately upon the arrival of a new rector a few months later. I unsuccessfully applied for a position at our cathedral in Albuquerque, New Mexico, at about the same time.

Life's events appeared to have reached some sort of equilibrium, which I hoped was set to continue for the next few years.

-25-

New Challenges – New Opportunities
(1980-1981)

Contrary to the final sentence of the previous chapter, life continued to become more active and less predictable.

Thalia, Noëlle, Monique, and I visited Thalia's family in the summer of 1980. It was the first and only European trip that included all four of us. We began our vacation in the London borough of Sutton with Thalia's younger brother Robin, his wife, and children. In addition to family time together, we ventured out to the City of London, Carnaby Street, and Windsor Castle.

Sadly, on June 30th, a day or two before our departure, Grandpa Solomon died. I could not play his requiem in Detroit on July 5th. The day before his funeral, however, I did offer prayers in his memory at a weekday morning Eucharist in a nearby parish church.

Before leaving Canada, I purchased a combined rail and rental car pass. It allowed us to board a train, ride to our next destination, pick up an automobile, use it, return it (not necessarily to the pickup point) and then continue by rail. After visiting Robin's family, we boarded a train in London and proceeded to Newcastle upon Tyne. Thalia thought that her old beau, John Maughan, the father of her child born in Connecticut in 1962, lived in the city. He was still unaware of his son's existence, and the main reason for stopping there was to try to make contact with him. We spent significant time in phone booths scouring phonebooks and called several people who shared his surname but had no success.

We picked up a car and drove from Newcastle to Thalia's parents in Cupar-Fife. It was Saturday, July 5th. We turned on the car radio during the fourth set of the epic John McEnroe-Björn Borg gentlemen's singles final at Wimbledon. Some sports analysts still consider this to be the greatest men's singles match in tennis history. I had never before heard play-by-play tennis broadcast on the radio. It was riveting.

We arrived in Cupar before dark and spent several days with Granny and Grump. While there, we visited Thalia's elder brother, Gordon, as well as Grump's sisters, Auntie Ag who lived in St. Andrew's, and Auntie Jean who lived in another nearby town. In St. Andrew's we also visited Thalia's childhood friend Virginia Nelson (née Reekie). At some point during the more than two weeks in Scotland, we decamped to East Kilbride (near Glasgow) to spend the better part of a week with Thalia's elder sister, Sonia, and her family. Noëlle and Monique immediately bonded with Sonia's kids. Monique, who has a particularly quick ear, picked up the local brogue. To this day, she can turn it on and off at will.

After our time with Sonia's family, we returned to spend several more days with Granny and Grump. Monique remembers that Granny's best friend, Phyllis, played musical spoons exceedingly well, to the delight of all. We all enjoyed trips around the corner for tasty pastries at Fisher & Donaldson's, as well as trips to the local fish and chip shop.

The four of us managed to spend a long day in Edinburgh. We visited Princes Street; saw the statue of Henry Dundas, Lord Melville (after whom our Canadian home town was named); walked down the

Royal Mile (at the foot of which I had the best fish and chips ever); visited Edinburgh Castle, and there purchased tickets to return in the evening for the Edinburgh Tattoo. Granny said that our trip was her vacation too, and inveigled us to drive her around Loch Lomond, close to a full day's excursion. We didn't want to do it, but it turned out to be a lovely family day. I can't remember whether we took the high road or the low road. ☺

As Thalia had bargained for a new kitchen when my studio was designed, I bargained to conclude our trip with a visit to France. I returned the rental car in Cupar, and after a good supper, we departed by train in the evening with overnight sleeper reservations.

Granny had prepared a bag of goodies for us to eat on the train, but Thalia was too embarrassed to accept it. I think she found bringing snacks to be rather low-class.

The train arrived in London around six o'clock the next morning. We were awakened by the porter and given a fresh pot of tea. Our train to the channel ferry at Newhaven was scheduled for just before eight o'clock. We had planned to buy breakfast in the train station but, alas, none of the restaurants opened until eight o'clock. We were a hungry lot as we boarded the train, and looked for food service, but there was none. At around eleven o'clock we arrived at Newhaven train station which was right next to the ferry dock: not a store in sight. Still hungry, we boarded the ferry, settled our luggage, and immediately looked for the restaurant. A sign on the door told us it did not open until noon. We went back to our seats and waited impatiently. When we finally presented ourselves. we discovered that the ferry operated on French time, one hour earlier than British time. Oh, how we wished we had accepted Granny's bag of goodies. The restaurant food was indifferent at best, but we didn't care after eighteen hours with only a cup of tea.

WE ARRIVED IN Dieppe mid-afternoon and almost immediately took the onward train. Most passengers would have been going to Paris, but we disembarked at Rouen. We had a layover of longer than an hour, enough time to venture outside where we purchased raspberry croissants from a street vendor. These were lovely, fresh and buttery with a cylinder of delicious raspberry jam down the middle. As I write more than four decades later, I have yet to find a similar treat. It was indeed one of life's small but memorable moments for all of us. We also managed to walk through Rouen Cathedral, an important part of my life as an exchange student twenty-two years previously.

We caught our connecting train and were in Yvetot in about an hour. My French father, Charles Bost, met us there. Ever the gentleman, he insisted that Thalia sit in the front passenger seat. Papa spoke clear but noticeably accented English. Thalia, who had resisted the idea of visiting France, was totally charmed. It was less than a 30-minute drive home to the Château de Lillebonne.[1] The property is situated at a high point overlooking the town of Lillebonne. It is surrounded by a combination of stone wall and brick fence. When we arrived at the entrance gate, Papa said, "*Dick, oeuvre la porte, s'il te plaît.*" (Dick, please open the gate.) I alighted from the car, opened the gate, waited for Papa to drive in, closed the gate, and hopped back into the car. We then drove another hundred or so metres around the back of the *donjon*, a 16th-

---

[1] For details about the chateau and my time there in 1958-1959, see Chapter 12: "An Exchange Student in France."

century war tower, and parked at the side door. As Papa led us up the stairs to the entrance, Thalia murmured to me, "It's a bloody castle." I'm not sure whether I replied, or just wished I could reply, "I told you so."

We passed through a mud room and entered a hallway with a grand staircase on the right, and the living room doors on the left. I have purposely avoided saying large this or large that: everything was large. Maman was waiting for us in the living room. After introductions and a brief conversation, she excused herself to serve supper. Gone were the days of a live-in maid. The current domestique's position was a day job. She had prepared supper in advance. While Maman was working, we stepped from the living room onto the front porch to look out over the property toward the horizon. The resident peacocks were roaming freely in the front yard. We could see the *donjon* directly to the left and, about 45 degrees toward the center, the ruined octagonal tower from the time of King Philip Augustus. Directly in front of us and to the right was a panoramic view over downtown Lillebonne, including the steeple of the 16th-century Gothic church. It was breathtaking in the early evening as sunset approached.

Once Maman had done whatever was needed in the kitchen, she served our meal in the dining room.

Thalia and I slept in Brigitte's former bedroom, the one I had occupied during my student days. Noëlle and Monique had bedrooms at the other end of the second-floor mezzanine which overlooked the grand staircase. The master bedroom, at the center of the mezzanine, was between the girls and us.

We spent the entire next day with Papa and sometimes Maman. Papa drove us to Étretat and then on to Pourville for afternoon tea. We were the only guests at a cordon-bleu school for pastry chefs. The bill was over $200. Cordon bleu indeed.

We departed from Yvetot early enough the following day to arrive in Paris at the Gare St-Lazare around noon. Our onward journey was from the Gare Montparnasse. We took a métro with buskers on board across the city, stopping for a full *déjeuner* (noon meal) at a sidewalk café near the train station. I wanted to impress Thalia and the girls. The meal was excellent as I remember. I inadvertently got rather drunk but successfully hid the fact from the rest of the family. We also managed to squeeze in a brief visit to my French sister, Brigitte, at her home on rue du Bac.

It was Thursday, July 31st, and it seemed as if everyone were simultaneously leaving Paris for their summer vacations. The trains were packed with people. Our next destination was Saumur in the Loire Valley where we would meet our friend Pol Corvez. The train was old and not air-conditioned. It had probably been brought out of retirement to handle the holiday traffic. We found seats for Thalia and the girls, but I stood most of the way. Being a French train, it arrived on schedule at Tours where we changed trains for Saumur. Pol was there to meet us, and we were whisked away to his home in Le Puy-Notre Dame, a village in Anjou.

Being in Anjou was particularly sentimental for me. While I attended the Lycée in Lillebonne in 1958, students were required to memorize a Joachim DuBellay sonnet, *Mal de Pays*, which is about the author's homesickness. In it, he wistfully pines for the gentleness of Anjou (*la douceur Angevine*) which he prefers to the grandeur of Rome. I can still recite it. I later set it to music for six-part choir, viola da gamba, baroque flute, and harpsichord. It may also be performed with cello and modern flute.

We arrived in Le Puy shortly after dark. At the time, Pol was a self-employed photographer. As we walked from the car to the house, we were surprised and delighted to see a photo of Noëlle and Monique, aged five and three, with their faces painted. Thalia and I had never before seen it. Pol had taken the picture while babysitting for us during his two years' teaching at McMaster University in Hamilton. The photo was a favourite of the townspeople who complained whenever it was not displayed in the studio window.

We were warmly greeted by Pol's wife, Melissa. (I don't think that either of their children had been born yet.) We had previously known her when Pol taught for two years at Allegheny College in Meadville, Pennsylvania, after his time at McMaster. The couple met when he was a faculty member and she an undergraduate. Such a relationship would be firmly prohibited now. After Pol returned to France, he realized he could not live without Melissa who, after graduating, was working in Washington, DC. He asked her to marry him, she accepted, and he was able to get a fiancé's visa to join her. They bought a 16th-century stone house in Le Puy at the suggestion of a couple who already lived there. At the time, there were no taxes on vacant property in France, so they were able to live and work in Washington while saving money to renovate their future home.

The main detail I remember of Friday was a drive into Saumur, likely to a market. I remember buying a Camembert. After that, we went to the nearby Château de Montreuil-Bellay, where Pol took colour photos of the four of us. We printed 200 copies of our favourite, and enclosed one with each of our 1980 Christmas letters. This was before the convenience of computers and the internet, so each letter was printed, and enclosed with the photo in a stamped, hand-addressed envelope before being mailed.

We departed on Saturday morning for Paris and the flight home, taking a taxi from the train station to the airport. Along the way we asked the driver to stop at a bakery where we purchased two loaves so we could have real French bread for breakfast at home the next morning. What a treat that was.

SOMETIME IN THE middle of 1980, Grant Avenue Studios was to record the musical soundtrack for a United Artists movie. They had been told I owned a clavichord, and they wanted to rent it. I started asking questions. Why did they need a clavichord? Why were they trying to rent a professional musician's instrument without hiring the owner? I discovered they were recording for a film called *Cutter and Bone*, a neo-noir thriller starring Jeff Bridges, John Heard, and Lisa Eichhorn. The music had been composed by future Academy Award winner Jack Nitzsche[2], then best-known in the film industry for writing the scores for *The Exorcist* and *One Flew Over the Cuckoo's Nest*. The soundtrack was for string quartet, clavichord, musical saw, and glass harmonica. After some conversation and negotiation, I led them to a better clavichord: the Wilson Barry instrument owned by my friend and student Dennis

[2] For whatever reason, I usually think of Jack Nitzsche (pronounced the same as the 19th Century German philosopher) as Buffy Sainte-Marie's husband, but they hadn't yet married.

Radesch. They rented his and hired me to play it for the movie.

Clavichords are seldom, if ever, played along with other instruments. One, therefore, does not usually bother to tune them to international pitch. Because this was an exception, I went over to Dennis' house and retuned his clavichord to A=440. By then, I had a copy of the music, and I ran through it there. It was easy.

When we got the instrument to the studio on the appointed recording day, the tuning was not fine enough for their purposes. A clavichord is exceedingly soft. For the movie soundtrack, the microphone was placed very close to the strings and soundboard, and the recorded sound is many times louder than reality. We spent the entire morning retuning while listening through earphones. The string volume was reasonable, but the tuning hammer placed on each tuning pin was deafening. At the time, I likened it to the sound of a garbage can being thrown into the Grand Canyon. As we lost the entire morning to tuning, Jack Nitzsche and the Grant Avenue people assumed we would be unable to finish the recording that day.

We broke for lunch and resumed in the early afternoon. I worked from the clavichord part. I did not have a copy of the full score, nor had I seen any of the movie. Through the stereo headphones I could hear only what had already been recorded, myself, and a click track to keep the tempo. The music was captured in twenty-four-track stereo, with each instrument recorded separately to give the composer and the recording engineers maximum control of the final mix. In my case, I was given two tracks: one for the right hand and one for the left.

I have three memories of the day. One passage in the film seemed particularly heartbreaking. When I commented on it, I was told that in the story, Lisa Eichhorn's character had just died. This is still a touching moment for me whenever I watch the film. Another memory is that the control room forgot to play my sound through the headphones on one of the takes. I could hear the other musicians and the click track, but not myself. When we finished that section, I told the control room and they were amazed. I had played well enough for them to keep my deaf recording for the final mix. As most of the recordings were first takes, we finished ahead of the original schedule.

Considering the small amount of work and preparation time, it was the best payday of my career. I received a fee of $1,000 US, plus a union pension fund contribution for my day in the studio. As mentioned, the movie is a neo-noir thriller. I am not a fan of the genre, but I occasionally watch my DVD to hear the music and relive the recording experience. I received residual cheques for at least five years. They were usually around $50-$60 US, and one year I was pleasantly surprised to receive around $250 US. I was however seriously disappointed that my name was omitted from the screen credits.

The film was the victim of interoffice disagreements at United Artists, and did not receive the promotion it deserved. The initial reception from daily newspapers was hostile. The studio panicked and withdrew the movie from distribution, after which good reviews came from periodicals. Some critics thought it to be among the best films of the year. It was eventually re-edited, retitled *Cutter's Way*[3], and reissued. Commercial distribution resumed, but the under-promoted film had limited success. It did, however, do well as a cult classic at film festivals.

---

[3] *Cutter's Way* - Wikipedia

EARLY IN 1981, I received a telephone call from Melrose United Church in Hamilton. Their organist and music director had taken seriously ill and was on an eight-week leave of absence. I was asked to fill in. Melrose is a large church, modelled on the ruins of Melrose Abbey in Scotland. The United Church of Canada was created in 1925 by merging the Methodist Church, the Congregational Union of Ontario and Quebec, the Association of Local Union Churches, and about 70% of Presbyterians.[4] The merger created a need for a larger building in the Kirkendall-Strathcona neighbourhood.

The new church was opened on Palm Sunday in 1929. It seated a congregation of 700-800 people and, I am told, had magnificent reverberant acoustics. The Canadian congregants, unaccustomed to the acoustics of a large gothic building, complained that they couldn't understand the spoken word. To dampen the reverberation, they hired an acoustical "expert" who, in those days, was usually someone selling acoustical tile. The ideal acoustical environment at the time was a radio studio where there was no reverberation at all. The Johns Manville company installed tiles on several walls, and when the job was finished, the workmen noticed several unopened boxes remained. They decided on their own authority to install the extra tiles on the untreated walls. The result was building acoustics that were deader than a doornail.

Melrose Church nevertheless developed a distinguished choral tradition, built largely on Anglican cathedral music. Some people described Melrose as high-church United. Cyril Hampshire, Director of Music for the Hamilton Board of Education, was their music director for twenty years (approximately 1933-1953). After his retirement,

---

[4] United Church of Canada - Wikipedia

numerous musicians came and went as the powers that be were never satisfied that anyone could fill his shoes. My closest friend and Monique's godfather, Michael Doran, lasted only ninety days. I was therefore leery of the place.

I nevertheless accepted the eight-week appointment. By the end of this time, the current music director was still not well enough to resume his duties. I was offered another eight weeks, which I accepted. He resigned during my second appointment. I was asked to become their permanent organist and director of music. Still, I hesitated. I requested and accepted a third eight-week contract. I warned them that, musically, I would throw everything but the kitchen sink at them — and I did. We sang and played Renaissance, baroque, modern, a rock-and-roll hymn on Easter Day, and electronic music. None of that scared them away. I therefore accepted the position and stayed for eleven years.

A contract for a minor, but significant, update in the organ's tonal design had been signed a year or so before my arrival. The fifty-stop three-manual Casavant organ was installed in 1930, the year after the building was opened. The sound was powerful but rather thick, as was then normal. In the new tonal revision, the mixture stops, among other things, were being reconstituted to make the instrument brighter and more flexible. I was able to amend the contract to brighten and soften the big tuba stop on the choir organ. We may have renamed it to more accurately describe its new sound. I was also able to add a great and choir reverse button so that whenever the organist so desired, the principal division (the great organ) could be played from the bottom keyboard rather than the middle one. The Melrose organ became, in my opinion, the most flexible organ in greater Hamilton.

The twenty-two-voice Melrose choir was comparable in skill to the Church of the Holy Saviour in Waterloo. The difference was that Melrose had paid section leader/soloists. The church's tradition was somewhat less flexible than Anglican parishes in that an anthem and a solo were expected every Sunday from September through June. Services moved from the main church into the chapel for July and August. There was one soloist, no choir, and a perfectly horrid little Rodgers electronic organ. The music director in the mid-seventies had sought my advice about purchasing an organ for the chapel but didn't accept it. He chose the Rodgers because it had more stops than the small one-manual pipe organ I had recommended. The larger size of the Rodgers was an illusion created by electronic manipulation. The chapel organ only had four different sounds at numerous pitches. I thought that only two of those sounds were decent.

One summer I obtained permission to place my Wilhelm portable pipe organ behind the chapel congregation. I thought it a great improvement, but people complained that the Wilhelm was white oak while the chapel was walnut. Oy vey!

THE NEW CHAMBER ORCHESTRA obtained an Ontario Arts Council grant to commission me to compose a piece for harpsichord and strings. Somewhere during the process, a significant number of the core members of the orchestra lost faith in the competence of the conductor and petitioned the board to replace him. The petition failed, and we were all fired. I completed the composition on 24 March 1980. The Ontario Arts Council paid me the contracted fee, but the New Chamber Orchestra refused to premiere my piece as required in the contract.

I therefore premiered it in November 1980 with the Te Deum Orchestra. It was titled *Suite for Harpsichord & Strings in A Minor*. The whole piece is modelled on the structure of a French suite for solo harpsichord. The first movement, *Prélude*, is slow and unmeasured, reminiscent of those of Henry Purcell or Louis Couperin for solo harpsichord. Mine is unique, at least in classical music, in that the string orchestra is given a barebones structure, and quietly accompanies a harpsichord improvisation. They proceed to the next chord at the nod of the harpsichordist's head. The second movement is a spritely set of variations called *Jeux de doubles* (Game of doubles). Thalia and I were tennis fans and I couldn't resist the play on words. In music, *double* is an old word for rhythmic variation. My variations were reminiscent of the *doubles* of the 16th to 18th centuries.

The third movement is a slow nostalgic piece called *Souvenir de Lillebonne* (Memory of Lillebonne) in homage to my life-changing stay there as an exchange student. The piece begins with a wistful harpsichord solo, the theme of which is then repeated and embellished by soloists and orchestra. The final movement is a French Baroque *rondeau*, consisting of a recurring theme with interspersed sections called *couplets*, which are about the same length as the rondeau. The rondeau theme came to me so quickly that I initially doubted it was my composition. I had to live with it for several days before I accepted it as my own work, as opposed to a memory of someone else's. Two of the couplets were each to be improvised by the principal cellist and the concertmaster. Michael Peebles and Nancy Mathis DiNovo were both shy about improvising in public, and wrote out excellent couplets. I have these and will publish them with the piece in case future performers are similarly shy.

The Te Deum audience, which rarely gave standing ovations or demanded encores, did so on this occasion. We played *Souvenir de Lillebonne* as an encore. During the subsequent applause, Grace Inglis, wife of a board member and mother of one of my harpsichord students, came forward from the audience to present me with a gorgeous floral bouquet. It was the first time in my life anyone had ever presented me with flowers, a forever precious memory.

A MAJOR BREAKTHROUGH later in the 1980-1981 season was our first Handel oratorio. For several years, Antony Hammond, one of the music critics for the Hamilton Spectator, had been agitating for us to perform Handel's *Messiah*. I resisted because both the Bach-Elgar Choir and the Mohawk College Community Choir performed *Messiah* almost every year. So I decided to take up the challenge by ending the season with something else by Handel: *Saul*. It is a great oratorio that is rarely performed. Saul is the eponymous villain in the piece; David is the hero. I hired James Bechtel, the great local bass-baritone with whom I had worked for many years, to portray Saul. He had previously sung for Te Deum, had been an occasional paid member of my choir at Temple Anshe Sholom, and was soloist/section leader at Melrose.

To portray David I hired countertenor John Ferrante, whom I had known since my Trinity College days. One Sunday in the early nineteen-sixties, he did me a favour and sang at South Congregational Church in Granby, Connecticut, where he chose to sing *O Lord, whose mercies numberless* from Saul. It knocked my socks off. That memory persuaded me to investigate *Saul* as my first Handel oratorio. John lived and worked in New York City, and we negotiated an affordable fee plus transportation and accommodation.

When I called him in January 1981 to discuss the rehearsal schedule and begin arranging his flights, he reacted angrily. His shocking diatribe took me aback. He accused me of being arrogant. Who did I think I was? How could Dick Smith suddenly become Richard Birney-Smith? He refused to fulfil the engagement. I was unaware that he was in the early stages of AIDS, a then-new affliction about which little was known.

I was in a serious pickle. What to do? The star of the show had quit on me. A countertenor is a male alto, and I had never before hired one to sing a solo role at Te Deum. I didn't know any other countertenor that I, at the time, thought had sufficient power and masculinity to carry the role. (I would think differently now.) I had been fascinated with countertenors since my second or third year of high school when I borrowed a library recording of Russell Oberlin and Charles Bressler singing John Blow's *Ode on the Death of Mr. Henry Purcell*. That recording also fanned my curiosity about recorders, harpsichords, and early music.[5] Nevertheless, I worried that my audience might not accept the sound of a man singing so high.

I can't remember if someone suggested the solution to my dilemma or if I figured it out myself. In the end, I hired the astounding Catherine Robbin to sing David. In the music business, a woman portraying a man

---

[5] I shared my excitement about the recording with my high school music teacher. He dismissed it all as needless antiquarianism: such music could be better performed using modern instruments and a female voice. Contrarian that I am, this further fuelled my curiosity.

is called a pants role. Cathy was at the beginning of her fame, and therefore affordable. She had just won at the Aldborough Festival in the UK. One music critic described her sound as burnished copper. Our first rehearsal was at her home in Toronto. Early on, I stopped her and asked that she not be so cautious. I wanted more ornamentation, especially cadenzas as they would have been performed in Handel's time. She was up to the challenge and went wild, but always in stylish good taste.

I was able to recruit two volunteers from the Melrose choir for the performance. One of them, Beverly Leslie, became the soprano section leader in the Te Deum Singers soon thereafter.

On the night, Cathy Robbin was magnificent beyond belief. Jim Bechtel was also magnificent. I can't say beyond belief because I had worked with him for years and knew what he could do. One female member of the audience came up to him after the performance and said something like, "Oh, Mr. Bechtel, you were so convincing as Saul that I just wanted to hiss." The newspaper review by Antony Hammond was ecstatic and, once again, called on us to perform *Messiah*.

The high-quality cassette tape recording of the concert no longer exists. A dear friend, who was dying of lung cancer some years later, asked to borrow it. Of course, I lent it to him and it really buoyed his spirits. Very quickly after his death, his family discarded and destroyed all the books and items around his bed. The memory of two of Cathy's arias, *O King, your favours with delight* and *O Lord, whose mercies numberless* haunt me to this day, but, alas, the evidence is gone.

After the triumph of *Saul*, we began planning our first *Messiah*.

The concerts were a total family activity: I conducted, Thalia managed the back of the house and was the de facto soprano section leader of the Te Deum Singers; Noëlle sang in the choir, while Monique took tickets and distributed programmes.

THE SUMMER OF 1981 took the family back to New England and New York City. In July, Thalia attended a twentieth-anniversary reunion of the Manchester (Connecticut) Girl Guides who had visited Cupar-Fife in 1961. This event provided the perfect excuse for a family trip. We visited friends in Sturbridge, Massachusetts, and Stoney Brook, Long Island, New York; showed the girls around the Trinity College campus and the chapel where Thalia and I had married each other eighteen years previously; and spent a long weekend in New York City. While in the Big Apple, we saw three Broadway plays. Together we saw *42nd Street*. On our second Broadway evening, I saw *Amadeus* while Thalia and the girls enjoyed the original cast production of *Woman of the Year* starring Lauren Bacall.

Summer wouldn't have been complete without time at Skycroft near the Rideau Canal, north of Kingston, Ontario; 1981 was our eleventh year there. We pitched our tent in the woods to enjoy the sun, sky, water, quiet, and Thalia's amazing campfire cooking.

IT WAS ALSO a big year for broadcasts on both CBC-AM and CBC-FM, now known as CBC Radio One and CBC Radio Two. The Te Deum Singers recorded their first of three annual Good Friday broadcasts for CBC's *Morningside*. The programme, recorded in Christ's Church Cathedral, featured music for Palm Sunday, Passover, Maundy

Thursday, Good Friday, and Easter Day. I then went into the Old Jarvis Street CBC studio to converse with host Peter Gzowski about the music. Some years our conversations were live to air, and other years recorded in advance. The Te Deum Singers shared a thrice-broadcast Christmas carol programme with the choir of the Cathedral Church of St. James, Toronto, and world-renowned actor William Hutt of the Stratford Festival. *An Organist's Life of Christ*, recorded there, alternated major organ pieces with spiritual reflections by author and producer, John Reeves.

In December, the Te Deum Singers & Orchestra performed Marc-Antoine Charpentier's *Messe de Minuit pour Noël* (Christmas Midnight Mass) at Christ's Church Cathedral. We had previously performed this wonderful piece twice before within Epiphany Eve Eucharists at St. James' Church in Dundas and the cathedral. But this was no longer practical because we were now selling tickets and charging admission to our concerts, which one cannot in good taste do for a church service.

Most concert performances of the Charpentier Midnight Mass just play the piece from beginning to end. I like to perform it in a manner that closely resembles a church service. I therefore begin with a prelude. In this case, I chose Archangelo Corelli's *Christmas Concerto* (Concerto grosso, opus 6, no. 8) for string orchestra and basso continuo. The concert performance continued with the Latin Gregorian propers for the day (introit, gradual, alleluia, offertory, and communion verse), interspersed with Charpentier's setting of the ordinary (Kyrie, Gloria, Credo, Sanctus & Benedictus qui venit, and Agnus Dei).

I hired the cantor from the Church of St. Mary Magdalene, Toronto, to intone the cantorial parts of the Gregorian chants and the priest's incipits. To my dismay, he came down with laryngitis the day before the dress rehearsal. I therefore chose to be cantor from the podium. Most of the audience wouldn't have known since my back was to them. The local critic, Hugh Fraser, did however, and compared my intake of breath to that of a beached whale. ☺ Ironically, radio producer John Reeves, also a composer, was so pleased with my cantillation that he recommended me to Elmer Iseler as cantor for the world premiere of John's oratorio, *Salvator Mundi*.

We ended the midnight mass performance with the French *noël, Les anges dans nos campagnes*, usually sung in English as *Angels we have heard on high*. The choir, with cello and organ continuo, sang each verse in French, with a literal translation provided in the printed programme. The audience and orchestra responded after each verse with the chorus: *Gloria in excelsis Deo*.

THALIA CONTINUED HER work as lunch programme coordinator at the Board of Education but was ready for a new challenge. She was more a creator than a maintainer. She also continued her volunteer commitment as a Pathfinder leader of the 12-15-year-old Girl Guides group. Both our girls were active Pathfinders and active members of St. James' Church. Noëlle, 15, was in grade ten at Parkside High School. She ran and skied on the cross-country teams, played trumpet in the band, worked on the yearbook, and took piano and dancing lessons. She occasionally slept in her spare time. Monique, almost 13 at the end of 1981, was in grade seven at Central Public School. She was in the school drama club, took piano lessons, and shared a weekly paper route with a friend.

Volume Two of Recollections & Reflections will be written and published as soon as possible.

Reflections

Reflection #1: Racism

"The struggle against racism is only legitimate if we are also fighting anti-Semitism, sexism, classism, etc. All of these isms are merely tools of oppression, which will continue to keep us fractured instead of united toward the common goal of a multicultural democracy." Irene Monroe[1]

Racism is but one form of discrimination. It may be characterized as one surface of a multi-faceted geometrical solid, whose other surfaces include nationalism, sexism, homophobia, biphobia, transphobia, anti-Semitism, Islamophobia, ableism, ageism, and many other ways that humans choose to separate themselves from one another. Human beings, as individuals and in groups, often look for ways to claim they are superior to those they deem to be inferior to themselves.

Racism is real. One of the easiest ways to practice it is to deny its existence. This denial may be explicitly intentional, saying things or behaving in a way that one knows to be untrue or inauthentic. But it may also be due to willful blindness, ignorance, or both. Either way, the denial helps to strengthen racism, ignore privilege, or both. We hear it both from ordinary individuals and, more sadly, from people in positions of power. I shall examine privilege in Reflection #3.

It is difficult to talk about one's own experience of racism because you risk being accused of inviting yourself to a self-pity party by those who don't want to hear about it. No matter how careful one is, those

---

[1] *Loving the Body: Black Religious Studies and the Erotic*, edited by D. Hopkins, (Palgrove Macmillan, New York, 2004) p. 130.

who do not want to listen will do their best not to hear.

This is my story. It is the only story I can authentically tell. Many Jews, blacks, Asians, and Indigenous peoples have suffered more than I have. Many have been killed. I firmly believe that the experience of racism wounds every survivor, and that each one interiorizes the experience in his or her own individual way.

Genetic research has demonstrated that race is a social construct. The human race is the only race. It cannot be objectively or scientifically subdivided.[2] The articles on race I read as a youth could not even agree how to divide humankind. Were there three: Caucasian, Negroid, and Mongoloid? Or were there five: white, black, brown, yellow, and red? Does a Dakota Sioux belong to the same race as a Japanese person? Are Moroccan Bedouins Caucasian like Spaniards, or do they belong to the same race as Tamils from Sri Lanka? Does a North American Inuit share the same race as a Tartar from Crimea? I could go on and on. The split hairs would get thinner and thinner.

We humans have conducted similar hairsplitting about language, nationality, religion, sex, and sexual orientation and used them as excuses for interpersonal discrimination and interpersonal violence, even war. But these are not the focus of this reflection.

So what is racism? At its simplest, it is illicitly focusing on another person or group's perceived racial difference from oneself or one's group. This is often based on a perceived difference in complexion. Two people may have 95 things in common, but these commonalities get overlooked because of skin tone. When certain individuals are too close to a dividing line, artificial tests are sometimes devised. For example, in

---

[2] https://www.nationalgeographic.com/culture/topics/reference/race-ethnicity/

apartheid South Africa, a comb might be drawn through the hair. If the comb passed freely, that person was declared coloured. If it got tangled in the hair, the person was declared black. In the United States, one drop of Negro blood qualified you as black. My mother was lighter than almost any Mediterranean European, but that one drop made her black.[3]

Racism is so deeply entrenched in human society that one can easily behave in racist ways without realizing it. Wearing blackface or brownface can be unintentionally hurtful to people who belong to those groups. Wearing a feathered headdress or a turban is cultural appropriation from those who have a right to wear those symbols. To my own embarrassment, I have removed an expression from this essay that was misappropriated from Indigenous culture.

Most of what I have said so far is abstract. I will now give concrete and personal examples. The first is about buying into someone else's racism and diminishing one's own sense of worth. My mother used to say, "If you're white, you're all right. If you're black, step back. If you're brown, stick aroun'." This showed up in a 1947 song by Big Bill Broonzy[4], but I am sure that various forms of the phrase had been around for a long time before then. The expression does several things at once, depending on the hearer. Broonzy was reporting a reality within which he lived. The expression, as used by my mother's generation, could introduce a feeling of hopelessness in a young hearer: "Why bother? The deck is already stacked against me." It could also instill a

---

[3] In the example of my mother, I am using the language of North American culture. There is no such thing as Negro blood. The human race has only eight types of blood: A+, A-, B+, B-, AB+, AB-, O+, O-. That's it. For a fascinating read about blood, see Lawrence Hill's 2013 *CBC Massey Lectures: Blood: The Stuff of Life*, (House of Anansi Press, Toronto, 2013).

[4] Song: https://www.youtube.com/watch?v=YSlNFMMqUs8

sense of defiance. In one individual, this feeling might express itself as violence; in another as a strong drive toward excellence; and in yet another as obsessive, even self-destructive overachievement.

Of course, one does not learn just one attitude or one piece of information. Life's decisions are based on a jumble of often contradictory attitudes and bits of information. So I learned, "If you're white, you're all right...," but at the same time, I also learned that I had to be twice as good to be equal. Michelle Obama learned this even more harshly from her father: "You have to be twice as good to go half as far."[5]

Another consequence of the "If you're white..." expression is a kind of conscious or unconscious hierarchy among blacks: a kind of individual self-loathing. A significant number of black people have spent a lot of money on bleach creams and other cosmetics to help lighten their complexion. I have read that this complexional hierarchy is particularly strong in Brazil.

I want to be clear about my own experiences of racism. They are real, but nothing like the soul-numbing day-in-day-out legal and societal segregation formerly practiced in the Southern United States or in apartheid South Africa. From birth until young married life, I lived in Michigan, Iowa, Ohio, Illinois, Missouri, Connecticut, and Massachusetts. With the exception of Missouri — a former slave state that did not secede from the Union at the time of the US Civil War — every place I lived in could be termed northern. I also had a five-month interlude in Normandy as an exchange student from Kansas City,

[5] Michelle Obama, *Becoming* (Crown Publishing Group, New York 2018). Michelle Obama has no idea who I am; we have never met. Her excellent first book is, in my opinion, an eye-opening read. I highly recommend it.

Missouri.

In spite of spending most of my youth in racially integrated situations, I have no remaining white friends from my junior high and high school years in Evanston and Kansas City, nor any from the group of Americans who travelled to Europe with me in 1958-1959, despite trying to maintain several of these connections. Thankfully, I do have my French siblings, numerous friends from Trinity College, and a couple from Harvard-Ratcliffe whom I met by accident on Thanksgiving Day in 1959. I also had my French parents and a schoolmate from Lycée, all now deceased.

The first time I remember coming into contact with racism in the news was the murder of Emmet Till in 1955.[6] He was a fourteen-year-old Chicago boy who was lynched for allegedly flirting with or whistling at a white woman while on vacation in Mississippi. I can't remember if this was extensively covered by *The Chicago Tribune* but pictures of his mutilated body were carried in *Ebony* magazine. Even though he was a boy my age from nearby Chicago, this blatant racist act did not seem connected to me at the time. I did not think, "That could have been me," even though it clearly could have. I relate to him and his story much more now than then.

In the summer of 1953, I attended Boy Scout camp for eight weeks with only a two-day trip home in the middle. I had really liked my four-week stay at Camp Wabaningo the previous year, so my parents seized the opportunity to simplify home life while my mother was undergoing major surgery. Wabaningo was the Western Michigan summer camp of Evanston Boy Scouts. I was a member of all-black Troop 30 that met at

[6] https://en.wikipedia.org/wiki/Emmett_Till

my former elementary school. In my first year there we had a charismatic Scoutmaster called Thomas Gibbs, an Amherst graduate. He, unfortunately for me, left Evanston to enter Episcopal Theological School, as it was then called, in Cambridge, Massachusetts. Scouts became quite boring after his departure.

Troop 30 normally attended camp for the third of the four two-week summer sessions. I spent the first four weeks of camp in 1953 with members of Troop 1, the oldest troop in Evanston. They met at St. Luke's Church. I don't remember my tentmates from the final two weeks.

I was familiar with St. Luke's; it was also only four blocks from Nichols Junior High School, and I had been taking organ lessons there since 1951. I really liked the boys in Troop 1 with whom I had spent time at summer camp and with whom, as of September 1953, I was attending junior high. I also liked their Scoutmaster, Keil Rieger. So with permission, I transferred to be with them. It was a very happy time for me. Unknown to me, some parents began complaining about the presence of a black scout. I suspect Mr. Rieger just dealt with this behind the scenes.

I completed all the requirements for the rank of Life Scout at camp in the summer of 1954. The next step was Eagle Scout, the highest rank. A candidate must pass a Board of Review after completing the requirements for promotion. This is part interview, part oral exam, and part performance evaluation. Several scouts were usually awarded promotions at a ceremonial Court of Honour after passing. My previous Boards of Review had always been rather routine and friendly. The 1954 board took place on a very comfortable screened-in veranda at one of the camp buildings. The person conducting the review was Dick Holden, a camp leader I had known and liked for a year or two. I was therefore totally unprepared for the hostile barrage I faced this time. I cannot remember the exact details, except the incredible sting of a totally unexpected negative experience. I was probably told I was arrogant or bossy. At a distance of more than sixty-five years, it is impossible to discern how much of this was honest criticism and how much was just putting an uppity black kid in his place. At the time, it never occurred to me that there might have been a racial component to what had just happened. I just recall the pain of being deemed unworthy of promotion and then having to attend the Court of Honour at which the other scouts were promoted. I am sure some of the criticism was justified but there was certainly no offer to help smooth out my rough edges.

I returned to Troop 1 in the fall that year only to discover that several boys did not return, and Mr. Rieger had resigned or retired as Scoutmaster. Is it possible he had been ousted? Dick Holden was the new Scoutmaster. A parents meeting was called; I doubt that my mother and father were invited. Instead of normal troop activities, the boys were sent to another room with no planned activity. We just sat on the floor and waited. One of my friends quietly told me that I was the subject of discussion. Basically, a substantial number of the parent group wanted me to leave Troop 1. The Rector of St. Luke's, the Rev. William T. St. John Brown, was in attendance and told them in no uncertain terms that he would not allow a segregated troop to meet at St. Luke's. The parents then voted to disband the troop. At that point, I left Boy Scouts.

Troop 1 went out of existence for more than a year and was later reactivated at another location. There is a lot that went on behind the scenes of which I am still unaware; the whole thing was a huge personal disappointment. My mother had been looking forward to the rose presented to the mother of a new Eagle Scout, but it was not to be.

When we moved to Kansas City, Missouri, in the summer of 1956, the schools had only been desegregated for one academic year. Lincoln High School, formerly the only high school for black students, was in a predominately black neighbourhood and therefore remained 99% black. My dad's parish church was southeast of Lincoln. I therefore attended Central High School, which was in the process of integrating. The student body included many white students bussed in from Independence, a town to the east of Kansas City. Off the top of my head, I would say that the student body was 70% white and 30% black. The general atmosphere was cordial and peaceful, and the two groups mixed comfortably in class — but never socially. I'm not aware of anyone trying to upset the status quo. The school had so-called literary societies (similar to fraternities or sororities) which invited only white students into their membership. There was no interracial dancing at school dances, and I am not aware of any interracial dating.

My first real taste of exclusion in Kansas City came in the spring or summer of 1957. I was walking in the downtown business district on a hot and humid day, on my way from the bus stop to the cathedral for an organ lesson. I was thirsty. Soda fountains, counters that served soft drinks and ice cream in drugstores and dime stores, were still common then. I entered a drugstore, sat down on a stool at the counter and ordered a Coke. It was served in a paper cup. I paid and inserted a straw.

I was immediately told that I could not drink inside. When I naively asked why, I was told that Negroes were not allowed to eat or drink in the store. I was crushed. I left and drank my Coke standing outside on the sidewalk in the sweltering heat and humidity.

My second taste of exclusion came about a year later in a completely different neighbourhood near the Kansas City Conservatory of Music. This occurred in a restaurant where I had previously eaten with other music students on several occasions. This time I entered alone, sat down, and was quickly informed by the manager that I could not eat there. They would, however, be happy to serve me in the kitchen. I told him that I had eaten there several times without problem. He informed me that I had come in before with other (he meant white) students and he had received complaints from other customers on those occasions. He said he had no problem with me but he could not afford to lose regular clientele because of my presence. I therefore got up quietly and left. This was even more crushing than the first experience.

My third exclusion was in Houston, Texas, in June of 1958, when I attended the National Convention of the American Guild of Organists. Five of us travelled together by automobile from Kansas City. I was the youngest in the group and the only black person. We would stop for meals between recitals and concerts in various parts of the city. We only had a problem on one occasion: a manager spoke to one of the other members of our group and told him that I would be welcome to eat in the kitchen but not in the dining room. The entire group quietly left and went to another restaurant where we were all welcome. This time I felt quietly victorious. If the restauranteur was willing to sacrifice five diners to maintain his policy, so be it.

I reiterate what I said earlier: my experience of overt racial discrimination is both limited and very tame compared to what those who lived in the Deep South had to endure daily. Even comparing my life in Evanston to Michelle Obama's life, less than thirty miles away on the southside in Chicago, shows that I lived a childhood of comparative privilege and racial integration.

I suspect there have been instances in my professional life where I did not make the short list for a church position, not even getting an interview because of race. This is a quiet form of discrimination that always seems to be lurking in the shadows where one cannot call it out. Like a virus, it is there, but you cannot see it.

I did experience overt discrimination just once in my professional career. It occurred in 1967. I was unhappy in Saskatoon after the arrival of Dean Patterson's successor[7], and started applying for positions in both Canada and the United States. In those days, applications were typewritten and mailed, decades before home computers and printers made photo applications normal. I was invited to interview for St. James' Episcopal Church in Milwaukee. Little did I know that the rector was a transplanted Southerner. When I arrived and he discovered I was Negro, he accused me of misleading him and the churchwardens because I had not informed them of this in advance. It never occurred to me that I should mention race in my application. Had I done so, it is clear I would not have been short-listed and flown down there at parish expense.

That said, I strongly suspect that I have had more professional opportunities in Canada than I would have had in the United States. This is a gut feeling rather than something that can be documented. I

[7] See Chapter 18: "Life in Saskatoon."

also feel that Indigenous and Caribbean Canadians are more obvious targets of discrimination than an African American import without a noticeable ethnic accent. I have never in my entire life applied for a position, been short-listed, received a face-to-face interview in competition with other candidates, and then been appointed. I have been specially called by particular priests who recognized I had skills they wanted, or called in temporarily to emergency situations and then asked to stay.

As a child and youth, I understood racism as peculiar to the Southern United States. Only as an adult have I learned that racism exists in many, perhaps most, parts of the world. British, French, Spanish, Portuguese, and Dutch colonialism had strong racist undergirding. Bringing civilization to the uncivilized is a racist idea. I was shocked to discover a hymn by Rudyard Kipling which includes the phrase, "lesser breeds without the law" was still in use in the Saskatoon Cathedral in 1966.[8]

As the United States and Canada became independent countries, colonial racial ideas persisted. The slave trade and the institution of slavery were part of both America and colonial Canada. Slavery was divisive, hotly debated, eventually leading to civil war in the United States. The idea that Indigenous people were less civilized than people of European ancestry, even less than people of African ancestry, is very

[8] *Recessional* by Rudyard Kipling, 1897. It appears as hymn 316 in the *Book of Common Praise* (Oxford University Press, Toronto 1938). Verse 4 reads as follows:

If, drunk with sight of power, we loose
Wild tongues that have not thee in awe,
Such boastings as the Gentiles use,
Or lesser breeds without the law--
Lord God of hosts, be with us yet,
Lest we forget--lest we forget!

deeply ingrained in North American societies. As a child, I played cowboys and Indians without hesitation. I even called myself a white man in those games because that's what the non-Indigenous people were called in the movies on television.

Canadians like to believe that racism is not part of our culture. This view is self-delusional. Our racism may differ from that in the USA, but it is no less present in our history. Why did Canada intern Ukrainians en masse as enemy aliens in horrible concentration camps during the First World War, while only a few Germans were charged with specific offences? Why were Japanese Canadians interned en masse during the Second World War, but only a few German Canadians charged with specific offences? Why did we intentionally try to assimilate Indigenous peoples in Indian Residential Schools and Indian Day Schools from before Canadian Confederation until 1996? Why did we collect a head tax on Chinese immigrants from 1885 until 1923, after which we abolished the tax and simply prohibited most Chinese immigration?

As recently as the early nineteen fifties, the Duke Ellington Orchestra could perform at Toronto's Royal York Hotel, but not stay there overnight. On our way to Washington, DC, in 1954, my family crossed the Niagara Peninsula from Detroit/Windsor to visit Niagara Falls. Somewhere along the way, my father got out of the car before the rest of us to ask a motelier if Negroes were welcome at his establishment.

Even while discussing the depth to which racism is ingrained in North American culture, I must acknowledge that huge forward strides have been made in the past century. I recently read a biography of Marian Anderson, a Philadelphia-born and raised African American classical singer of world renown.[9] She, like numerous other African American performing artists, found greater success in Europe than was possible in the United States.[10] In America, her managers had great difficulty organizing concert tours. Auditoria large enough to accommodate her audiences — at Constitution Hall in Washington, for example — barred non-white performers from their stages. Even the Metropolitan Opera in New York City did not allow non-white solo singers until 1955.[11]

Each of us, in many ways, stands on the shoulders of those who went before us. Citing only the racial dynamic, Jackie Robinson might not have been invited to break the colour bar in baseball without heavyweight boxing champion Joe Lewis preceding him. Metropolitan Opera star Leontyne Price stood on the shoulders of Marian Anderson. Martin Luther King, Jr. stood on the shoulders of Jackie Robinson and Marian Anderson. Barack Obama stood on the shoulders of them all.

It has been more than five hundred years since Europeans began to invade North America. The racial attitudes that came along with colonialism persist both overtly and beneath the surface. Indigenous peoples and the descendants of those brought here against their will continue to suffer. The descendants of the Chinese who came to North America as cheap labour to build the railroads continue to suffer. Chinese people of more recent immigration are often treated as second-class citizens, as are others of Asian, Caribbean, and African extraction.

Things are getting better, but far too slowly.

[9] Raymond Arsenault, *The Sound of Freedom: Marian Anderson's Historic Concert at The Lincoln Memorial* (Bloomsbury Press, London 2009) - also a highly recommended read.
[10] Sydney Bechet and Josephine Baker are first to mind but there are many others.
[11] Both Marian Anderson and Robert McFerrin, Bobby's father, made their Metropolitan Opera debuts in January, 1955. https:/wikipedia.org/wiki/Robert_McFerrin

Reflection #2: Assimilationism

This reflection could have been titled *Racism, Part Two*. I wrote part one before I read *Stamped from the Beginning* by Ibram X. Kendi and *Caste* by Isabel Wilkerson.[1] These two books have profoundly changed my understanding of the depth of racism in North American and European societies.

What I wrote before still stands, and I have decided to leave it be.

I also want to state that I am who I am, and am comfortable in my own skin. I think that throughout my life I have, on most occasions, made the best decisions I could at the time with my then-available knowledge and understanding. That notwithstanding, I have, since about the age of fifty, said on numerous occasions, "If I had known then what I know now, I would have made a different decision."

I remind the reader that this is a book about my life and my experience. While I must make some broad statements for contextual reasons, I am not trying to write a definitive history of racism or assimilationism.

In the racism chapter, I said that I grew up understanding that I had

---

[1] Ibram X. Kendi: *Stamped from the Beginning – The Definitive History of Racist Ideas in America*, © 2016, Bold Type Books, New York. Isabel Wilkerson: *Caste – The Origins of our Discontents*, © 2020 Random House, New York. I consider Wilkerson's Book the most important I have ever read, with Kendi following a close second. I read Kendi first and suggest the curious reader do the same. They employ completely different approaches. The first is a history book about the evolution of an idea; the second is about the dehumanizing impact of social stratification. What startled me most about Kendi's book was the revelation, to me at least, that American racism was not the result of racist ideas. Racist ideas grew, and evolved over time, to justify the status quo.

to be better in order to be equal. I think this competitive strategy carried a hidden agenda of assimilating as much as possible into the majority culture. The United States has long described itself as a melting pot. This has meant that many Irish-Americans, Italian-Americans, and Polish-Americans, to name just three immigrant groups, have worked hard to lose the hyphenated prefix to become simply American. Canada, by contrast, describes itself as a cultural mosaic. This means Canadians of European ancestry are more welcome to acknowledge their roots than their American counterparts. It is clear from almost daily news that the Indigenous peoples who welcomed Europeans to these shores and taught them how to survive the unforgiving winters have long been victims of discrimination, cultural genocide and forced assimilation, beginning almost as soon as Europeans had sufficient numbers to turn the tables.

I was born in the United States and lived there until I was twenty-four. My youthful approach to life was therefore shaped by the melting pot ideal: assimilate into the majority and therefore become a non-hyphenated American. Americans of European ancestry can do this because, after a generation or two, their foreign accents disappear. Individuals of African ancestry may lose their distinctive accents, but only a small minority can lose that most distinctive marker, darker skin. Asian Americans may also lose their accents after a generation or two, but retain distinctive physical features that prevent them from totally assimilating.

One of my favourite television programmes is *Finding Your Roots* on PBS.[2] This show features well-known Americans searching for and

2 PBS: Public Broadcasting Service in the United States.

discovering information about their personal ancestries. A common thread in the series is that grandparents and parents are frequently unwilling to share family information with their descendants. They just do not want anyone to know that their predecessors were poor Sicilians, or persecuted Ashkenazi Jews, or slaves. One might say that this practice implies, "We are Americans now and that's all you need to know."

Assimilationism is a form of cultural nationalism. For visible minorities, assimilationism is also a form of racism. The European American just assimilates into the dominant social stratum: white America. For most black Americans, skin colour makes it impossible to do the same. Many of us nevertheless try to overcome the obstacles in front of us.

Being better to be equal is a form of unwittingly accepting the assimilationist ideal. Without realizing it, my family bought into it. Neither of my grandfathers nor my parents spoke with any noticeable black accent. I remember once recounting to my dad and stepmother my fascination with the varieties of black English, previously unknown to me, enumerated in the BBC/PBS television series: *The Story of English*.[3] My stepmother, retired chair of the English Department at Tuskegee University, briskly replied, "There is no such thing as black English. There is the King's English, and there is the language of ignorance."[4]

[3] Robert McCrum; William Cran; Robert MacNeil: *The Story of English* © 1986 Faber & Faber and BBC Publications, London. The television series and the book were a single project. The book has since been twice revised: 1993 and 2002.

[4] My stepmother Ada was a warm and wonderful person. Born in Maine, she was proud she had no slaves in her ancestry. This may or may not have been true, but she believed it so. I, for one, could not understand this pride since one has no control over one's ancestry. She, to her credit, more than once attempted to register to vote in

Before seeing *The Story of English*, I would have agreed with her. Stated baldly, our behaviour, dress, and language were as white as possible. My grandparents and my parents would likely be horrified to hear me say this, but I now think it is true. It simply had not occurred to me earlier in life that we were pursuing a white ideal.

In 1944, Swedish economist and Nobel Laureate Gunner Mydahl wrote, "It is to the advantage of American Negroes as individuals and as a group to become assimilated into American culture, to acquire the traits held in the esteem by the dominant white Americans."[5] I believe that this is the view held by most American liberals since the time of early 19th-century abolitionists. While segregationists and white supremacists believe that black people are inherently inferior to white people — assimilationists, whether unwittingly or intentionally — regard black people as inferior, but capable of improvement with education and hard work.

Judeo-Christian teaching says that all individuals are equal in the eyes of God. The Declaration of Independence stated, "We hold these truths to be self-evident, that all men are created equal, that they are endowed by their Creator with certain unalienable Rights, that among these are Life, Liberty and the pursuit of Happiness." That seems

Alabama. The deck was of course stacked against any black person. The test consisted of copying a paragraph from the US Constitution. The given text included spelling errors. If you corrected the errors, you were failed for not copying the given text. If you did not correct the errors, you failed for incorrect spelling. If you were white, it did not matter what you wrote unless the examiner held a personal grudge against you.

[5] Gunner Myrdal: *An American Dilemma: The Negro Problem and Modern Democracy*, vol. 2, pp. 928-929, as quoted by Kendi on p.3. This study was commissioned by the Carnegie Corporation in 1944. The most recent publication or republication, seems to be © 1996, Transaction Publishers, New Brunswick, New Jersey.

perfectly clear, but, in early practice, "all men" included only white men with property. Women, white men without property, Indigenous people, and blacks were excluded from these unalienable rights. It was also common and legal to exclude Roman Catholics (especially the Irish), Jews, and other non-Anglo-Saxon, non-Protestant people.

Many immigrants in North America have willingly self-sacrificed and overworked to make a better life possible for their children and their grandchildren. I now believe that many assimilated blacks have self-sacrificed, overworked, self-censored, and self-deprecated for various reasons. Among these driving motivations would be to improve the race (as if it were somehow defective), or to persuade society that we earned the right to be treated equally (as if equality needed to be earned). The practice of trying to earn respect in society by good behaviour is known as *uplift suasion*. After more than a century of effort, it clearly does not work.

I have lived most of my life trying to demonstrate that I have earned, by education and acquisition of professional skill, the right to be treated equally. Sometimes this was misconstrued as arrogance; sometimes I was indeed arrogant. I have forgotten more about classical music and jazz than most people will ever learn. I did not learn until after the age of sixty the wonderful wisdom, usually attributed to Theodore Roosevelt: "People don't care how much you know until they know how much you care." This observation arrived as a thunderbolt.

This disjointed essay poses more questions than it answers. I am still wrestling with the idea of assimilation.

Much that I have been taught and much that I have learned includes assumptions that I now question. The history to which I have been exposed has always had a Western-European bias. The colonization of North America was initiated mostly by Western Europeans. The United States Declaration of Independence and the Constitution were heavily influenced by the French Enlightenment. My education at Trinity College, Hartford, valued logic over emotion but failed to teach — me at least — that logical reasoning which begins from a faulty premise, risks yielding a faulty conclusion.[6]

Television and the mainstream media taught me to appreciate European ideals of beauty, whether talking about music, art, literature, or women. Early in high school, I took to the French language like a duck to water. This later grew to include French organ music, French art, and French cuisine. Again, I remind the reader that I am talking only about my experience. Neither am I apologizing for who I am.

I have gained a lot of knowledge, experience, and pleasure because of my Eurocentricity, but I cannot help but wonder how much I have missed along the way because of it. I also note that I have been attracted to high culture more than popular culture, whether European or North American. My family moved to Kansas City in 1956. While a suitable rectory was being purchased and renovated, we were temporarily housed next to an African Methodist Episcopal minister who was very knowledgeable about Negro Spirituals. I failed to seize this as a learning opportunity because I did not respect them as important music. I had been taught they were primitive or ignorant compared to Bach, Beethoven, and the great European classics. It simply did not occur to me that I was comparing apples to oranges by believing one was superior to the other.

[6] See John Ralston Saul, *Voltaire's Bastards: The dictatorship of Reason in the West*, © 1992 Simon & Schuster, New York.

This kind of thinking was common in books I read. Fortunately for me, when Alistair Cooke and Leonard Bernstein introduced me to jazz[7], I was able to follow my own intuition rather than the classical prejudices of some of the musical authorities I was reading.

I know some white people who are uncomfortable in a majority-black situation. I know some black people who are uncomfortable in a majority-white situation. I only attended a majority-black school from the middle of grade two until the end of grade six. I only lived in a majority-black neighbourhood until the end of high school. It has never bothered me to be one of few blacks, or even the only black, living or working in a majority-white situation.

This has been difficult to write because my understanding of assimilation changed after reading Kendi. I think I have likely gained more from my own personal, mostly voluntary, assimilation than I have lost. It is clear that my assimilation is different from that experienced by Indigenous peoples, who were forcibly removed from their families, communities, and languages and placed in residential schools. I also confess that I have looked down on other black individuals who have chosen a more Afro-centric path than I. No more!

Human freedom means that every individual should have the right to choose their own path. I have been privileged to have that freedom.

Many haven't.

[7] *Omnibus: "The World of Jazz, 1955* – available by subscription: https://www.medici.tv/en/documentaries/leonard-bernstein-omnibus-the-world-of-jazz/
or purchase recording:
https://www.amazon.ca/s?k=omnibus+jazz&ref=nb_sb_noss

Reflection #3: Privilege

Privilege is having an advantage over another person because of the accident of one's birth or other circumstances. Some advantages (a university degree or on-the-job experience, for example) are earned; the kind of privilege I am writing about here is not.

The discussion of privilege is more complicated than that of racism because most privileged people, including me earlier in life, do not recognize they have it. It is easy to assume that one's maleness or white skin is a neutral fact while navigating society. But such facts are not neutral. It is far easier to point out someone else's privilege than to recognize one's own. If one fails to do the latter, one will still benefit from, and perhaps even unwittingly, take advantage of it.

Rather than give abstract examples, I will talk about the privilege I have enjoyed. As I began grappling with this idea around the year 2000, I found I benefitted from a shocking amount.

Male privilege is the most obvious. Society gives me an advantage over a woman in job applications. The prospective employer knows, amongst other things, that I will never get pregnant. The glass ceiling is real. Women, in general, are paid less than men for doing the same job. Change started many years ago, but it is painfully slow. One glimmer of hope is that some men, in jurisdictions where permitted, are beginning to share in post-natal parental leave. Many people, both men and women, now recognize that a limitation on anyone's freedom is a limitation on everyone's freedom.

I remember when I was first introduced to McDonalds in 1960. We didn't use the word restaurant anywhere near fast-food outlets back then. Part of McDonalds' amazing early success was due to four policies: no hot dogs, no item on the limited menu could be personalized (for example, you could not order a hamburger with ketchup and onion but no pickle), no place to sit, and no female employees. The exclusion of female employees was blatantly sexist, yet my friends and I accepted it as a reasonable business policy.

White privilege is very real.[1] Throughout North American history, people who belonged to the dominant social stratum, White Anglo-Saxon Protestants (WASP), often feared that immigrants, black people, and Asians would have a competitive advantage because the non-WASP was usually willing to work for a lower wage just to survive. Of course, the non-WASP's frequent choice was to accept that lower wage or not get the job.

While I cannot claim White privilege, I now realize that I have benefitted because of my light complexion. It is easier for some people to overlook my café-au-lait skin than it would be for them to overlook the skin colour of someone who is chocolate brown or licorice black. This advantage is also enhanced because my father insisted that I speak proper grammatical English without an accent. I was called out from time to time by other black kids for "talking white." My manner of speaking was also sometimes characterized as "uppity".

I had a white college friend from Arkansas who, back then, very

[1] "White Privilege: Unpacking the Invisible Knapsack" © 1988 Peggy McIntosh. https://www.pcc.edu/illumination/wp-content/uploads/sites/54/2018/05/White-privilege-essay-mcintosh.pdf This essay is excerpted from *White Privilege and Male Privilege: A Personal Account of Coming To See Correspondences through Work in Women's Studies* (1988), by Peggy McIntosh, available from the Wellesley College Center for Research on Women, Wellesley MA, 02181.

patiently tried to explain to me that I was nothing like the Negroes where he came from. For him to accept me, he had somehow to make me exceptional.

Married privilege is also real, even though prospective employers in most jurisdictions are now forbidden to ask about an applicant's marital status. In the past, as a married man and presumed breadwinner, I would have had an advantage over a female applicant, and likely over a single male. I remember a situation in 1965 where the fact I was married was considered an asset. The departing employee was single, and the employer thought a married man would be more stable and dependable. This was entirely legal back then, and I did not question it. Today, such a consideration would be widely illegal and unethical. I suspect that, even though unspoken, married people still have that advantage.

Couple privilege is also a widely-practiced form of social dis-crimination. Members of a couple will invite other couples into their home more easily than single friends. This may be done on purpose or unconsciously. In its most grievous form, divorced or widowed individuals find they are no longer invited to gatherings that normally included them in the past. The excuse is that single people might not be comfortable around couples. The truth is more likely that one member or other of the host couple finds the single person to be a threat to their relationship. Single people, by implication, are assumed to be on the hunt for a new partner.

Heterosexual people often have an advantage in being accepted in society or the workplace over gay, lesbian, or trans individuals (LGBTQ+). Some LGBTQ+ people are immediately visible because of the way they walk, talk, or dress. Others can stay in the closet and hide their sexual orientation, just as some light-complexioned black people can pass for white. Everything I have read or learned in face-to-face conversations indicates that closeted people pay a high emotional price when hiding behind a false façade.

Ableism is yet another kind of privilege. An able-bodied person will often have an advantage over a physically-challenged individual of equal or greater ability. This can be true of access to education or employment opportunities, but is most blatantly obvious in restaurants, bars, and theatres where the washrooms are down a steep set of stairs.

I hope this chapter will encourage and enable the reader to examine their own privilege. Unless you are a poor, single, BIPOC[2] female, you almost certainly have unseen privilege. Until we can eliminate the invisible knapsacks of privilege that most of us carry, our aspiration to live in a society of equals will never be realized.

[2] BIPOC = Black, Indigenous, Person of Colour.

Reflection #4: Romantic Love and Relationship

Love and relationship are two different things. Ideally, we want them to be simultaneously healthy and life-giving.

Love exists in many forms. Some languages have numerous distinct words for various aspects of love, but English is lacking in this respect. I will limit myself to three Greek words because I am not writing an exhaustive treatise about love in all its forms and aspects.

First, there is *philia*, sometimes called brotherly love (an outdated term as we try to adopt more inclusive language), or friendship. This is what we feel for people with whom we are acquainted and with whom we value connection.

Some acquaintances are casual, may be occasional, but are still significant to retain. I have dozens of high school and college friends who fit this description. I may send them my annual letter around Christmas time because I want them to know what is happening in my life. Some will reply with their news, and some won't. I do not judge them one way or the other. I will see some of them periodically at class reunions or other gatherings. I value our connection but am not involved much in their day-to-day lives. I also have blood relatives and relatives by marriage with whom my connection is occasional.

Some people are close friends or relatives because we have shared, and continue to share, significant life events. These are people with whom I talk on the telephone or share a video call from time to time. Some friends are so close that they seem to be family. I may visit their homes, even travel hundreds of kilometres, to spend a few hours or several days with them.

Second, there is *eros*, which is usually called romantic love. This is the love immortalized in song by Tin Pan Alley and whatever its modern successors are called, the love that makes the world go round. It makes the sun, moon, and stars seem brighter, colours more vivid, and life more exciting. Romantic love may or may not include sexual desire. It is, in my opinion, a common misconception that romantic love must include physical yearning. One of my favourite descriptions is, "Love is friendship caught on fire." I have no idea who said it first, as the quotation has been attributed to dozens of people on internet memes.

Third is *agape*, a triangular relationship between you and God, you and others, God and others. In Latin, it was *caritas* which became charity in English. This is love in community. The modern use of charity in English has become quite limited, often meaning giving money to worthy causes. Agape is the love that includes "Love your enemy; do good to them that hate you" or "You cannot love God and hate your neighbour". This love connects you to the most despicable dictator or criminal, an ordinary stranger, or any unlovable acquaintance. It is the love that causes you to volunteer in a hospital, prison, or long-term care facility; tutor struggling students; coach a team of disadvantaged youth; or help people understand and exercise their voting rights. The list could go on and on. In short, agape impels you to help those who need help, to listen to people who need to be heard, and to care for others when there is no gain for you, other than perhaps a warm feeling.

Relationship is the ongoing connection between you and another. We are in a relationship with every other human being on the planet, every animal, every plant, and the planet itself. Mother Earth is our home. If we don't care for her, humankind will become extinct. The word stranger also describes a relationship. How we treat strangers is indeed a hallmark of our character.

Now that I have defined words, I want to focus on romantic love and the interpersonal relationships that are associated with it. Such relationships include, but are not limited to, marriage, cohabitation, monogamy, and ethical non-monogamy. Such relationships may be heterosexual, same-sex, or relationships between or among non-binary individuals. One of the main impediments to loving relationships is our hesitancy, certainly in the English-speaking world, to talk about them. Relationships are deemed private, which they are, but our society has confused privacy with willful ignorance. As the late John Lennon said, "We live in a world where we have to hide to make love, while violence is practiced in broad daylight."

Romantic love may give us the feeling that we want to share the rest of our lives with someone. Many fairy tales end with the words "...and they lived happily ever after." That is what most of us desire, but we are not trained to do the work to achieve that goal. The idea that "happily ever after" is a destination rather than a process is a misconception. The idea that love alone can sustain a healthy relationship is equally false. We are engaging in a process similar to a journey along a bumpy road that traverses numerous, and often unexpected, peaks and valleys. Sometimes, the road may narrow to a pathway or even disappear altogether.

The key to navigating this journey is communication, and the key to communication is trust. The things that you fear talking about the most are the things that you most need to talk about. "I can't discuss this with my partner[1] because they will never understand" is probably the biggest red flag that will ever enter your field of vision. Pay attention: danger.

That silence may seem small at first, but if untended, it is a wound that will become infected over time and may become fatal to the relationship.

If the most important part of navigating the relationship journey is communication, then listening is the key. Some Indigenous peoples have a tradition of passing a feather. The person with the feather speaks. Everyone else listens without interrupting. When the speaker is finished, the feather is passed on. Another useful technique is for that next person to summarise what they heard. It is not unusual for problems to be solved at this stage. Many supposed disagreements are not disagreements, but rather misunderstandings of what the other person is saying or thinking.

We must be careful not to put ourselves down because we have certain feelings. Feelings are real as well as irrational, they are ours and we ignore them at our peril. I do not mean all our feelings are equally important; after we accept that they belong to us, we can better monitor and evaluate them. If we encounter a bear while hiking in the wilderness, our fear is justified, and we should not spend more than a split second validating it. If we are deathly afraid of a bear attacking us while we are shopping for groceries, we need to examine that fear carefully. Are we being paranoid? Are we perhaps really fearing

[1] The word *partner* as I use it in this reflection always includes the plural. It quickly became tedious to write partner(s). This chapter does not assume monogamy to be the only possibility.

something else?

How we respond to our feelings is critically important. We can work to change, to respond less to certain kinds of crippling fear (for example, going to work every day, fearing we are going to be fired) while cultivating an increased reaction to positive feelings such as empathy.

We must be even more careful to avoid negatively judging other people's feelings. The idea that someone has no right to feel a certain way should unfurl a brilliant red flag.

Sometimes, our rational thoughts and our emotions line up with each other; often they will not. It is helpful to know your Myers-Briggs Type Indicator (MBTI)[2] and that of your partner. The MBTI helps us understand how we and they process information and make decisions. Many interpersonal misunderstandings arise simply because individuals process information and communicate differently.

I personally am an INFP.[3] This means, among other things, that I process information and make decisions intuitively and then confirm, if possible, with logic. I spent at least forty years of my life thinking that I was, above all, logical. In other words, I was living life backwards.

The seventh commandment is, "You shall not commit adultery." Unfortunately, the word *adultery* was not clearly defined in Hebrew scripture. It has, in my opinion, been too closely wedded to genital exclusivity.

I believe that adultery is about emotional infidelity. The key to a

[2] Myers-Briggs Type Indicator: https://eu.themyersbriggs.com/en/tools/mbti/mbti-personality-types/

[3] INFP: https://introvertdear.com/news/10-type-secrets-of-the-infp/
This article is illustrative rather than clinical. INFP individuals share numerous characteristics but we are not all the same. For example, I am not particularly an outdoor person.

healthy interpersonal relationship is trust, knowing one's partner is telling the truth. Trust can be assassinated by a lie or a secret between partners. Once gone, it is almost impossible to recover.

No one can make another person happy. It takes all the partners working together and working hard to achieve a healthy relationship. Flexibility and compromise are important tools in relationship building. Compromise can only be achieved when all sides understand the other's position, and then find a middle ground acceptable to all involved. This is seldom easy and seldom quick. In the past, I have mistakenly thought that I was compromising when, in fact, I was foregoing what I wanted, and giving the other person what I mistakenly thought they wanted (which they did not). This failed because I had skipped over the necessary communication and negotiation, and failed to do the work of finding out.

Another useful tool is to know the difference between a "put up with" and a "deal breaker." I learned this when I was well past sixty from a Chicago columnist named Dan Savage. Every partner has quirks and idiosyncrasies. We learn how to live with these because the relationship is more important than almost anything else in life. People in intimate relationships need to understand each other's deal breakers. As an ethically non-monogamous person who believes in open relationships, secrecy violates that openness. This is something that irreparably goes against my core values. A deal breaker for me would be a secret personal relationship.

Every relationship is unique. There is no guidebook for yours. While there are many good books on love, relationship, and sex, no one has all the answers. Make the best decisions you can with the information you have, but never stop gathering more. Admit your mistakes; learn and grow from them. Communicate with your partner. Get outside help when you need it.

Above all, live with joy. The joy of a good relationship is the payoff for all the hard work necessary to keep it healthy and in good repair.

I wish I had known this when I was twenty.

Image Gallery

Dial phone like we
had in Dayton.

Candlestick telephone
like we had in Keokuk.

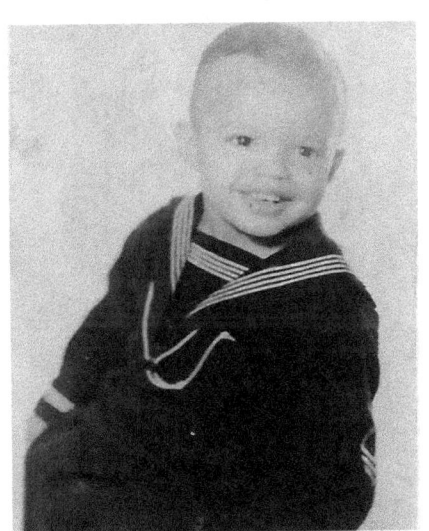

Richard, c. 1943-44

Dad, seminary graduation,
1946

Birney III, Marris, Richard, Mother and Dad, c. 1958

Mother with Richard, Birney and Marris, c. 1948

Grandpa Smith's cross, obverse

Richard, high school graduation, 1959

Grandpa Smith's cross, reverse

Château de Lillebonne, autumn

St. Augustine's Church, Kansas City, MO.

Dad led the congregational to build this
in the early 1960s.

Organ console, St. Sulpice, Paris

Organ case, St. Ouen, Rouen

Carillonneur playing a carillon.
The bells are in the tower above
him. The bottom half of the
keyboard is duplicated by a
pedalboard.
He plays with both hands & both
feet.

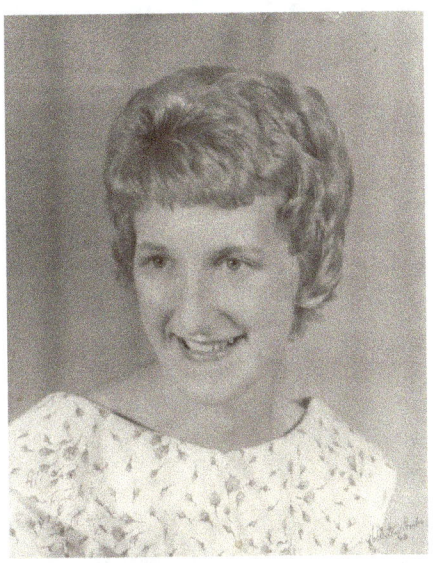

Thalia's engagement portrait,
1963

Thalia & Richard
wedding reception, 1963

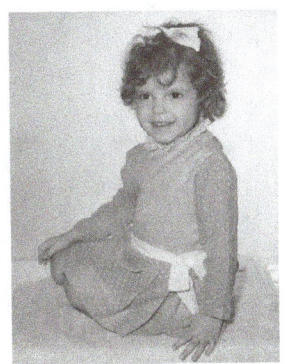

Noëlle at age 3 or 4.

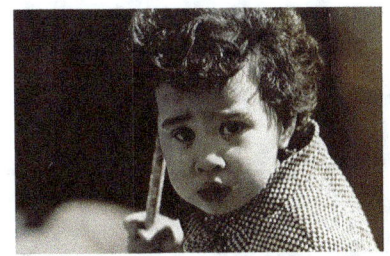

Monique at age 3 or 4.

Soundboard detail of Ross
harpsichord

My 1969 William Post Ross
harpsichord.

My 1973 Karl Wilhelm
portable positive organ

Keyboard detail of Ross
harpsichord

Andreas Ruckers
harpsichord enlarged by
Pascal Taskin.
Instrument collection of
Paris Conservatoire

Keyboard view of my Wilhelm organ

Grandma Ruth Smith,
c. 1906

Grandma Pansy & Grandpa
Solomon with friends behind,
c. 1918

Grandma Eva & Grandpa
Solomon, c. 1933

Monique,
Richard,
Grandma Marge,
Grandpa Smith
with violin &
Noëlle, Brighton
1969

Grandpa Solomon, center, at work

Dad & Ada wedding toast 1974

Grandpa Smith at 70, 1954

Dad at 70, 1982

Dad & Mother in front of St. Augustine's Church, Kansas City, 1956

105 Victoria with studio
addition, c. 1979

Noëlle, Richard,
Monique, Thalia,
Château de Montreuil-
Bellay, France, 1980
(Photo: Pol Corvez)

Organ, Trinity College Chapel
Hartford, Connecticut

Organ console, Trinity College
Chapel

Glossary

This glossary is for readers of this book. I explain pipe, for example, from an organist's point of view but, do not include how a plumber or a bagpiper would use the same word. Similarly, I explain tribune from an organist's point of view rather than the way a journalist might use the same word. - rbs

a cappella – Adjective that describes singing without instrumental accompaniment: unaccompanied.

acolyte – Specifically, an altar server who carries a candle. When I was a child, this term was used for all altar servers.

aleatory – An old adjective related to the throw of dice. In music, aleatory music is sometimes called chance music. In such a composition, many decisions are left up to the performer(s).

Anglo-Catholic – A member of one of the churches of the Anglican Communion who leans more toward the Catholic heritage of Anglican worship rather than the Protestant heritage. Anglo-Catholics like rich ceremony, colourful vestments, and often Gregorian chant, holy water and incense. Anglo-Catholics are often called high church. Many often use the word mass in preference to Eucharist or Holy Communion.

aspergillum – A holy water sprinkler.

Barker levers – A small pneumatic pouch that exhausts to minimize the weight (or resistance) of a mechanical-action organ key. Barker levers were usually only available on the great organ (grand orgue) in France. They were used when the grand orgue had several other divisions coupled to it. The Barker levers were part of the key action inside the organ console. They were turned on by depressing a foot-operated lever, called *appel machine* or ventil, on the console.

Baroque music – Music that evolved from Florentine opera. Baroque music (1600-1750) sought to express emotion in particular stylized ways. This allowed emotion to be expressed through certain forms that were different from the cool objectivity of Renaissance music. The Baroque era included such composers as Corelli, Vivaldi, Purcell, Bach, Telemann, Handel, Couperin, and Rameau.

The Baroque era gave way to the Classical era (1750-1828) which evolved into the Romantic era (1828-1900). Classical and romantic music expressed emotion more through dynamics (loud and soft) rather than form. There was also a Baroque era in art and architecture.

basso continuo – The harmonic undergirding of baroque music (approximately 1600-1750). A bass instrument or instruments (such as cello, viol, or bassoon) combined with a chord-playing instrument or instruments (such as harpsichord, organ, or lute) to create the continuo. The piano and bass in a jazz band or the rhythm guitar and bass in pop music serve a similar function. The basso continuo, however, disappeared from classical music in the late eighteenth century.

boat boy – Usually a young altar server in training who assists the thurifer by carrying a container of incense. The container is shaped somewhat like a boat. Since altar service is no longer strictly male, an inclusive term might be *boat bearer*.

café au lait – A breakfast beverage consisting of scalded milk and strong coffee.

carillon – A large musical instrument consisting of 23 or more tuned bronze bells. It weighs tons and is usually in a tower. It is played from a mechanical manual keyboard and a mechanical pedal keyboard located below the bells. See the photo section.

catechism – A question-and-answer form of teaching.

Cathedral or cathedral church – The mother church of a diocese. It is so named because the bishop's official chair (the cathedra) is located there.

Catholic – The word means universal. It is popularly used to refer to the Roman Catholic Church but is never used that way in this book. Roman Catholics, Easter Orthodox Christians, Anglicans, and, to some degree, Lutherans consider themselves part of the One, Holy, Catholic, and Apostolic Church. Their respective understandings of these words vary.

click track – The sound of the rhythmic beat, played through earphones, which allows separate musicians to record individually. If all conform to the click track, the various recordings may be mixed to sound as if the musicians were playing together rather than separately. The recording engineer thereby has ultimate control of the finished product.

console – The key desk upon which the organist plays. A very small organ may have only one keyboard of 54 or 56 keys. A more typical small to medium-sized organ may have two or three keyboards of 54, 56, or 61 keys. A large organ may have four or five keyboards. Most organ consoles also include a pedalboard which is played with the feet.

People often look at a console and incorrectly call it an organ. The organ is the instrument that makes sound: the windchests and pipes. The console is the control desk.

continuo – see *basso continuo*

countertenor – An adult male alto. Countertenors are normal in British choirs of men and boys. They continue in many British choirs that now include girl sopranos. In the Germanic tradition (for example, the Vienna Boys Choir) the alto part is sung by boys rather than men.

coupler – A control on an organ console that enables an organist to play two or more divisions simultaneously.

deacon – The first of the three major orders of Catholic ministry. In ascending order: deacon, priest, bishop.

déjeuner – The midday meal in the French language: the main meal of the day eaten in the early afternoon.

département – An administrative unit of the French government, similar to a county in England. French departments were created under Napoleon to replace the much larger provinces. The provinces continue in French culture but no longer have administrative functions. Normandy, for example, was divided into five departments.

division – A chorus of organ pipes played from a particular keyboard or the pedalboard. Each division should contrast with and complement the other divisions, allowing them to be played separately or combined.

electro-pneumatic action – An organ system for transmitting an organist's finger or foot action from the console to the pipes. It was the dominant system for the first three-quarters of the twentieth century. The organ key would transmit an electromagnetic impulse to pneumatic pouches beneath the chosen pipes. The air in the pouch would exhaust to open the air channel beneath the requisite pipes. See entry for mechanical action.

Evensong – An Anglican word meaning sung Evening Prayer.

Erev Shabat – Sabbath eve: Friday evening.
    The Book of Genesis says, "… it was evening and it was morning, the first day. A Jewish or Christian liturgical day therefore always begins in the evening. For example, Christmas begins at sundown on December 24th: Christmas Eve. Secular society routinely misuses the term for the entirety of December 24th, but Christmas Eve technically does not begin until sundown. The same is true of Easter, All Saints (All Hallows Eve or Halloween), or any other Jewish or Christian liturgical day.

Eucharist – The main service of worship in Christian tradition. The word, derived from Greek, means Thanksgiving. The service includes the reading of scripture and the blessing of bread and wine (communion) for the congregation to eat and drink. The Eucharist is also called Holy Communion, the Divine Liturgy or the mass in different Christian traditions.

fauxbourdon (literally: false burden) – The word has a long history in music. In this book, it always refers to a harmonized variation of Gregorian chant in which the melody is carried by the tenors.

4-foot pitch – The ensemble sound of an organ depends on the effective blending of stops of various pitches. A stop that matches piano pitch is described as 8'. For example, Trompette 8'. A stop that is an octave higher is described at 4'. One that is an octave lower is described as 16'.

fondue suisse – Swiss fondue is gruyère and Emmenthaler cheese melted in dry white wine with a splash of kirsch. One eats it by dipping bite-sized bits of bread into a common pot.

great organ (*grand orgue*) – The main division of an organ with more than one keyboard. The term is also, somewhat confusingly, used to refer to the entire gallery organ in a French church. In this book, I have tried to use the terms great organ or gallery organ separately to minimize such confusion.

For the detail-oriented, you may search for terms such as pipe organ, swell organ, choir organ, or pedal organ, to name just a few. WARNING: This rabbit hole is huge. Some of us have spent a lifetime learning these things.

harmonium – A pipeless organ that produces sound by sucking air through reeds. In North America, these were often called pump organs or reed organs. The French harmonium is tonally superior to the North American variety.

incipit – The opening phrase of a prayer, hymn, or psalm chanted by a priest or cantor, before the choir joins in. Four examples: *Gloria in Excelsis Deo, Glory be to God on high, Magnificat anima mea Domino, My soul doth magnify the Lord.*

improvisation – Music composed and performed on the spot. It is neither played from a written score nor from memory. While good improvisations usually adhere to a plan, they are spontaneous compositions.

introit – an entrance anthem chanted at the beginning of the Eucharist.

mass – See *Eucharist.*

meantone – The notes of the twelve-note chromatic scale used in European music are in a precise mathematic relationship to each other. This is called just intonation. Unless one is satisfied playing every piece in the same key, just intonation is impossible on any keyboard instrument. Meantone is a system for tuning keyboard instruments to play in various keys. Some intervals are more in tune than others. Meantone, or variations of it, was the dominant tuning system during the Baroque era (1600-1750). Meantone was gradually replaced by equal temperament, the dominant tuning system of today. In equal temperament, every interval is equally out-of-tune except the octave. Most people accept this as normal. Some of us prefer to play and hear earlier music in the temperaments of their times.

mechanical action – A method of transmitting instructions from the organist's fingers and feet to the relevant organ pipe(s). All organs before the mid-nineteenth century were mechanical. Since then, other systems have been invented. Most organists today prefer more modern computerized systems. I still prefer mechanical action. Among other things, it has a longer life expectancy, thereby requiring less frequent rebuilds. For contrast, see *electro-pneumatic action.*

missal – A book with the texts and prayers for the mass (Eucharist).

mission status – In the Episcopal Church USA, a mission is partially subsidized by the diocese. A parish is financially self-supporting.

nave – The main body of a church building where the congregation sits.

mattins – another name for Morning Prayer in the Anglican communion. Spelt with only one t, matins is one of the monastic daily offices.

mixture – A compound high-pitched organ stop consisting of several rows of pipe sounding simultaneously.

NBC – Abbreviation for National Broadcasting Company in the USA; one of the major radio and television networks.

petit déjeuner – Breakfast in the French language. In my experience, it consisted of café au lait and bread & butter or jam. Occasionally, one might have hot chocolate instead of coffee or a croissant instead of normal bread.

pontifical – An adjective describing a service at which a bishop presides.

portative organ – A very small pipe organ light enough to carry and play while walking in procession.

positif, positiv, or positive organ – In this book, a small one manual pipe organ that rests on the floor. The term distinguishes it from a portative. The term is also used elsewhere as the name of a secondary division of a multi-manual organ. This distinguishes it from the great organ or other divisions.

propers of the mass – The texts that change from day to day.

organ pipe - A cylindrical or conical metal tube, or rectangular or square wooden tube, into which air is gently blown to make a musical sound. Each pipe makes only one sound, which cannot be varied while playing.

rood screen - The partition separating the nave from the chancel (or great choir) and altar. In medieval times, only clergy, monks, and choir members sat on the east or altar side of the rood screen. In modern times, many congregation members, especially for sparsely attended weekday services, will sit in choir rather than in the nave. A rood screen in a medieval building was quite solid and one to two metres thick. Remember that a pipe organ atop the rood screen weighed several tons. Modern church architecture would not normally include a rood screen.

server – A person who assists the priest at the altar. When I was a child, only boys were allowed to serve. They were also popularly known as altar boys.

stop – A matched set of pipes of graduated length producing a particular tone colour: one pipe for each key. A flute stop or a trumpet stop, for example, will each have 54, 56, or 61 pipes, depending on the number of keys on the keyboard.

Sousaphone – An musical instrument invented by American bandmaster and composer, John Phillip Sousa, to replace the tuba in marching bands. Its tubing winds around the head and shoulders of the player. It is easier to carry than a tuba.

string bass – The lowest-pitched member of the string section in an orchestra. It is properly called a bass viol. It is sometimes called a stand-up bass or bull fiddle in jazz or pop music. For the detail-oriented, it is technically a member of the viol family rather than the violin family.

terce - The third of the daily monastic offices. For the detail oriented: Canonical hours - Wikipedia

tonal finishing – The process of adjusting the speech of each pipe to suit the building. It must be done after the organ is installed. It cannot be done in the organ factory prior to delivery and installation.

torchbearer – An acolyte who carries a candle atop a wooden pole.

thurifer – An altar server who manages the thurible: a metal pot on chains in which incense is burned upon hot charcoal. The thurifer prepares the thurible for the priest to cense the altar or the deacon to cense the gospel book. At other times, the thurifer censes the priest, other clergy, choir and servers, or the congregation. He would also swing the thurible in a liturgical procession.

titular organist – In my youth, the principal organist of the gallery organ in a French church or cathedral: organiste titulaire au grand orgue. Today, a major church or cathedral may have several organistes titulaires for the gallery organ and several more for the chancel organ (organiste titulaire à l'orgue de choeur).

tonic sol-fa – A method for sight reading music. The notes of the scale are called do-re-mi rather than C-D-E.

tracker action – See mechanical action.

tribune – The gallery or balcony upon which the large organ (grand orgue or orgue de tribune) is placed. The tribune was usually at the west end, over the main doors, of a French church or cathedral. It could also be placed on a side wall. Prior to Vatican II, the grand orgue was used only for solo music and improvisation.

trompette en chamade – Most organ pipes stand vertically on a windchest. Pipes en chamade are mounted horizontally, which makes the tone richer and brighter. Trumpet stops are the most common pipes en chamade, but it is also possible to have a cromorne or other reed pipe en chamade.

tuba – The lowest bass member of the brass family of musical instruments.

ventil – A foot-controlled lever on an organ console by which a pre-determined battery of stops may be held in reserve until the organist presses it. Ventils were especially important in the pre-computer age. In the second half of the 19th-century, they made stop control easier on the mechanical-action French organs. For example, if an organist wants to hold the great organ reeds and mixtures in reserve, he or she will prepare by pulling the desired stops on, but leaving the ventil off. At the desired moment in the music, one would depress the ventil (appel anches du grand orgue) and the chosen stops would be added to those already sounding. Think of it like a circuit breaker. One can turn a lot of light switches on but there are no lights until the circuit breaker is also turned on.

ADDENDA

On page 6, I said that my dad's brother, Carter, had a long and successful career working at the River Rouge plant of the Ford Motor Company. Cousin Ruth Ezell tells me that her elder brother, Bill, worked there at least one summer during the late nineteen-sixties while a student at Eastern Michigan University. Uncle Carter maintained and supervised just-in-time part delivery to the assembly lines. Draftsmen often sought his advice on design problems. Bill was very impressed by the high esteem in which Uncle Carter was held by both white-and-blue-collar workers alike, irrespective of race.

I mentioned seminarian Congreve Quinby on page 64 and wondered if he might still be alive. Cousin Ruth found his obituary. I discovered three striking details:

1) He served as Canon Pastor of Grace and Holy Trinity Cathedral in Kansas City, where I had taken organ lessons during my high school years.

2) He served as priest-in-charge, presumably between rectors, at my dad's former parish: St. Augustine's in Kansas City.

3) Con, a white man, marched with Martin Luther King Jr in Selma in 1965. He was a lifelong advocate for civil rights and social justice.

The full obituary is online at:

https://www.nny360.com/news/obituaries/congreve-quinby/article_aef2e7c7-9a32-50bb-a539-b9f65eb73c94.html

---

I told of the marriage of my dad and Ada Peters on page 235. I have since found the following: Ada was either the first black woman or one of the first black women to graduate from the University of Maine. "…Ada V. Peters was the first person of color to join Phi Beta Kappa at UMaine, the oldest and most prestigious academic honors society in the country. Even in high school, she was at the top of her class, with a

Richard Birney-Smith

nearly perfect average according to the Bangor Daily News article linked in the images. She was the daughter of Black Canadian immigrants, themselves descended from enslaved people who escaped to Nova Scotia, Canada, generations earlier, and returned home following the Civil War.

"Ada graduated in 1927 from the University of Maine with a degree in French. By 1930 she was living in Alabama, teaching at Booker T. Washington's Tuskegee Institute. She later received her M.A. from Columbia University."

Source: *A History of Black Student Success on Campus* - Clio (theclio.com)

Acknowledgements

Thank you to my colleague Christopher Dawes, who served as Director of Music at St. James' Church in Dundas from 2010 until 2013. I told him a story while attending an end-of-season patio potluck at the home of one of the choir members. He suggested that I should write a book. *Recollections & Reflections* is the result.

Thank you to Mark Vorobej, who proofread early drafts of every page and made helpful suggestions, especially when I was ambiguous or had lapsed into professional jargon.

Thank you to Julia Kollek (www.juliakollekcreative.ca) for editing the entire book after my rewrite.

Special thanks to my beta readers: Cathryn Baird, Roger C. Bond, Rosemary Eden, Ruth Ezell, and Lorhel White, who scrutinized every punctuation mark, spelling, capital letter, and verb tense in the edited text.

Extra-special thanks to: JS Veter (shoestringhouse85@gmail.com) for formatting and proofreading; Esther van Bokhorst-Beentjes (www.merakicoverdesign.com) for the cover design; and Meggan Larson (www.megganlarson.ca) for publishing and liaison with Amazon.

All final decisions rested with me. I take full responsibility for any errors that managed to creep through. I wonder why no one warned me that writing the book was the easy part.

Thank you, dear reader, for acquiring a copy of volume one. I look forward to sharing volume two with you within the next year or two.

www.ingramcontent.com/pod-product-compliance
Lightning Source LLC
Chambersburg PA
CBHW051003140626
46546CB00016B/121